DEVELOPMENT OF SCHEDULED CASTE

DEVELOPMENT OF SCHEDULED CASTE

Anil Bhuimali

SERIALS PUBLICATIONS
NEW DELHI

First Published - 2007

ISBN: 978-81-8387-123-5

Published by

SERIALS PUBLICATIONS
4830/24, Prahlad Street, Ansari Road
Darya Ganj, New Delhi-110002 (India)
Phone : 23245225 Fax : 91-11-23272135
E-mail: serials@satyam.net.in

CONTENT

1.	Introductory Overview		1
2.	Discrimination and inequality: Theoretical Reflections	*D.K. Verma*	11
3.	On The Status and Well-being of Rural Agrarian Women in India: The Influence of Socio-economic and Socio-cultural Factors	*Hillol Kumar Chakrabarti*	42
4.	Income Inequality and Poverty Among Scheduled Castes and Scheduled Tribes in Selected States in India	*Maniklal Adhikary*	58
5.	Gandhi, Jinnah and Dr. Baba Saheb Ambedkar: Reflections on Their Role in the Nation-making of India	*Dr. I. Sarkar*	74
6.	Development and Empowerment of Disadvantaged People of India	*Anil Bhuimali*	82
7.	Disadvantaged Migrant People on Balasan River Bed	*Sri. Samar Kumar Biswas and Mr. Somenath Bhattacharjee*	101
8.	Development of Primary Education Among Scheduled Castes in Andhra Pradesh	*D. Pulla Rao*	117
9.	Rights and Privileges of The Scheduled Castes Community of India	*Tapan Kumar Ghosh*	135
10.	Genesis of Scheduled Castes and Constitutional Safeguards For Them	*Sidhartha Sankar Laha and Anil Bhuimali*	160

11.	Literacy Rate among The Scheduled Castes With Reference To West Bengal	*Biplab Chakraborty*	177
12.	His and Her Syndrome in Political Reservation of Women: An Analysis in The Present Socio-legal Framework	*Biswajit Chatterjee*	188
13.	Scheduled Caste Women in Decision-making: A Study of Darjeeling Municipal Administration	*Padam Nepal* *Namrata Pariyar*	200
	Index		213

ABOUT THE CONTRIBUTORS

D. K. Verma, Professor, SC, ST, OBC Development Dr. Babasaheb Ambedkar National Institute of Social Sciences, MHOW (MP).

Hillol Kumar Chakrabarti, Professor of Economics (Rtd.) Department of Economics, University of North Bengal.

Maniklal Adhikary, Professor of Economics, Department of Economics University of Burdwan.

Ritwik Mazumdar, Research Scholar, Department of Economics, University of Burdwan.

I. Sarkar, Reader in History, Department of History, University of North Bengal.

Anil Bhuimali, Professor of Economics, University of North Bengal.

Anil Kumar Biswas, Lecturer in Economics, P. D. Women's College, Jalpaiguri, West Bengal.

Samar Kumar Biswas, Lecturer Department of Anthropology, University of North Bengal.

Somnath Bhattacharjee, Research Scholar Department of Anthropology, University of North Bengal.

D. Pulla Rao, Associate Professor Department of Cooperation and Applied Economics, Andhra University.

Tapan Kumar Ghosh, Lecturer in Economics A. C. College Jalpaiguri, West Bengal.

Sidhartha Sarkar Lala, Senior Research Fellow Department of Economics, University of North Bengal.

Biplal Chakraborty, Project Fellow, SAP-DRS Department of Economics, University of North Bengal.

Biswajit Chatterjee, Lecturer Department of Law, University of North Bengal

Padam Nepal, Lecturer in Political Science St. Joseph's College Darjeeling, West Bengal.

Namrata Pariyar, Lecturer in Political Science Darjeeling Government College, Darjeeling, West Bengal.

1

INTRODUCTORY OVERVIEW

I

INTRODUCTION

Indian society is based on caste system with massive inequalities in social, economic and political spheres. The caste system is, in fact, a two-tier construction. In one end, there is upper caste consisting of Brahmin, Kshatriya and Vaishya and in another, there is lower caste consisting of Sudra and Outcaste. The institution of caste had formulated some laws and regulations which, in effect, alienated a section of the society from the mainstream. Social relationships separated from the production relationships in the domain of economic activity were largely depended and governed by the divine superstitution of rights. Here lies the fundamental source of social exploitation. The upper caste enjoyed rights and privileges more than its contributions to the society. The lower caste, on the other hand, had been denied rights and privileges equal to its contributions. This practice started for about 3,500 years ago. This has been continuing even today in one form of other. Therefore, the division of the society according to privileges enjoyed by the people points carefully the picture of social exploitation of the lower caste by the upper caste.

Since independence, the Government of India have provided some constitutional safeguard to the people who are socially, economically and culturally backward. The objective of such a policy is to benefit the weaker sections of the society. This has been administered by the Central and the State Governments. The policy package consists of a set of goals. It tries to remove social and religious inabilities of the lower caste. It provides facilities in education, employment, parliament, state legislators and locals bodies and finally, the policy safeguards the deprived class from all sorts of social injustice and exploitation.

The untouchable castes were listed in 1931 Census. They were officially defined as deprived castes in 1932. The expression "scheduled castes and scheduled tribes" was first created by the Simon Commission and incorporated in the Government of India Act of 1935. Before 1935 they were known as untouchables, depressed classes or exterior castes. The Government published a list of scheduled castes under the Government of India (Scheduled Castes) Order, 1936.

The Government, since 1950, has been providing some benefits to the lower caste (especially the scheduled caste and tribe) especially in the fields of education and occupation. As a result, many deprived people have enjoyed educational and other benefits and sought employment opportunities. A section (although meagre) of them has been in a position to seek entry in urban occupation. Naturally, a change in the life pattern has been noticed. It has enjoyed benefit for about fifty years and a legislation extending reservation for a further 10 year period beyond 2001, has been passed. Experience tells that the majority of benefits has enjoyed by the people having economic affluence. The people at the lowest strata of this section cannot enjoy the opportunities provided by our Constitution. Majority of them live in the rural and slum areas who have so far been denied even the basic requirements of decent living. Certainly the first priority for them is food, shelter and clothing. There is no food security for them. As a consequence, they have been denied education, health and nutrition. A few, who have been successful in coming out of the poverty trap, have had to pay a heavy price for this. Thus, considering social, economic and cultural backwardness of the least privileged section of the society we plead that reservation policy should continue at least for further twenty five years with proper implementation and wide coverage.

A section of people is of the opinion that in the age of liberalisation, globalisation and privatisation the reservation policy may not improve the social, economic and political upliftment of the lower caste people. They argue that reservation benefit will maintain their backwardness by taking away all the urge for competition and development. It is also believed that reservation benefit deteriorates quality. Naturally, as set of questions come up in our mind. Should reservation continue? If the answer is 'yes', then how long will it continue? Is it necessary to change the modus operandi? Dose it benefit the actual beneficiaries (lowest strata)? Is there any bottleneck in its implementation? To get satisfactory answers of all of the above queries it needs detailed investigation. In this born we will try to point out some of the important aspects of the reservation policy.

According to 1991 Census, lower caste (excluding OBC) account for about 25 per cent of the total population of the country. The OBC account for about 40 per cent. Therefore, the lower caste (including OBC) account for about 65 per cent of the total population. According to a rough estimate, of the total 40 crore people living at present below the poverty line, 75 per cent belong to lower caste (SC, ST and OBC). Reservation in Government, semi-Government and educational institutions for OBC is a recent phenomenon in some states. But the states of North India, Gujarat and Maharashtra have reservation policy for the OBC since the mid-seventies of the last century. In the North Indian states especially Kerala, Andhra Pradesh, Karnataka and Tamil Nadu there is reservation for OBC for more than 60 years. For proper implementation, the extent of reservation has reached there almost to saturation point. In those states there is no need of further extension of reservation policy to those who have enjoyed benefits for two or more generations. This should continue to those states which still are lagging behind in implementing the provision due to bureaucratic and administrative bottlenecks.

The implementation of reservation policy should be flawless. For this, the existing policy needs a thorough revision. Stress should be given at the grass roots level. The children of the disadvantaged families will be provided food, shelter, clothing, education, nutrition and health facilities in an integrated manner. This requires hugs funds. This can only be possible by proper utilisation of the existing funds meant for the development of weaker section of the Indian society.

We clearly find two distinct divisions of the lower caste on the basis of economic capability. Relatively economically developed category people enjoy the opportunities of reservation package. The least-privileged sections are far from sharing effective social, economic and political powers. Even after more than half a century of preferential treatment only negligible portion of this section can be found in professional and white color jobs. The utilisation rate of reservation in Government, semi-Government and educational institutions is much more less than the allocations made. For example, the selection committees for selection of reserved candidates very often come to the conclusion : "NONE FOUND SUITABLE". The ultimate result is that seats have been dereserved and filled in by the people of upper caste. For allround development of the society the weaker section needs to be brought on par with others by equipping them with talent and tool. To attain this, the NGOs, the Government and the society as a whole should play a dominant role.

The provision of reservation is not enough. For reservation to improve the life chances of the socially under-privileged other components of the policy will have to show higher operational efficiency. Higher operational efficiency depends on the rate of utilisation. The higher the rate of utilisation the higher will be the rate of operational efficiency and vice versa. The low rate of utilization is one of the causes of poor performance of entire policy package. For improving operational capacity effective performance of other aspects of the policy is equally vital. For this, it is necessary to improve the level of literacy. Improvement in the level of literacy certainly will increase the capacity of receiving benefits of reservation. To attain the moderate level of literacy of the vast section of people living below poverty line is almost impossible task.

If we want equitable and allround development of the society stress should be given for the development of 40 crores unfortunate people living below the poverty line (of which lower caste represents 30 crores and upper caste represents 10 crores). They are so poor that the many infrastructural and other facilities for development lie beyond their reach. The problem of poverty renders them helpless inspite of the development taking place in many sectors of the economy. The goods and services produced do not reach to them in the present competitive economic system. Poverty is, now-a-days, discussed in terms of relative deprivation. In our case, poverty means denial of the right to survive to 40-crore who are in need of bare minimum necessaries. Poverty is a social product. If clings to families over generations as an inherited legacy which has struck not only the lower caste people but also a sizable section of the upper caste component as well.

To have an egalitarian society it is necessary to ensure the right to opportunity of education and upward social mobility through acquisition of knowledge and skill to every member of the society. In this context we want to make some important suggestions for better implementation and greater coverage of reservation policy. We propose that the reservation policy should continue with better implementation and without any leakage. The objective of the policy should be more social rather than political. We also propose that there should be reservation for the people living below the poverty line in upper caste category too. More opportunities will be provided to those who actually belong to the lowest strata of the lower caste category. There will be no reservation benefits for those who have taken advantage for two generations.

Huge funds are spent as stipend for scheduled caste and scheduled tribe students taking higher education. But 10 per cent (roughly) of them are actual beneficiaries. This means that the rest *i.e.* 90 per cent who are enjoying the financial benefit have ability to bear with the expenses. If the present form of reservation policy continues it will further deteriorate the socio-economic position of the lowest strata of the lower caste; since the social benefits received by this section is much less than the social cost incurred. Therefore, the policy should be more social benefit maximizing and social cost reducing.

II

The book starts with the analysis of discrimination and inequality. It is the discrimination by a section of society to other part of the community over centuries which is the root cause of inequality in the Indian economy and society . D. K. Verma's paper provides a theoretical foundation of discrimination and inequality in the Indian context. In the discussion of the issues of discrimination and inequality the author tries to explain economic and social inequalities and says that although it is possible to quantity and measure economic inequalities it is just impossible to quantity and measure social disabilities. He shares the view that the gap between the rich and the poor is the most obvious sign of inequality, but it is also true that equality cannot be made possible by lowering down this gap. Some important issues such as social change, social movements rights, gender discrimination, untouchability, globalisation and liberalisation, science and technology have been discussed to analyse discrimination and inequality.

There is wide gender gap within and between most of the developing countries of the world including India. In this context it needs empowering women socially, economically and politically. Reduction in gender gap urgently requires reducing the gap between men and women in primary, secondary and higher education. Not only this it needs improving health conditions, reducing diseases, poverty, overcoming hunger, lowering child mortality and so on (HDR, 2003). H. K. Chakrabarti's paper examines the status of rural agrarian woman majority of whom belong to disadvantaged community (scheduled castes, scheduled tribes, other backward community and minority community people). He has also examined the conditions of their well-being under the changed circumstances of global order. In the discussion of this important issue the author not only does consult with the existing literature but also he relies on primary data collected from three villages of West Bangal.

Developing countries are afflicted with the problem of income inequality, poverty and unemployment. India, being a developing nation, is equally confronting with those problems. Even after sixty years of independence and fifty-six years of planning we fail miserably to reduce curse of mars poverty. Almost one-third of our total population still live under abject poverty and hunger. This section of population cannot even manage the minimum conditions for existence. Largest number of illiterates and mat-nourished people are found from them. A study reveals more than one in three Indians spend less than one dollar per day (Bhaduri, 2005). Maniklal Adhikary and Ritwik Mazumdar's paper provides a clear description of income inequality and poverty among scheduled castes and scheduled tribes in some states (like Andhra Pradesh, Bihar, Maharashtra, Madhya Pradesh, Orissa, Tamil Nadu, Uttar Pradesh, and West Bangal) of India. Their presentation is based on data collected from a sample of 33, 230 rural households drawn from sixteen states. The survey was conducted by the NCAER in May 1994. Comparisons of data between SC, ST, and other groups have been made on the basis of computed measures of poverty and inequality. Head count ratio, Sen's index and Foster-Green-Thorbeck index have been used to measure poverty.

To free India from the clutches of the British regime many political and socialist leaders took part in the freedom movement. They had countless contributions in the nation-making of India. The article by I. Sarkar makes a comparative study of three personalities Gandhi, Jinnah and Ambedkar and finds that Dr. Bhimrao Ramji Ambedkar's (1891-1956) contribution in uplifting the untouchable is marvellous and outstanding. He founded the Depressed Classes Institute and led a satyagraha to establish the rights of the dalits to draw water from a public tank. It was a herculean task because it was a private property of the upper caste Hindus. No harijan was allowed to lift water from the tank. He won the case in the Bombay High Court in 1937. In those days the dalits had no right to enter into temples. Again Ambedkar fought to establish this right. He dedicated his whole life for the cause of the untouchables. Dr. Sarkar's proper attempts to make a comparative study of the three nationalist leaders and shows how Dr. Ambedkar had some exceptional qualities as a "free man" and with these qualities he fought for universal justice, emancipation from any social bond for all people, rich and poor, high caste and low caste, young and old, men and women.

Since independence and even before independence of India (especially since 1931) a number of states had been taken to uplift the social, economic and political conditions of the untouchables. Anil Bhuimali and Anil Kr. Biswas's paper investigates the development and empowerment of the disadvantaged people, who, constitute almost one-fourth of the Indian population on the basis of their performance in education, employment and representation in the political bodies. Their development prospects and empowerment have also been discussed.

Most of the polluted and hard working activities are performed by the people of disadvantaged community. Samar Kumar Biswas and Somenath Bhattacharjee, in their investigation, have presented untold misery of disadvantaged migrant people who took shelter on Balason river bed near Siliguri township area and readily accepted the low-paid job of stone crushing. The working environment of the stone crushing people and its impact on their health and some other related issues have nicely been represented here.

Indian Constitution makes provision for primary education to all. This is because of the fact that our constitution-makers, like many other socialist thinkers and political leaders, thought education as one of the powerful instruments of social and economic changes. Education brings about development of the quality of population which again improves the level of production and productivity (Sarkar, 1986). Dr. Rao in his paper has presented the conditions of education among scheduled castes in Andhra Pradesh. Projects taken up by the Government of Andhra Pradesh such as operation Black Board, Andhra Pradesh Primary Education Project, District Primary Education Programme, Chaduvula Panduga, Aksharn Sankranti, Sarva Shiksha Abhiyan, Vidya-Volunteer Scheme, Mid-day Meal Scheme, etc. have some affirmative impact on enrolment, and recruitment of teachers of communities including scheduled castes. Dr. Rao's paper examines the impact of those government-aided programmes on primary education of children belonging to scheduled caste community.

Since 40s of the last century, the Government of India came forward to uplift the disadvantaged sections of the community-socially, economically and politically. Special provisions have been made in the constitutions to protect the rights and privileges of the downtrodden especially the scheduled castes and scheduled tribes. Tapan Kumar Ghosh's paper depicts the privileges assigned for the development of the scheduled caste community through the reservation package.

A similar analysis on scheduled caste community regarding their genesis and constitutional safeguards provided by our government has been provided by Sidhartha Sankar Laha and Anil Bhuimali. Their paper makes an indepth analysis about the genesis of scheduled castes and a comprehensive list of scheduled caste in different states. A comment on the constitutional safeguards has also been made in the end.

To improve literacy among the children aged upto 13 years it needs greater allocation of public expenditure on basic education especially in the context of developing economies. The share of public expenditure on basic education has been consistently higher in east Asia than elsewhere and the share of public fund meant for tertiary education has tended to be low. The average was 15 per cent during the past three decades (Washington D.C.; the World Bank 1993). Biplalu Chakraborty's paper represents a trend of literacy among the scheduled caste community of different states of India. It also makes a comparison of literacy among the general category and scheduled caste. A rural-urban literacy among the scheduled caste has also been shown. The impact of Sarva Shiksha Abhiyan on the literacy of scheduled castes community has also been clearly discussed.

Women in every society are less represented in political institutions. Even in societies where women enjoy greater freedom in every sphere, but they are ill-represented in political bodies. In this context, Indian women's position is even worse. What is more alarming is that their representation in politics has been declining (Vats, 2004). Biswajit Chatterjee's paper analysis, in detail, about reservation for women. It also discusses about reservation within reservation *i.e* whether there should be any reservation for scheduled caste and scheduled tribe women in Assembly and Parliament. The issue still remains unsettled and is under consideration. Why this is so has been spelt out by the author.

Padam Nepal and Namrata Pariyar in their paper have presented a quite similar topic. It is a case study on scheduled caste women and their participation in municipal administration. The paper includes that the government has established multi-tier administrative structures decentralised in nature to ensure the participation by the marginalised groups especially the disadvantaged women belonging to scheduled caste community. But the fact is that their influence in the decision-making process is still negligible.

REFERENCES

Aggarwal, S., Kumud Khanna and Surjeet Malhan (2003), Quality of life of Farm Women. Abhijeet Publications.

Bhaduri, A. (2005): Development with Dignity. A Case for Full Employment. National Book Trust.

Bhuimali, A. (2003): Rural Cooperative and Economic Development. Sarup and Sons.

Bhuimali, A.(2004): Education, Employment and Empowering Women (Ed). Serials Publications.

Bhuimali, A. and Sampa Poddar (2005): Development of Rural Women through Education and Empowerment. Abhijeet Publications.

Bhuimali, A. (2005): Poverty and Human Rights of Women. Serials Publications.

Meier, G.M. and James E. Rauch (2000): Leading Issues in Economic Development. Oxford University Press.

Sarkar, S. and Anil Bhuimali (2005): Disadvantaged Women in Informal Sector. Abhijeet Publications.

Sen, A. (1962): Choice of Techniques. Oxford University Press, Bombay.

Sen, A. (2005): The Argumentative Indian. Allen Lane an imprint of Penguine Books.

Sen, A. (2006): Identity and Violence. The Illusion of Destiny. Allen Lane an imprint of Penguine Books.

Tilak, J. B. G. (1986): Education and Regional Development (Ed). Yatan Publications.

United Nations Development Programme (UNDP). (2003): Human Development Report 2003, Oxford University Press.

Vats, P. (2004): Political Participation and Attitudinal Transformation of Rural Women. Abhijeet Publications.

Vats, S. (2004): Women's Participation in Rural Development. Abhijeet Publications.

2

DISCRIMINATION AND INEQUALITY: THEORETICAL REFLECTIONS

D.K. Verma

DISCRIMINATION

Discrimination is one of the major factors, which operate against equality. Segregation is a form of discrimination and it has appeared in all parts of the world where there are multiracial or multicaste communities. Social segregation is the practice of restricting people to certain circumscribed areas of residence or to separate institutions (e.g., schools, religious and common places) and facilities (parks, playgrounds, restaurants, restrooms) on the basis of alleged caste or race. Social segregation provides a means of maintaining the economic advantages and superior social status of the politically dominant group, and in recent times it has been employed primarily by the higher caste populations to maintain their ascendancy over other groups. Though several steps have been taken by the state to eliminate various discriminatory and unequal treatment practices, the manifestations of these social evils are still evident in many areas and forms in all the longitudes and latitudes of the country. The caste system has been denounced illegal in India for more than fifty years, but it continues to haunt people's lives.

The higher castes control the economic resources and possess power whereas the lower castes remain confined to menial jobs like and land-less labourers, scavenging and unskilled low paid occupations. The Government of India and various State Governments in the country continue to take measures after measures to rid the country of the caste system and preceding evils, but still practices of discriminatory and unequal treatment practices are wide prevalent. The 21st century will witness some new forms of discriminatory practices. Earlier the power, and wealth were used to be controlled by land ownership and restricted occupation. Now it is the knowledge and technology, which give the power and wealth. The land and particular occupation had subjective values supported by the religious sanctity. Thus, the discriminatory practices were/are more or less transparent of identify the discriminated groups. While the future discriminatory practices based on knowledge and technology will be in subtle forms discriminating anybody who happens to be a non-beneficiary in the process. The reflects a wide scope for discussion on forms, extent and magnitude of discriminatory practices against our future generations.

INEQUALITY

Rousseau regards the inequality between men not as a separate problem but as one of the features of the long process by which men become alienated from nature and from innocence. Inequality is not just antonym of equality. Because inequality is not just a physical and mathematical disproportion which can be compared with a single/ or a fixed set of indicators. Inequality can be justified by all means by the supporters of inequality as well it can also be condemned at any level by its opponents. Because the assessment of inequality depends more on the qualitative and subjective ends than quantitative and objective means.

In my opinion, equality is not just reduction in the range of inequality. The gap between rich and poor is a most obvious sign of inequality but equality cannot be achieved by bridging that gap. Equality is the empowerment of the poor with those opportunity which the rich enjoy to become rich. Inequality will always remain decided by the market force based on demand and supply and the equality can always be achieved by eliminating disabilities imposing and/or restricting opportunities to compete with the market forces. The gap should not be treated as inequality but the economic diversity as it exists in nature as biodiversity where no physico chemical-biological-ecological disability is imposed against any organism be it is lowest among low.

All are free to compete. Of course, the nature controls those who go beyond the ecological cycle causing imbalance. They can even be wiped out by the nature. Extinction of Dianasaurs can be placed as an example here. The recent placement of computer engineers and management graduates from some intuitions in India were given appointment with a minimum salary of 1.5 lakhs per month. While I have come across some engineering graduates and masters in computer science who are ready to serve for any salary even less than Rs. 2000 per month! Many a times we discuss the problem of brain drain or non-payment of minimum wages or gender inequality. In fact these inequalities aries due to lack of opportunities. Opportunities to get highest levels of learning, accessibility to best possible facilities, access to latest information, ability to produce the best performance and so on.

We have several plans to reduce inequalities and provide opportunities to students belonging to weaker sections. For example, scholarships are paid the real expenditure on education. Can this together with the lack of accessibility to best educational institutions, teachers and libraries, will help in reducing the inequality. Today on an average one is required to pay more than Rs. One lakh per annum as education cost to become a software engineer earning Rs. one lakh per month. How can one compete for economic equality with total family income of less than Rs. one lakh per annum?

This is just a reflection in the beginning of the 21st century and one can imagine the situation in years to come. Earlier the inequality used to be manifested mainly on social grounds. Now the inequality will be manifested with a more and compounding impact of economic disabilities.

BROKEN PEOPLE: THEIR COUNTRY-WIDE STATUS

The recent report of the National Commission for Scheduled Castes and Scheduled Tribes (1997) and the report of the Human Rights Watch (Broken People, 1999) underscore that the impositions of social disabilities on person by reason of their birth in a particular caste is still widely practiced in many forms throughout the country. Social manifestations of caste based discrimination reported in these reports reveal the centuries old picture of discrimination.

Reports mention that untouchables are still not allowed to draw water from common wells, they cannot sit on their cots when a higher caste person passes by, they cannot enter into temples, they are forced to use their own or separate crockery and cutlery in tea shops and food stalls, barbers and others service provides refuse to entertain them, they are still abused with derogatory words and not considered of carrying any social dignity in the society even if they are by protective discrimination holding the power. The United Nations Commission (1996) Committee also reports these discriminatory and unequal treatment practices in rural India. The Committee reports gross violation of articles of the Convention on the elimination of all forms of Racial Discrimination. No doubt, there has been a perceptible change in condition of backward people still the goal of an egalitarian society is miles and miles away. Several empirical studies conducted by Indian and Foreign scholars also confirm that the backward people face more or less similar kinds of disabilities as they used to face in the early part of the 20th century.

More than a dozen empirical research studies conducted by the Institute on problems like social segregation, aspirations and achievements of scheduled castes in last five decades, atrocities on SCs & STs, untouchability, universalisation of primary education, PCR Act, rehabilitation of scavengers, primitive tribal groups, impact of various welfare progrommes including SCP, IRDP, social forestry, post-matric scholarship, handcraft artisans, value crisis among neo-Buddhists, infant mortality, tribal migration and migration of Chhattisgarh region of MP etc., also confirm the above observations with regard to the status of backward people. The welfare and development of backward people need more concerted efforts. Some new strategies are required to understand and eliminate the ever growing menace of discrimination and inequality.

THEORETICAL REFLECTIONS

Discrimination and Inequality are the basic concerns in the theoretical discussions on social development and justice. Economic inequalities are easy to measure and explain, but social disabilities are very intricate and complex because they remain hidden in the human behaviour and thus cannot be objectively measured. In India, it is the caste systems which has given rise to most forms of disabilities and inequalities. The reality of caste system is so complex that one gets perplexed in understanding its network as well as intra and caste dynamics. In the following discussion an attempt is made to understand the theoretical reflections on discrimination and inequality.

Various forms of discrimination and unequal treatment practices are basically related to the rights to individuals in the society by the religious and political authorities. Rights are the concern of justice. The concept of right can be traced to ancient Greece and Rome, where it was closely tied to the pre-modern natural law doctrines of Greek Stoicism. The school of philosophy founded by Zeno of Citium, which held that a universal working force pervades all creation and that human conduct therefore, should be judged according to, and brought into harmony with the law of nature. It was not until after the Middle Ages, however, that natural law doctrines became closely associated with liberal political theories about natural rights. In Greco-Roman and medieval times, natural law doctrines taught mainly the duties, as distinguished from the rights, of "Man". Moreover, as evident in the writings of Aristotle and St. Thomas Aquinas, these doctrines recognized the legitimacy of slavery and serfdom and, in so doing, excluded perhaps the central most ideas of human rights as they are understood today— the ideas of freedom (or liberty) and equality.

The scientific and intellectual achievements of the 17th century— the discoveries of Galileo and Sir Isaac Newton, the materialism of Thomas Hobbes, the rationalism of Rene Descartes and Gottfried Wilhelm Leibniz, the pantheism of Benedict de Spinoza, the empiricism of Francis Bacon and John Locke— encouraged a belief in natural law and universal order, and during the 18th century, the so-called Age of Enlightenment, a growing confidence in human reason and in the perfectability of human affairs led to its more comprehensive expression. Particularly to be noted are the writings of the 17th-century English philosopher John locke- arguably the most important natural law theorist of modern times- and the works of the 18th-century Philosophers centered mainly in Paris, including Montesquieu, Voltaire, and Jean-Jacques Rousseau.

Rousseau, Jean–Jacques begins his Discours sur I'origine de I'inegalite (1755; Discourse on the origin of inequality) by distinguishing two kinds of inequality, natural and artificial, the first arising from differences in strength, intelligence, and so forth, the second from the conventions that govern societies. It is the inequalities of the latter sort that he sets out to explain. Adopting what he thought the properly "scientific" method of investigating origins, he attempts to reconstruct the earliest phases of man's experience of life on earth. He suggests that original man was not a social being but entirely solitary, and to this extent he agrees with Hobbes's account of the state of nature. But in contrast to the English pessimist's view that the life of man in such a condition must have been "poor, nasty, brutish and short," Rousseau claims that original man, while admittedly solitary, was healthy, happy, good and free. The vices of men, he argues, date from the time when men formed societies.

Rousseau thus exonerates nature and blames society for the emergence of vices. He says that passions that generate vices hardly exist in the state of nature but begin to develop as soon as men form societies. Rousseau goes on to suggest that societies started when men built their first huts, a development that facilitated cohabitation of males and females; this in turn produced the habit of living as a family and associating with neighbours. This "nascent society", as Rousseau call it, was good while it lasted ; it was indeed the "golden age" of human history. Only it did not endure. With the tender passion of love there was also born the destructive passion of jealousy. Neighbours started to compare their abilities and achievements with one another, and this "marked the first step towards inequality and at the same time towards vice." Men started to demand consideration and respect; their innocent self-love turned into culpable pride, as each man wanted to be better than everyone else.

The introduction of property marked a further step towards inequality since it made it necessary for men to institute law and Government in order to protect property. Rousseau laments the 'fatal' concept of property in one of his more eloquent passages, describing the "horrors" that have resulted from men's departure from a condition in which the earth belonged to no one. Civil society, as Rousseau describes it, comes into being to serve two purposes: to provide peace for everyone and to ensure the right to property for anyone lucky enough to have possessions. It is thus of some advantage to everyone, but mostly to the advantage of the rich, since it transforms their *de facto* ownership into rightful ownership and keeps the poor dispossessed. It is a somewhat fraudulent social contract that introduces government since the poor get so much less out of it than do the rich. Even so, the rich are no happier in society than are the poor because social man is never satisfied.

Rousseau's social contract begins with the sensational opening sentence: "Man was born free, but he is everywhere in chains," and proceeds to argue that men need not be in chains. If a civil society, or state, could be based on a genuine social contract, men would receive in exchange for their independence a better kind of freedom, namely true political, or republican, liberty. Such liberty is to be found in obedience to a self-imposed law.

John Rawls in his theory of justice explains the social contract as a hypothetical contract. The basic idea of Rawls's Social contract theory, as expressed in 'Justice as Fairness', is that a practice is just if it is in accordance with the principles all who participate in it might reasonably be expected to propose or to acknowledge before one another when they are similarly circumstanced and required to make a firm commitment in advance. For Rawls a social contract is a hypothetical not an historical contract. Thus, Rawls does not claim that people actually agree to particular set of morally defensible principles of justice. Rather Rawls claims that people would agree to such principles under certain specific conditions. Later in 'Distributive Justice' and subsequently in A Theory of Justice, Rawls makes it explicit that the most relevant condition required for this hypothetical contract is a veil of ignorance which deprives people of the knowledge of the most particular facts about themselves and their society. According to Rawls, morally adequate principles of justice are those principles people would agree to in an original position which is essentially characterised by this veil of ignorance.

Rawls maintains that social and economic inequalities are to be arranged so that they are to the greatest benefit of the least advantaged and are attached to offices and positions open to all under conditions of fair equality of opportunity. All social values – liberty and opportunity, income and wealth and the bases of self-respect— are to be distributed equally unless an unequal distribution of any, or all of these values is to the advantage of the least favoured.

The post-modern theory of justice argues that human beings can and should build systems of justice; systems of law; systems of social control. It is the just that the architecture of such systems should be explicitly political; that they should be open to collective critique, collective change and accommodating of diverse social forms. Stuart Henry and Dragan Milovanovi (1991) have set out constitutive theory in general. They explain that a post-modern approach to both knowledge and society emphasizes the provisional and situated emergence of truth. While the sociology of law and justice is most complex still the general point can be made that law and the principles of justices upon which law is grounded follow the political and economic arrangements of the social order in which they are found. Modernist justice systems make much of routine, rationality and uniformity in treatment before the law. Post-modern justice systems, grounded upon chaos/complexity theory make room for creativity and variety in both the making and the enforcement of law. Chaos theory teaches us that efforts to predict and to control fade and fail as ever more chaotic regimes appear. The vast efforts to control the effects of racism, gender violence, class inequality and corporate hegemony over the production and distribution of essential social goods are, if social processes are indeed non-linear, these efforts are doomed to failure.

SOCIAL CHANGE

The sociological perspective on equality, liberty and right are based on the ideas of social change. Several ideas of social change have been developed and basic among them are the idea of decline or degeneration, or in religious terms, the fall from an original state of grace; the idea of cyclical change, a pattern of subsequent and recurring phases of growth and decline, and the idea of continuous progress. The concept of progress, became the most influential idea, especially since the 18th century Enlightenment. Social thinkers like Anne Robert, Jacques Turgot and the Marquis de Condorcet in France and Adam Smith and John Millar in Scotland advanced theories on the progress of human knowledge and technology.

Progress was the key idea in 19th century theories of social evolution and evolutionism was the common core shared by the most influential social theories of the century. Evolutionism implied that mankind as a whole progresses along one line of development; that this development is predetermined and inevitable. The most encompassing theory of social evolution was developed by Herbert Spencer, who unlike Comte. (laws of three stages) linked social evolution to biological evolution. According to Spencer, biological organisms and human societies follow the same universal, natural evolutionary law: "a change from a state of relatively indefinite, incoherent, homogeneity to a state of relatively definite, coherent, heterogeneity." In words, as societies grow in size, they become more complex; their parts differentiate, specialize into different function, and become, consequently, more interdependent.

Marx and Friedrich Engels were highly influenced by evolutionary ideas. The Marxian distinctions between primitive communism, ancient slavery, feudalism, capitalism, and future socialism may be interpreted as a list of stages in one evolutionary development. Engels were impressed by Morgan's anthropological theory of evolution, which became evident in Engels' book Der Ursprung der Familie, des Privateigentums und des Staats (1884; The Origin of the Family, Private property and the State). The originality of the Marxian theory of social development lay in its combination of dialectics and gradualism. In Marx's view, social development was a dialectical process; the transition from one stage to another took place through a revolutionary transformation, which was preceded by increasing deterioration of society and intensifying class struggles. Underlying this discontinuous development was the more gradual development of the forces of production (technology and organization of labour).

Durkheim and Max Weber showed ambivalence towards the ideas of progress. Durkheim regarded the increasing division of labour as a basic process, which was at the roots of modern individualism, but could also lead to 'anomie,' or lack of moral norms. Weber rejected evolutionism by arguing that the development of western society was quite different from that of other civilizations and therefore historically unique. It was characterized, according to Weber, by a peculiar type of rationalization, which had brought modern capitalism, modern science, and rational law, but also, on the negative side, a "disenchantment of the world" and increasing bureaucratization.

Evolutionary theories were criticized on empirical grounds because of their determinism and Western-centered optimism. Theories of cyclical change that denied long-term progress gained popularity in the first half of this century; these included the theory of the Italian economist and sociologist Vilfredo Pareto on the "circulation of elites" and those of Oswald Spengler and Arnold Toynbee on the life cycle of civilizations. Although the interest in long-term social change never disappeared, it faded to the background, especially when, from the 1920s until the 1950s, functionalism, emphasizing an interdependent social system, became the dominant paradigm both in anthropology and in sociology.

From the 1950s and increasingly through the 1960s and 1970s there was a revival of interest in long-term social change. Neo-evolutionist theories were proclaimed by several anthropologists, including Ralph Linton, Leslie A. White, Julian H. Steward, Marshall D. Sahlins and Elman Rogers Service. These authors hold to the idea of social evolution as a long-term development of mankind, which is patterned and cumulative in some respects. Neo-Evolutionism differ from 19th century evolutionism in that it does not assume that all societies go through the same stages of development; much attention is paid to variations between societies as well as to relations of influence among them. The latter concept has come to be known by the term acculturation. Moreover, social evolution is not regarded a pre-determined or inevitable but is rather conceived in terms of probabilities. Finally, evolutionary development is not equated with progress.

The revival of interest in long-term social change has been partly induced by the problems of the so-called underdeveloped countries. In order to explain the inequality as gaps between rich and poor countries, western sociologists and economists in the 1950s and 1960s elaborated modernization theories. These theories implied a covertly Western-centered evolutionism insofar as they assumed that poor countries had stagnated on a relatively low level of development and could and should develop, or modernize, in the direction of a western-type society. Modernization theories have been criticized for their lack of attention to international power relations, in which the richer countries dominate the poorer ones. These relations have been brought into the center of attention by more recent theories of international dependency or, in Immanuel Wallerstein's terms, the "world capiltalist system."

MECHANISM OF SOCIAL CHANGE

Conflict, competition and cooperation are the major mechanisms of social change. Group conflict has often been viewed as a basic mechanism of social change, especially of those of radical and sudden social transformations identified as revolutions. Marxists in particular tend to depict social life in capitalist society as a struggle between a ruling class, which wishes to maintain the system, and a dominated class striving for radical changes; social changes then is the result of that struggle. These ideas are basic to what Dahrendorf has called a conflict model of society. Competition is also put forward in individualistic theories, which conceive social change as the result of the actions of individuals pursuing their self-interest. With the help of game theory and other mathematical devices, it has been shown that individuals acting on the basis of self-interest will cooperate, given certain conditions, in widening social networks. In structural functionalism, social change is regarded as the adaptive response to some tension within the social system.

When some part of an integrated social system changes, a tension between this and other parts of the system is created, which will be resolved by the adaptive change of the other parts. An example is what the U.S. sociologist William Fielding Ogburn has called cultural lag, which refers in particular to a gap that develops between fast-changing technology and other slower paced sociocultural traits. Some social changes are to be regarded as the result of the diffusion of innovations, such as technological inventions, new scientific knowledge, new beliefs, or a new fashion in the sphere of leisure. Diffusion is not automatic but selective; an innovation is only adopted by people if they are motivated to do so and if it is compatible with important aspects of their culture. One reason for the adoption of innovations by larger groups is the example of higher status groups, which are reference groups for other people. Successful innovations, which affect the majority of the people of a society, tend to follow a pattern of diffusion from higher to lower status groups.

Social change may be, to a certain extent, the result of goal-directed, large-scale social planning. The possibilities of planning by government bureaucracies and other large organizations have increased in modern societies. Most social planning is short-term, however; the goals of planning are often not attained, and, even if the planning is successful in terms of the stated goals, if often has unforeseen consequences. The wider the scope and the longer the time span of planning, the more difficult it is to attain the goals and to avoid unforeseen and undesired consequences. This has become especially clear in Communist societies, where the most serious efforts have been taken to put the ideal of integral and long-term planning in to practice. Large scale and long-term social developments in any society are still largely unplanned.

Planning implies institutionalization of change, but institutionalization does not imply planning. Many unplanned social changes in modern societies are institutionalized; they originate in organizations permanently oriented to innovation, such as universities and the research departments of governments and private firms, but their social repercussions are not controlled. It is in the fields of science and technology especially that change is institutionalized, producing social change that is partly intended and partly unintended.

These mechanisms of social change are not mutually exclusive. On the contrary, some of them are clearly interconnected. For example, innovation by specialized organizations is stimulated by competition. Several mechanisms may be combined in one explanatory model of social change. Social structure and social change are central theoretical concepts of the social sciences that refer to basic and complementary characteristics of social life in general-permanence, continuity, and repetitiveness on the one hand, dynamics and changeability on the other. Both concepts are interconnected: the social structure cannot be conceptualized adequately without some notion of actual or potential change, and social change as a more or less regular process is inconceivable without the notion of continuity. To the degree that change processes are regular and interconnected, social change itself is structured. Any separation of the two concepts, as though they refer to divergent fields is, therefore, misleading.

SOCIAL MOVEMENTS

The discriminatory and unequal treatment practices have time to time been rejected, resented and revolted by the social movements including reformatory and revolutionary movements. A commonly used but highly subjective distinction is that between "reform" and "revolutionary" movements. Such a distinction implies that a reform movement advocates a change that will preserve the exiting values but will provide improved means of implementing them. The revolutionary movement, on the other hand, is regarded as advocating replacement of existing values. A reactionary movement advocates the restoration of a previous state of social affairs, while a progressive movement argues for a new social arrangement.

A conservative movement opposes the changes proposed by other movements, or those seeming to develop through cultural drift, and advocates preservation of existing values and norms. All movements tend to be either political or religious in character, depending upon whether their strategy aims at changing political structures or the moral values of individuals. In its earliest stages, the strongest influence on a movement is likely to be the charismatic leader who personally symbolizes its values. At some point, intellectuals play a leadership role by contributing to the developing ideology of the movement. And if a movement endures and grows for any length of time, administrative leaders arise who are concerned with the practical matters of organization and strategy.

Changes due to movements may tend in either of two general directions. It may emphasize personal transformation, bringing about social change by converting a majority of society to implement the values by their actions. Or it may emphasize a strategy of societal manipulation, changing social institutions so that the program may be implemented without regard to the number of people favouring the new order. Strategy and changes in strategy are strongly influenced by the relationship of the social movement to the larger society and to other social movements. The social structure and the prevailing belief system may suggest either that change can be brought about by changing the hearts and minds of the individual members or that individuals have little effect on the social order.

More general theories of the origin of social movements, such as those of Smelser, Turner and Killian, suggest that social change may result in strains or conflicts in one or more crucial aspects of the social order. Other theories like the resource mobilization theory, take as its starting point a critique of those theories that explain social movements as arising from conditions of social disorganization and strain and as finding their recruits among the isolated and alienated in society.

By contrast, research mobilization theorists argue that the success of social movements rests mainly on the resources that are available to it; this means forming coalitions with already-existing organizations, securing financial support, and mounting effective and organized campaigns of political pressure. As a result of this emphasis, resource mobilization theorists downplay the factor of ideology— and irrational factors generally— in the study of social movements. Another of social movement derives from an intellectual dissatisfaction with the predominantly Marxist view that treats social movements as reflecting a fundamental struggle among classes organized around economic production. That theory, it is argued, has become less relevant as these classes have been drawn into collective bargaining, the welfare system, and other social advancements within the state. The end products of social movements as collectivities attempting to change the social order cannot be analyzed simply in terms of success or failure. Failure may come as a result of ruthless suppression of the movement or through widespread apathy. A movement may wither away because too few take it seriously and it does not develop enough power to force its program on society. Sometimes the remnants may linger for a long time as cult, oriented inward toward the gantifications that the members obtain from participation but making no serious effort to change the social order.

Success is most apparent when a movement manages to have its power legitimized as authority. In a successful revolution, the social movement becomes the new source of authority and respectability, and opposition to its values is defined as counterrevolutionary. In other instances, the movement achieves power through secession. Failing to compel acceptance of its values in the larger group or society, the members withdraw into a new social system in which they can attempt to implement the values separately from a hostile or indifferent society. A less obvious form of success is the institutionalization of the values or same part of them. Accepting the legitimacy of the movement's values, the traditional associations in the society incorporate them into their own values and implement them without a transfer of authority to the movement. Sometimes the social movement itself is institutionalized by being accorded authority as the legitimate custodian of the new values. The movement is then transformed into a bureaucratic association, as happened with the American labour movement of the early 20th century and the Congress Party of India after British rule ended.

RIGHTS

Human rights refer to a wide continuum of value claims ranging from the most justifiable to the most aspirational. Human rights partake of both the legal and the moral orders. Sometimes indistinguishably. They are expensive of both the "is" and the "ought" in humans affairs. Human rights represent individual and group demands for the shaping and sharing of power, wealth, enlightenment, and other cherished values in community process, most fundamentally the value of respect and its constituent elements of reciprocal tolerance and mutual forebearance in the pursuit of all other values.

Consequently, they imply claims against persons and institutions who impede realization and standards for judging the legitimacy of laws and traditions. At bottom, human rights limit state power. Three generations of human rights can be identified. The first generation of civil and political rights derives primarily from the 17th-and 18th-century reformist theories noted above, which are associated with the English, American, and French Revolutions. Infused with the political philosophy of liberal individualism and the economic and social doctrine of laissez-faire, it conceives of human rights more in negative("freedoms from") than positive ("right to") terms.

Belonging to this first generation, thus, are such claimed rights as are set forth in Articles 2-21 of the Universal Declaration of Human Rights, including freedom from racial and equivalent forms of discrimination; the right to life, liberty, and the security of the person; freedom from slavery or involuntary servitude; freedom from torture and from cruel, inhuman, or degrading treatment or punishment; freedom from arbitrary arrest, detention, or exile; the right to a fair and public trial; freedom from interference in privacy and correspondence; freedom of movement and residence; the right to asylum from persecution; freedom of thought, conscience, and religion; freedom of opinion and expression; freedom of peaceful assembly and association; and the right to participate in government, directly or through free elections. Also included is the right to own property and the right not to be deprived of one's property arbitrarily, each fundamental to the interests fought for in the American and French revolutions and to the rise of capitalism. The second generation of economic, social and cultural rights finds its origins primarily in the socialist tradition that was foreshadowed among the Saint-Simonians of early 19th-century France and variously promoted by revolutionary struggles and welfare movements ever since. In large part, it is a response to the abuses and misuses of capitalist development and its underling, essentially uncritical, conception of individual liberty that tolerated, even legitimated, the exploitation of working classes and colonial peoples.

Illustrative are the claimed rights set forth in Articles 22-27 of the Universal Declaration of Human Rights, such as the right to social security; the right to work and to protection against unemployment; the right to rest and leisure, including periodic holidays with pay; the right to a standard of living adequate for the health and well-being of self and family; the right to education; and the right to protection of one's scientific, literary, and artistic production. Most of the second-generation rights necessitate state intervention in the allocation of resources because they subsume demands more for material than for intangible values according to some criterion of distributive justice. Second-generation rights are, fundamentally, claims to social equality. Partly because of the comparatively late arrival of socialist-communist influence in the normative domain of international affairs, however, the internationalization of these rights has been somewhat slow in coming; but with the ascendancy of the Third World on the global stage, intent upon a "revolution of rising expectations," the second-generation rights have begun to come of age.

The third generation of solidarity rights, while drawing upon, interlinking , and reconceptualizing value demands associated with the two earlier generations of rights, are best understood as a product, albeit one still in formation, of both the rise and the decline of the nation-state in the last half of the 20th century. Foreshadowed in Article 28 of the Universal Declaration of Human Rights, which proclaims that "everyone is entitled to a social and international order in which the rights set forth in this Declaration can be fully realized" it appears so far to embrace six claimed rights.

Three of these reflect the emergence of Third World nationalism and its demand for a global redistribution of power wealth, and other important values: the right to political, economic, social and cultural self-determination: the right to economic and social development: and the right to participate in and benefit from "the common heritage of mankind" (shared earth-space resources; scientific, technical, and other information and progress; and cultural traditions sites, and monuments). The other three third-generation rights-the right to peace, the right to a healthy and balanced environment, and the right to humanitarian disaster relief— suggest the importance or inefficiency of the nation-state in certain critical respects.

The ideology of human rights is probably the only one which can be combined with such diverse ideologies as communism, social democracy, religion technocracy and those ideologies which may be described as national and indigenous.

DISCRIMINATION AND INEQUALITY: ISSUES

Social Discrimination and Untouchability

More than one-sixth of our country's population live in a precarious existence, shunned by higher castes because of their rank as Dalits. They are discriminated, denied access to land, forced to work in degrading conditions and routinely abused at the hands of the higher caste groups. Villages in many States of the country still remain segregated by caste. Legislative and constitutional protection serves only to mask the social realties of discrimination and violence faced by the Dalits. Despite the fact that the untouchability has been abolished under the

Constitution in 1950, the facts of inposition of socials disabilities on persons by reason of their birth in certain castes remain very much part of our society particularly in rural areas.

Besides banning untouchability, the Constitution also provides these groups with specific educational and vocational privileges and grants them special representation in the parliament, Educational Institutions and Public Services. In support of these efforts the Untouchability (Offences) Act (1955) and the Scheduled Castes & Scheduled Tribes (Prevention of Atrocities) Act, 1985 provide penalties for preventing anyone.from enjoying a wide variety of religious, occupational, and social rights on the grounds that he/she is a Harijan, or abusing him/her in any manner derogatory to social dignity. Despite such measures, the traditional divisions between pure and polluted caste groups persist in some levels of Indian society, making full emancipation of these groups slow to come about. After five decades of the adoption of the Constitutions, the untouchables are still subjected to many social restrictions in independent India, which is increasing in substantial and subtle forms day-by-day. In many cases, they are segregated in villages or towns, they are forbidden entry to many temples, to well from which higher castes draw water.

Today, lowest among the low Dalits are acutely facing the age-old social disabilities. The laws creating special provisions for the upliftment of dalits reach only to a very small percentage of these sections. The lowest among low still remain untouched by these measures and face acute problems resulting from their social discrimination. This has led many untouchables to seek some degree of emancipation through conversion to Christianity, Islam, or Buddhism. But the studies conducted in the Institute on the converted scheduled castes particularly Neo-Buddhists conclude that conversion in not the answer for their plights as their socio-economic condition has not changed rather they are now facing a cultural and value crisis.

On the other hand, lacking access to a normal life and increasingly frustrated with the peace of reforms, Dalits have begun to resist subjugation and discrimination in peaceful as well as violent struggles. In some states notably Bihar guerilla organization advocating the use of violence to achieve land distribution have attracted Dalits supports. Naxalites (a term derived from Naxalbari in Northern region of West Bengal, where under the leadership of Kanhu Sanyal, the concept of forcible protest against the social order relating to holding of property and sharing of the social benefits originated) have implanted deep roots in other states including Madhya Pradesh, Bihar, Andhra Pradesh and Maharashtra. The recent killings of police officials in MP is an example of this outburst.

Gender Inequality

The most significant social development in the 20th century was the integration of women into the economic, social and political life of man dominant society. Yet this revolution is unfinished–gender equality remains an elusive goal. Our challenges, our responsibility and our opportunity to become an egalitarian society is to build on the momentum of recent decades and to ensure that the 21st century offers women the opportunity to participate fully in the making of the history. In so doing, we will ensure that our legacy is one of equality, opportunity, freedom and progress.

At the dawn of the 21st century the genius of half of humanity is still largely untapped. Tremendous opportunities have been opened for millions of the world's women. Many of the most egregious disparities and violations of basic human rights have been bridged. Nonetheless, significant challenges remain unmitigated for the Indian woman particularly those belonging to weaker sections. With vigilance, foresight and an unwavering commitment to the human rights, the 21st can be, and indeed must be, the century in which gender equality becomes a global reality.

One hundred years ago, few of the world's women enjoyed even the right to vote. Flowing from this basic lack of political rights, women's educational opportunities were significantly constrained, and few females had any role in the worlds of commerce and trade. For many women, childbearing began at a young age and continued for upto two decades. The incidence of death due to complications associated with childbirth was frighteningly high. Women on the other hand, were responsible for educating and rearing the children, duties that were added to, not substituted for, agricultural obligations and/ or other household responsibilities, such as cooking and cleaning. Women now account for a substantial portion of all earned income and have been making steady gains in work force participation. Woman have taken their place in Parliaments, and a few-too few-have ascended to the head-of-state level. Educational opportunities have been expanded dramatically and good per cent of girls can now count on a primary education. Women have entered social life as never before— participating in the Olympics, contributing to the arts, and leading in the development of non-governmental organizations and community groups.

Women however, continue to earn far less than their male counterparts in the workplace— a gap of more than 70 per cent. While women now are able to hold public office but they can be counted on figures. A woman bearing a child still has a risk of losing her life as a result of the lack of proper health care. Illiteracy among women is a great challenge. And the face of poverty is distinctively feminine. Most of the perils of the poverty are faced by women. And violence and abuse of the human rights remains a troubling reality for millions of women and girls— including such atrocities as sexual outrages, female genital mutilation and vicious beatings.

All of the world's women are recognized by an international framework for human rights that includes: the United Nations Charter; the Universal Declaration on Human Rights; the Covenant on Civil and Political Rights as well as the Covenant on Economic. Social and Cultural Rights; and the Convention on the Elimination of All Forms of Discrimination Against Women (CEDAW). In response to these basic freedoms and opportunities, women have taken greater control of their lives. Educated women tend to marry late, have fewer children and are more likely to take part in economic enterprises. Maternal mortality has been reduced. Women are not only important beneficiaries of development, but essential engines for it. Enhancing the status of women is essential for social, political and economic progress. Moreover, in recent years it has been realized that even the most concerted development efforts will not be successful without corresponding attention to the powerful role that women can play as agents of change and progress. Women produce more than half of all the food grown in our country. She is the major work force in farm activities. One of the considerable concerns has been the more or less steady decline in the sex ratio during the current century from 972 females per thousand males in 1901 to 927 in 1991. The factors responsible for this continued decline are as yet not clearly identified. However, it is well-recognized that the adverse sex ratio is a reflection of gender disparity.

Most of the inequalities and disparities with regard to gender are related with the reproductive behaviour which is affected by an extremely complex set of economic and social variables. Although it is difficult to derive precise relationships between these variables and the inequalities, some of the linkages are well-accepted in qualitative terms. In particular female illiteracy, infant mortality rates, average age at marriage and labour force participation rate for women are believed to exert considerable influence on gender inequalities. It is therefore, very important that a special emphasis is placed on basic minimum services and on empowerment of women. A more holistic approach to women's reproductive health must be pursued. Quality reproductive health care is aimed at ensuring healthy pregnancies, reducing maternal morbidity and mortality and alleviating suffering and disease. Women must be given the opportunity to participate equally and equitably in the great struggle to create a better future. Women represent half of the human population and contribute enormously to environmental, economic and human well being–governments can no longer countenance, or afford, their treatment second-class citizens in too many parts of the world. Moreover, men must accept and fulfil their responsibilities as husbands and fathers— and as parliamentarians, where they still vastly outnumber women and must understand the imperative of reproductive health.

Economic Inequality

Despite the fact that there has been a decline in the incidence of poverty over the past two decades, millions continue to live below the poverty line, a large proportion of whom reside in rural areas. The thrust of the new industrial policy announced in July 1991 has been on substantial reduction in the scope of industrial licensing, simplication of procedures, rules and regulations, reforms in the Monopolies and Restrictive Trade Practices (MRTP)

Act, reduction of areas reserved exclusively for the public sector, disinvestment of equity of selected Public Sector Enterprises (PSEs), raising the limit of foreign equity participation in the domestic industrial undertakings, liberalisation of trade and exchange rate policies, rationalisation of duties, etc. with a view to promoting growth and increasing efficiency and international competitiveness.

It is now an accepted fact that it is not possible to reverse the direction of the new economic reforms. The markets have become very important. The future of the weaker sections and the problems they face much depend on the markets be it education market or job market. An important principle of economics, which has largely been ignored is the sanctity of the contract. To get the most out of the market strong institutions which enforce voluntary contracts between individuals are essential. There are exceptions to this principle. We must make sure that the contract does not adversely affect uninvolved outsiders. The feasibility of credible contracts is the backbone of a modern economy. In the United States, graduate education is very expensive. Yet, lots of people acquire it. They manage this only because it is easy to get long-maturity loans. Banks give long-maturity loans only because they know the borrower is contractually bound to repay the loan.

If the judiciary were inefficient and took very long to book a defaulter or if it were "kind" and permitted borrowers to get away without repayment on a variety of grounds— such as that they are less well-off than the lender or that, in retrospect, the initial terms seem too harsh— then banks would either not lend or charge a very high interest rate to cover default risks. One reason why the Indian worker is so much poorer than developed nations is that our law and the judiciary make it so difficult for workers and employers to sign credible contracts which have a severance clause. Both parties know when the time comes to enforce such a contract, there are a variety of ways to renege. This inability to sign contracts has kept the demand for labour (and therefore wages) low India. True, state laws cannot be changed in a hurry. However, since the judiciary in India is strong enough, it can help not only with the maintenance of law and order, but also contribute to the progress of the Indian economy.

GLOBALISATION

Globalisation is the progressive emergence of a single worldwide economic system and the simultaneous reduction in global cultural and political differences. A presumed result of globalisation would be the merging of previously separate political entries and the growth in power and prestige of international institutions. Globalisation of the economy is a new kind of cooperate colonialism visited upon poor countries and the poor in rich countries. The German economic philosopher Wolfgang Sachs argues in his book. The Development Dictionary that the only thing worse than the failure of this massive global development experiment would be its success. Although common trends are making the world a smaller place and affirming the sense that we are all global citizens, the concept of the planet as a global village hides as much it illustrates about the new state of global affairs. Hidden behind the one-world scenario is the deepening global divide between the economically privileged, market-skilled, and internet-wired on one (the strong sections), and the disadvantaged, unskilled, and unconnected on the other side of the world (the weaker sections). Increasingly evident at all latitudes and longitudes is the steady deterioration of ecological systems that have sustained the population and the economic growth of the last millennium.

Production, marketing, and finance-aided by new communications technology have been increasingly integrated by globe-girdling corporations and Banks. Globalisation has made the world a smaller place but one deeply split by sharp economic divides. Economic polarization, financial contagion, environmental plunder, and the destruction of social contracts have become the defining characteristics of today's global economy. We are now being asked to believe that the development processes that have further impoverished people and devastated the planet will lead to diametrically different and highly beneficial outcomes, if only they can be accelerated and applied everywhere, freely, without restriction: that is, when they are globalized.

Impact of the globalisation can simply be seen in the phrase that "Words don't feed the poor". A political and legal system that is blindly anti-rich actually hurts the underprivileged. The present economic policy is not democratic because it is not for the people. The consumerism and profligacy of the wealthy are jarring. The ever-increasing consumption cannot be sustained forever. Anti-poverty programmes should be specifically designed for generation of both self-employment and wage-employment. A holistic approach need to be adopted with an integration of the exiting sub-schemes. Efforts should be made to bring about a greater integration between the poverty alleviation programmes and the various sectoral programmes as well as the area development programmes within the umbrella of the Panchayati Raj Institutions (PRIs).

Land Reforms

Land reform programs should become more comprehensive and encompass much more than the reform of land tenure or land distribution. Reformers have often faced hard choices: to promote and sustain private ownership with inequality or to institute public or collective ownership with equality but with restrictions on the individuals' private interests; to spread employment by supporting labour-intensive, low-productivity techniques or to promote high productivity through capital-intensive, efficient methods; to pursue gradual "repair and maintenance" reform that is basically ineffective, or to promote revolutionary, comprehensive, effective but disruptive reform. In capitalist reforms these contradictions have usually been resolved in favour of the first set of options; in socialist reforms, in favour of the second Land tenure reform seems to have been of little significance in creating substantive economic change, although it has been important for improving the status of peasents and maintaining social and political stability. Most reforms have narrowed the gap between reform beneficiaries and other farmers through land redistribution and tenancy control, but only the comprehensive socialist reforms have narrowed the gap between agriculture and other sector of the economy.

Land redistribution programs have had limited success for several reasons. They often have deprived the farm of the former landlord's contributions without providing a substitute. They have inhibited mobility of labour by giving the present a stake in the land, through only in the form of an inefficient minifarm. They have provided compensation for the expropriated land and hence left wealth and income distributions largely unaffected.

They have been conditional upon peasant participation in Social and Political activity and cooperative organisation, even though the peasant was unprepared for these activities. Moreover, the redistribution of land has rarely been fortified by protective measures that could prevent reconcentration of ownership and the recurrence of crises. India concentrated on abolishing intermediaries who prevailed as survivals of traditional and feudal tenures. The tenants have become hereditary holders, with the title vested in the state.

In India reform was at the level of the states and emphasized peaceful and compensatory methods; hence the results have varied from one state to another. In contrast, after the communists came to power in China, private ownership was eliminated and the peasants were organized in village communes. Extensive supplementary measure have been tried, and the role and organization of the commune have varied according to the pressures on the economy. The most recent innovation in China's agriculture has been the "production responsibility system," which allow the commune to contract with its members for quotas of output; the members are free sell the surplus in the open market. The change is seen as an incentive generator, but land cannot be rented, bought, sold, or used expect as authorized by the commune. The effects of China's agrarian policy on peasant living conditions and the Chinese economy have been generally accepted as positive, genuine and impressive.

Educational Inequality

The current literacy rates (1991) are 52.1 for total population 37.41 for SCs and 29.60 for STs. The Literacy Rates of SCs and STs in terms of the gains and gaps show that while the literacy rate among general population (including SC & ST) increased by 77.28% during 1971-1991, it increased 155.01% among SCs and 161/95% STs. The gap between SCs and the general population has remained constant around 14.78-14.85 during 1971-91 but this has been increasing among STs from 18.15 in 1971 to 22.61 in 1991. This is very alarming as the gap is increasing between tribals and general population. (Source: Educational Development of SCs and STs. Department of Education 1995).

Female Literacy Rate in 1991 was 39.29 for total population and it was 23.76 for SCs and 18.19 for STs. The gap between the female literacy rate of SCs and of all Communities was 15.53. It was 18.92 in 1981 and 15.53 in 1971. While for STs this gap was 21.10 in 1991 and it was 21.81 in 1981 and 17.12 in 1971. The data reveals that the female literacy rates in respect of SCs and STs have increased substantially from 6.44 per cent and 4.85 per cent in 1971 to 23.76 per cent and 18.19 per cent in 1991, respectively. Besides, the most encouraging sign was the increase in the female literacy rate amongst SCs and STs and the reducing gap between the female literacy rates of SCs and of the general population during 1981 to 1991. However, the female literacy rates of these communities as a whole continued to be very low requiring focused attention.

The enrollment ratios of SC and ST girls and boys have continued to slow progressive trends alongwith the rest of the population. The other revealing factor was the better pace of progress maintained by STs at primary level (43.0%) over SCs (29.7%), especially that of ST girls (49.0%) over SC girls (37.3%) during 1981 to 1996. Above all, the overall progress made by SCs and STs in terms of enrollment ratios at primary and middle levels between 1980-81 and 1995-96 has been impressive, as they could prove much better than the general population. The figures for 1990-91 in class I-V (6-11Yrs) general were 114.0 (Boys), 85.5 (Girls and 100.1 (Total). For SCs 122.7 (Boys), 80.6 (Girls) and 102.2 (Total). For STs 126.8 (Boys), 78.6 (Girls) 103.4 (Total). For SCs these were 127.6 (Boys), 95.1 (Girls) 111.9 (Total). For STs these were 30.0 (Boys), 94.9 (Girls) and 113.0 (Total).

The drop-out rate, which is a crucial indicator in the field of education also reveals that there has been a steady decline in the drop-out rates of SCs and STs. Drop-out rates amongst SCs and STs at various stages of Education were 58.70 and 48.08 in classes I-V for general population in 1981 and 1991 while these figures for SCs were 60.16 and 49.03 and STs 75.66 and 63.81. For classes I-X the figures during the same period were 82.46 and 71.34 for general; 86.91 and 80.58 for SCs and 91.18 and 86.00 for STs. The problem appears to be the worst with regard to STs with a very high drop-out rate of 86 per cent for classes I to X during 1990-91).

Education ranks among the most cost-effective investments for reducing population growth and enhancing social development. Inadequate education is a powerful determinant of high fertility and stymies the ability of individuals to live up to their full potential: to themselves or their countries. All over the country, education must be a vital component of development strategies and the gap between educational opportunities for girls and boys must be eliminated.

SCIENCE AND TECHNOLOGY

Information Technology (IT) is fast emerging as the technological infrastructure for global integration and rapid development of all sectors of economy. It broadly includes all sub-sectors dealing with the generation, transmission and utilization of information like telecommunications, computers, consumer electronics, media infrastructure etc. The impacting of technological progress with agriculture is a complex subject. For example, where good soils and assured sources of water existed, markets worked well in the spread of the Green Revolution. It is now increasingly recognized that hunger and deprivation were minimized in areas where widespread agricultural growth took place, generally supported by market incentives. However, in the absence of these favourable initial conditions, it appears that growth did not occur. The performance of areas with low and/or uncertain rainfall regimes remained poor and uneven.

After the agricultural and industrial revolutions we are now at a point of ecological revolution. The future generations will look back on these initial years of the twenty first century and call it the time of the Great Turning. It is the epochal shift from an industrial growth society, dependent on accelerating consumption of resources, to a life-sustaining society. While the agricultural revolution took centuries and the industrial revolution took decades, this ecological revolution took just a few years. Such a revolution has to be more thorough-going and will involve not only our political economy, but also our attitudes and habits that sustain it.

CONCLUSION

The discriminatory and unequal treatment practices have deep roots in our society. Even the disposal of the dead, which is considered most polluted thing, is discriminately done in our caste ridden society. There exist separate cremation and burial grounds for separate castes among Hindu in many places. This reflects the extent of the discrimination done in our society. Sex determination and the female foeticide is the recent from of gender inequality which shows that even the unborn generations are not spared from the practice of unequal treatment. Thus the ultimate analysis show that an integrated strategy involving changes in the attitude and behaviour of people particularly the higher castes and empowerment of capabilities of lower castes would be required to fight against the menace of discriminatory and unequal treatment practices. The concept of sustainable development ensures this intergration, if taken in its true sprit because it calls for meeting the basic needs of the present generation without compromising the ability of the future generations to meet their own need.

BIBLIOGRAPHY

Ashby, H. R. (1968), "Variety, Constraint the Law of Requisite Variety." P. 135 in Buckley, Modern Systems Research for the Behavioral Scientist. Chicago: Aldine.

Barry B. (1989), Theory of Justice. Harvester-Wheatshef, London.

Beteille A. (1965), The Future of Backward Classes: the Competing Demand for Status and Power. Perspectives, Supplement to the *Indian Journal of Public Administration*, 11.

Beteille A. (1966), Caste, Class and Power. Changing Patterns of Stratification in a Tanjore Village. Oxford University Press, Bombay.

Beteille A. (1992), The Backward Classes in Contemporary India. Oxford University Press.

Brown A. (1986), Modern Political Philosophy, Theory of the Just Society. Penguin.

Buchanan A. E. (1982), Marx and Justice. The radical critique of liberalism. Rowman and Littlefied.

Cohen J. (1986), Review of Spheres of Justice. *Journal Philosophy*, 83.

Crush Janathan (1995), Power of Development. Roultedge, London.

Dalton D. (1967), The Gandhian view of Caste and Caste after Gandhi. In India and Ceylon: Unity & Diversity. Oxford University Press.

Das B. (1982), Unsociability, Scheduled Castes and Nation Building. Social Action, 32 p. 269-282

Deal, Anthony. (1994), Part 1. The Science of Law. Legal Research Project. Macquarie University. Page 1.

Deliege Robert (1999), The Untouchables of India. (Translated from French by Nora Scott) Berg Publishers, Oxford.

Doyal L and Gough I (1991), A Theory of Human Need. Macmillan, London.

Dworkin R. (1981), What is Equality? Part I: Equality of Welfare. Part II: Equality of Resources. Philosophy of Public affairs. 10 185-246 & 283-345

Dr. Babasaheb Ambedkar Writings & Speeches (1989): Unpublished writings Untouchables and Unsociability- Socio-Political-Religious. Volume 5. Education Department, Government of Maharashtra, Bombay.

Dubey S. (1955), Indian Village. Rouletdge & Kegan

Dunont L. (1962), Tribes and Castes in India. Contributions to Indian Sociology. 6, 120-2.

Dumont L. (1966), Homo Hierarchicus: essai sur le susteme des castes. Gallimard, Paris (Translated in English : Homo Hierarchicus: The Caste system and its implications by Mark Sainsbury, Loius Dumont and Basia Gulati. Chicago Press, 1980)

Fried C. (1983), Distributive Justice. Social Philosophy and Policy., 145-59.

Galanter Mark (1984), Competing Equalities. Low and the Backward Classes in India. Berkley CA. University of California Press.

Ghurye GS (1975), Caste and Race in India. Popular Prakashan, Bombay.

Ginsberg M. (1965), On Social Justice. Penguin.

Gleick, James (1987), Chaos: Making New Science N. Y.: Penguin

Government of India. Census of India, 1991, Office of the Registrar General, New Delhi.

Harvey D. (1989), The Condition of Post-modernity. Basil Blackwel, Oxford.

Human Rights Watch (1999), Broken people. Caste violence against India's Untouchables. March, 1999. New York

Hume D 91739, Ed L A Selby-Bigge (1960), A Treatise of Human Nature. Oxford University, Press

Hutton J (1946 reprint 1973), Caste in India. Its nature, functions and origins. Oxford University Press, Delhi.

IPPR (1993), The justice gap. Institue for Policy research, for the Commission of Social Justice.

Jatav D. R. (1988), Social Justice in India. INA Shree Publishers, Jaipur.

Kelly, J.M. (1992), A Short History of Western Legal Theory. Oxford. Clarendon Press.

Kukathas C and P Pettit (1990), Rawl's– A Theory of Justice and its critics. Polity Press, Oxford.

Lynch O. (1969), The Politics of Untouchability: Social mobility and social change in a city of India. Columbia University Press.

Mandelbaum D (1970), Society in India. Univ. of California Press

Markovie, Mihailo (1974), From Affluence to Praxis. Boston. Beacon.

Mill JS. (1983), In M Warnock, Ed. 1962). Utilitarianism, On Liberty, essay on Bentham. Collins, London.

Myrdal G. (1968), Asian Drama: An inquiry into the poverty of Nations. Pantheon, New York.

Namboodripad E. (1976), Economic Backwardness of Harijans in Kerala. Social Action Scientist, 4.

National Commission for Scheduled Castes & Scheduled Tribes (1997). National Crime Records.

Bureau (MHA) Statement showing cases registered with the police under different nature of crimes and atrocities on scheduled castes and scheduled tribes from 1994 to 1996. Government of India, New Delhi.

National Commission for Scheduled Castes & Scheduled Tribes (1999), Highlights of the Fourth Report. Government of India, New Delhi.

National Police Commission (1980), Police and the weaker sections of society. Third report of the National Police Commission. Government of India, New Delhi.

Omvedt G. (1987), Dalit literature in Maharashtra: Literature of Social Protests and Revolts in Western India. South Asia Bulletin, 7.

Rawls J. (1971), A Theory of Justice Harvard University Press.

Roberts, J.M. (1993), History of the World. New York. Oxford University Press.

Russel R. and Hira Lala (1916 reprint in 1975), Tribes and Castes of the Central Provinces of India. Cosmos, Delhi.

Sachchidananada (1976), The Harijan Elite: a study off the status, networks, mobility and role in the Social Transformation. Thompson Press, Delhi.

Sen A. (1973), On Economic Inequality. Oxford University Press, Delhi.

Sen A. (1973), Expanded Third Impression, 1999), Inequality Reexamined. Oxford University Press, Delhi.

Sen A. (1973), On Economic Inequality. Oxford University Press, Delhi.

Sen A. (1996), Radical Needs and Modern Reforms. In Indian Development. Selected Regional Perspectives. Eds. Jean Dreze and Amartya Sen. Oxford University Press, Delhi.

Smith David (1994), Geography and Social Justice. Blackwell Publishers, Oxford.

Srinivasan M. N. (1962), Caste in Modern India and Other Essays. Asia Publishing House, Bombay.

Srinivasan MN and A Beteille (1965), The Untouchables of India. Scientific American, 213.

UNDP Human Development Reports, 1990-1998. Oxford University Press, Oxford.

UNICEF (1998), The Progress of Nations.

Verma DK. (1993), Intergenerational Equity. Environmental right of the child, AJSDJ, Vol. 3, 163-168.

Verma D.K. (1993), *"Samajik nyaye aur vikas mein paryavaran shiksha ki bhumika"* (in Hindi). Dr. Ambedkar Samajik Vigyan Shodh Patrika.

Verma D.K. et. al. (1993), Participatory micro-level model of social action for sustainble resource management and development: an approach paper on Manpur Cluster Project, Mhow (MP). AJSDJ, Vol. 3. 11-16.

Verma D.K. (1994), Ecoethical approach for sustainable development and justice. JSDJ 1994.

Verma D.K. (1994), Role of social forestry in conservation and management of forests, Vanyajati. Vol XLIII (I), 20-22.

Verma D.K. (1995), Ecological sustainability in Social Development. In Social Development & Justice Eds R.G. Singh & R.D. Gadkar, Radiant Publishers. New Delhi.

Verma D.K. (1997), Dr. Ambedkar's views on Planning, Development and conservation of environmental resources. AJSDJ, Vol. 5, 1-8.

Verma D.K. (1998), Role of Social Forestry Programme in the development of Schedule Castes & Scheduled Tribes. AJSDJ, Vol. VI, 53-69.

Verma D. K. (1999), Concept and Dimensions of Social Environment needed for Sustainable

Development in Social Environment & Sustainable Development Ed. Y.G. Joshi and D.K. Verma, Rawat Publishers, Jaipur.

Verma D.K. (2000), Sustainable Development MPISSR Journal. Jan 2000.

Waldorp, M. Mitchell (1992), Complexity: The Emerging Science at the Edge of Order and Chaos.

New York. Touchstone Books; Simon & Schuster.

Young, T. R. (1992), Chaos Theory and Human Agency. In Humanity and Society. November. 16:4. p. 441-460.

Zelliot E(1992), From Untouchables of Dalit. Essays on Ambedkar Movement. Manohar Publications, Delhi.

3

ON THE STATUS AND WELL-BEING OF RURAL AGRARIAN WOMEN IN INDIA: THE INFLUENCE OF SOCIO-ECONOMIC AND SOCIO-CULTURAL FACTORS

Hillol Kumar Chakrabarti

It is a well-known fact that in india the populace is found mainly in rural areas and engaged in primary economic activities. Even after a decade of economic reforms, three-fifths of India's total workers are employed in agriculture, and most female workers are involved in agriculture. (Census, 2001). In fact, agricultural operations are found largely dominated by women in almost all states of India (Banerjee, 1997;). But most of the women work force engaged in agriculture are agricultural labourers rather than cultivators. In India despite impressive economic development in recent years, poverty is still very much widespread, and poverty is considered mainly as a rural problem. (Rani, 2005). According to Census 2001 incidence of poverty in rural areas is very high at 25.6% and the evidences show that poverty is on increase as some sections of the poor, especially rural agrarian women, are excluded from the process of growth (Rani, 2005). The rural agrarian women constitute more than three fourths of the rural poor in India (Agarwal, 2000).

The question of gender discrimination and deprivation of women has received considerable importance in recent years and this is well-reflected in the importance given by UNDP gender related measures of attributes of development like GDI and GEM in its range of development indicators. But it should be noted that such measures are based on national aggregates and averages or macro-variables (Tisdell, C. *et al,* 2001). Of course such measures are quite useful in ascertaining the status and well-being as well as deprivation of women as a class, the value of many of UNDP's development indices becomes limited because of the lack of attention to disaggregated data and absence of socio-economic-cultural surveys (Tisdell, C.& R. Gopal, 2005). They need to be supplemented by micro type surveys of households of the type emphasized by Boserup, E. (1970). This has been attempted in this paper by analyzing and interpreting the result from a survey of 179 rural agrarian wives including divorced women and widows, undertaken in three villages of block situated in the Dooars region of West Bengal (India) in 2003-04. Before we analyse and interpret the data collected from the survey, a brief description of some of the factors affecting the status and well-being of the rural women, particularly of those who are connected with agrarian activities (see Chakrabarti, H.K., 2002 for a detailed discussion) may be undertaken.

That the demographic imbalances between women and men continue to exist in general in spite of a slight increase in the total female population are well-documented in the existing Indian data covering various aspects of women problems. Thus, over the decade 1991-2001, female population rose from 407.1 million to 495.7, life expectancy at birth rose from 59.7 years in 1989-93 to 65.3 years in 1996-2001, and sex ratio from 927 in 1991 to 933 in 2001 (Census, 2001). All evidences suggest that male child in India is generally preferred to female child as females are considered 'non-bread earners' in future as well as their incapability of giving any security to the parents at their old age. Among various reasons, subsequent marriage of the female child is perceived to be the main cause for such preference for a male child in Indian society. Moreover, even if girl child is born she is destined to face discrimination from birth till death which may incidentally rise if she is born in a poor family. Her position of the society becomes precarious due to a host of other factors like gender discrimination in all walks of life, her low level of education and work participation, poor nutritional and health status, sexual harassment and violence against women, lack of access to food and health care. Moreover, Indian women are generally viewed as economic burdens and the contributions they make in the spheres of production remain mostly invisible as their contribution to their family is often overlooked (Chakrabarti, H.K., 2002). In addition, it is also important to note that women constitute 35.9% of total employment in agriculture & allied activities, 19.07% in service sector and 12.43% in the industry sector (Q.E.R., April-June, 2000). Hence, it is evident that the distribution of occupation among women points to the fact that there exists gender segregation of tasks, and the underlying reality of high illiteracy among female workers which confines them to low paid, unskilled jobs compared to males (Chattopadhyay, A. 2005). In the informal or unorganized sector, women constitute 90% of the total workers where 80% are found in agriculture and the remaining 10% in activities other than agricultural. Of the total rural unskilled workers, women constitute roughly 90%. It is also evident that almost all the poor women, especially the BPLs, are to perform domestic duties and also to supplement the family income. As they are unskilled, they do not have any principal occupation and are subjected to economic exploitation with low and discriminatory wages (Chakrabarti, 2002). In all developing countries generally domestic and farm activities undertaken by women remain unremunerated. But these activities make significant and vital contribution especially to the poor rural agrarian economy (Chakrabarti, 2002). It is also observed that poorer the family is, greater have to be hours of work performed by women and their contribution to the family as such also tends to be greater (Sharma, 2001). It is perhaps important to mention the fact that technological improvements have produced rising demand for female agricultural labours in recent times (Chakrabarti, 2001) but such increased employment due to increased demand might have affected leisure time available to female agrarian labourers (Chakrabarti, 2001) and might compel them to perform arduous agricultural activities which from the point of view of ILO's definition may not be decent. The deplorable condition of the women and particularly of the rural agrarian women is further compounded by the fact that most of such women has no title to land, and even if they enjoy ownership of land they may not have effective control over it (Agarwal, 1994. 2001). Hence, a rise in female work participation does not necessarily empower a women. Together with this, it is also to be understood that women have hardly any ownership of resources and autonomy to spend their income and to take any independent decision (Chakrabarti, 2002). It is thus observed that it is the male head of the family who would decide in which type of activity and particularly what type of agricultural jobs shall be performed by the female members. We might capture the deplorable condition of women from another angle. The status of rural women would be adversely affected so long as men receive resources and agricultural extension training (Sharma, 2001). In such circumstances, benefits would rarely 'trickle down' to women.

One of the peculiar circumstances to which rural agrarian women are often subjected to is that new crop varieties are rarely demonstrated or tested on agricultural land owned by women. And hence the problems generally associated with introducing new crop varieties are little known to them. This would invariably affect their productivity. Such gender discrimination is bound to affect adversely the status of rural agrarian women (Chakrabarti, 2002).

The gender discrimination is also largely visible when the formal institutions advance credit to agriculture, for ownership of land is largely vested in male households in India. And hence males are supposed to make cropping and input utilization decisions. As a result credit is obviously granted to the male households. We have already stated that even when ownership of land is granted to a women, she may not have effective control over it. And hence, in a male dominated society, women's land is used as a collateral by a male to get credit from the formal credit agencies (Chakrabarti, 2002).

PART II

Having briefly stated some of the aspects of gender inequalities and consequently deprivation of women in general and rural agrarian women in particular, we may now set forth the objective of undertaking our village survey. Our main purpose has been to point out how various indicators of the well-being of rural agrarian women as gauged from our studies are related to certain selected economic, social and cultural factors. We have tried to incorporate as many economic, social and cultural factors that indicate the status of rural agrarian women and a few indicators depicting their deprivation. This is presented in Table-1. The three villages from where data were collected, are all dominated by scheduled castes with no tribal population. All the scheduled and non-scheduled castes were found to be Hindu by religion. The socio-economic and socio-cultural indicators depicting the status enjoyed by the agrarian rural women *perse* have been arranged seriatum in accordance with their group or personal character. Thus indicators I-VIII are group-specific and IX-XI are specific to personal attainments.

We have explored deprivation or rural agrarian women in terms of their accessibility to health, food, title overland and decision-making power over cash expenditure of the family. The absence of accessibility to these could surely be considered as indicators of deprivation. Women who were deprived in terms of these indicators were categorized in accordance with their existing status in respect of the following variables:

GROUP SPECIFIC

I. Scheduled Castes/Other Status.
II. Perceived Economic Status of the Respondent Women.
III. Contribution of Respondent Women to Total Cash.
IV. Level of Education of the Respondent Women.
V. Type of Work of the Respondent Women.
VI. Command over Agricultural Inputs of the Respondent Women.
VII. Level of Accessibility of Respondent Women to Agricultural Extension Training.
VIII. Access to Credit of the Respondent Women.

PERSONAL ATTAINMENTS

IX. Respondent women's contact with the family.
X. Participation of respondent women in woman's SHGs.
XI. Level of participation of respondent women in decision-making.

It should be made clear that although deprivation of rural agrarian women in terms of these indicators varied in accordance to differences in caste status as revealed by our survey we have not sub-categorized the levels of such deprivation by caste-wise in Table-1. Our initial discussion proceeds instead by grouping all agrarian rural women who are either wives, divorced women or widows together irrespective of caste differences. At the end of our discussion, we have captured caste-wise deprivation in respect of the indicators by sub-categorising them according to the existing status enjoyed by them.

It should also be noted that we have refrained from calculating levels of income because of difficulties in accurately measuring rural income. Hence, we have taken 'perceived' economic status as a *proxy* for delineating the relative economic positions of the agrarian women. The respondent women were thus asked to assess whether their family is belonged either to the top, middle or bottom level in terms of their economic conditions.

Similarly, the respondents were categorised into three groups in accordance with their levels of education, viz., (i) No formal education, (ii) Upto primary level, and (iii) Secondary level and above. None among the agrarian rural women reported that they were educated 'above secondary level'.

The respondent women were also categorised in terms of the type of work they were found to perform. Here the type of work was classified by whether the work was arduous or non-arduous. The ILO's definition of 'decent work' would apply in the case of work which guarantees rural agrarian women with (i) freedom of association, (ii) scope of social dialogues, (iii) social protection, & (iv) access to income and employment together with the power to take spending decision and to select the type of employment. Hence, our category of non-arduous work would capture several aspects of 'decent work'.

We also categorised respondent women in terms of their command over agricultural inputs. This was included to see to what extent women are compelled and directed by males when their lack of command over agricultural inputs relates to deprivation.

The respondent women were also asked whether they participate in agricultural extension training to see the extent of empowerment of rural women as a group.

We included accessibility of credit as an indicator by categorising women on the basis of the availability or non-availability of such access. This was done in order to determine indirectly the relative impact of credit access (both formal and informal) in affecting deprivation of rural agrarian women.

The respondent women in our survey as stated as earlier comprised wives, divorced women as well as widows, and hence the extent of their contact with their family seemed to us to be an important factor for categorising the impact of marital/familial status on the respondent women. It was anticipated that this would enable us to see to what extent contact with family helps to reduce deprivation of women within the family at a personal level.

The status of rural agrarian women in terms of their personal attainments could also be captured by categorising them on the basis of their participation in women's SHGs. It may be noted that one of the important factors determining the degree of personal participation and involvement in SHGs is the personal qualities of the women concerned. A destitute woman might thus participate voluntarily as well as actively in the SHG which would enable her to remove her destitution.

We have finally taken the level of participation of women in decision-making to categories our respondents in terms of the extent of their empowerment *vis a vis* the indicators of deprivation. In needs to be emphasized in this context that empowerment is multi-dimensional and refers to the expansion of freedom of choice and action in all spheres of one's life as well as the capability of a person to gain control over recourses and to take decisions independently (Chattopadhyay, 2005).

As regards indicators of deprivation of women and for that deprivation of rural agricultural women, we have taken the access of women to basic needs as well as their control over resources of the family. Access to medical care (health) and food (nutrition) are the basic needs. It is found that in many rural agrarian families of India, males generally enjoy relatively more access to health and food than females (Tisdell and Roy, 2000). Hence, absence of access to these two basic needs would surely show the extent of deprivation of the women. Two other indicators like ownership of land (holding land title) and control over cash expenditure of the family were taken with a belief that members of the family who control resources have greater empowerment in the family (Tisdell and Regmi, 2005). Hence, absence of such control would also indicate the extent of deprivation of women in the family.

PART III

We shall now present the results of our survey and, in the process, we shall try to discern the interrelationships if any, between the indices determining the status of rural agrarian women and the selected indicators of deprivation. Since the percentile differences are striking and significant specific testing for statistical significance was deemed unnecessary for analyzing the data (all the Tables are given at the end of our article).

It is evident from Table-1 that from the standpoint of access to basic needs and control over resources of the family, the deprivation of the scheduled caste women was higher than those of women belonging to other status. This observation might support Indian Government policy of formulating socio-economic programmes for the upliftment of the scheduled caste population where in rural agrarian women could claim special attention.

A further look to Table-1 would show that the perceived economic status of the respondent women could not exert much influence on the extent of their accessibility to resources of the family. But such could determine to a large extent their deprivation in respect of their access to basic needs. Deprivation in terms of accessibility to basic needs as well as control over resources was found to be higher; lower was the contribution of respondent women in total cash income of the family. It could be inferred from the Table-1 that even a poor agrarian rural woman could empower herself in a family through gaining control over resources if she contributes more cash income to the family. This would necessarily emphasize the need to see that women are not confined only to domestic work and childcare. Although the level of the respondent women's level of education seemed to be less important in accessing land but could determine their deprivation in respect of their accessibility to control over cash in a significant way. At the same time their accessibility to basic needs would be substantial among the literate women. It could be said that higher level of income of the family would enable the women to receive education which would be instrumental in their realization of need to raise their nutritional as well as health standard.

Type of work of the responded woman was seen to be an important factor in influming the extent of deprivation of women. Arduous in the type of work performed by rural agrarian woman, their deprivation interms of their access to basic need, and control over resources of the family increases. It could be inferred from the Table-1 that incidence of the arduous type of work would be

Table 1
Deprivation Of The Rural Women In Agriculture
(In Percentages)

Socio Economic & Socio -Cultural Status of Rural Agrarian women	*1* No Access To Medical Care	*2* No Access To Food	*3* Holding No Land Title	*4* No Control Over Cash Expenditure
I. ScheduledCastes/Other Status				
I. Non-Scheduled Castes (64)	23.4 (15)	28.1 (18)	67.2 (43)	71.9 (46)
II. Scheduled Castes (115)	70.0 (77)	75.7 (87)	92.2 (106)	84.3 (97)
II. Perceived Economic Status				
I. Bottom Level (103)	66.0 (68)	75.7 (78)	94.2 (97)	98.1 (101)
II. Middle Level (66)	33.3 (22)	39.4 (26)	65.2 (43)	53.0 (35)
III. Top. Level (10)	20.0 (2)	10.0 (1)	90.0 (9)	70.0 (7)
III. Contribution of Respondent Woman To Total Cash Income of The Family				
I. Up to 50% (149)	57.1 (85)	61.1 (91)	91.3 (136)	83.2 (124)
II. Above 50% (30)	23.3 (7)	46.7 (14)	43.3 (13)	63.3 (19)
IV. Level of Education of the Respondent woman				
I. No formal Education (125)	68.8 (86)	76.8 (96)	77.6 (97)	84.8 (106)
II. Primary Level (49)	12.2 (6)	18.4 (9)	95.9 (47)	71.4 (35)
III. Secondary Level and Above (5)	0.0 (0)	0.0 (0)	100.0 (5)	40.0 (2)
V. Type of Work of the Respondent Woman				
I. Non-Arduous (39)	0.0 (0)	0.0 (0)	41.0 (16)	46.2 (18)
II. Arduous (140)	65.7 (92)	75.0 (105)	95.0 (133)	99.3 (125)
VI. Command Over Agricultural Inputs				
I. Responding 'Yes' (36)	0.0 (0)	0.0 (0)	36.1 (13)	0.0 (0)

Contd......

Socio Economic & Socio -Cultural Status of Rural Agrarian women	1 No Access To Medical Care	2 No Access To Food	3 Holding No Land Title	4 No Control Over Cash Expenditure
II. Responding 'No'(143)	64.3 (92)	73.0 (105)	95.1 (136)	100.0 (143)
VII. Level of Accessibility to Agricultural Extension Training				
I. Non-Participating (130)	70.8 (92)	80.8 (105)	86.9 (113)	96.2 (115)
II. Participating (49)	0.0 (0)	0.0 (0)	73.5 (36)	36.7 (18)
VIII. Access to Credit				
I. Unavailable (130)	70.8 (92)	70.0 (91)	100.0 (130)	97.2 (127)
II. Available (49)	0.0 (0)	28.6 (14)	38.8 (19)	32.7 (16)
IX. Respondent Woman's Contact With the Family				
I. Frequent & Close (143)	49.0 (70)	61.5 (88)	81.1 (116)	82.5 (118)
II. Moderate (29)	55.1 (16)	55.2 (16)	93.1 (27)	86.2 (25)
III. Infrequent (4)	75.0 (3)	25.0 (1)	75.0 (3)	0.0 (0)
IV. Non-existent (3)	100.0 (3)	0.0 (0)	100.0 (3)	0.0 (0)
X. Participation in Women SHGs				
I. Responding 'Yes' (46)	2.2 (1)	0.0 (0)	34.8 (16)	82.6 (38)
II. Responding 'No' (133)	68.4 (91)	78.9 (105)	100.0 (133)	78.9 (105)
X I. Level of Participation in Decision Making				
I. Non Existent (102)	88.2 (90)	76.5 (78)	100.0 (102)	100.0 (102)
II. Passive (41)	4.9 (2)	65.8 (27)	100.0 (41)	100.0 (41)
III. Active (36)	0.0 (0)	0.0 (0)	16.7 (6)	0.0 (0)

Source: Figures in the bracket indicate absolute nembers.

substantial among these women who were found Illiterates; most of them belonged to poor families. Similarly, non-participation of women to agricultural extension training as well as absence of their command over agricultural inputs was found to raise deprivation among them. It was pointed out earlier that agricultural extension training is generally imparted to males in Indian society (Chakrabarti 2002). Such training would obviously be not imported at all to such women who do not enjoy any title over land. Deprivation interms of the absence of control over land could explain non-participation of women in agricultural training activities. The non-participation of women in such training would be substantial as long as women enjoy no real control over land.

Taking now the factor, access to credit we could see that some of the women to whom credit was available, used to sacrifice food for their family. Their perceived economic status was stated to be at bottom level. The Indian rural custom favouring gender discrimination in respect of food intake in the rural agrarian community, might explain such behaviour of women. Moreover, availability of credit to women having no title over land would suggest in an indirect way the presence of informal credit as stated earlier, and the extent of availability of such credit might indicate to some extent the relative importance of such credit in our rural economy and consequently to rural agrarian women also. Whatever might be the source of availability of credit as a whole to rural agrarian women was found to affect their control over cash expenditure. Their control over cash expenditure was found to be higher; was their accessibility to credit.

Taking now all the group specific attributes together, we could say that deprivation of women in respect of basic needs and control over resources was found substantial among rural agricultural women having lower level of family income, lower level contribution to family cash income, lower level of education, type of work arduous, absence of command over agricultural inputs, and participation in agricultural extension training as well as availability of credit was nil.

Having discussed the influences of group-specific indicators on the level of deprivation of women in rural agrarian economy, we shall now state deprivation of women interms of their personal attainments. In order to facilitate our discussion the indicators of deprivation are arranged row-wise and and personal attributes column-wise. This is presented in Table 2.

It is evident from Table 2 that proportion of deprived women interms of their access to health care was high among those women whose contact with the family stood at low ebb. It might be inferred from this that close contact of a woman with her family would likely to empower her within her family (Dyson & Moore, 1983). But the same was not found true in the case of those deprived women who had no access to food. The impact of marital/familial status on the respondent women level of contact with the family might explain non-deprivation in terms of food access.

The Table 2 also shows that higher proportion of non-participating women in SHGs were deprived of basic needs. And similarly, proportion of deprived women in terms of their power to control cash expenditure of their family, remained substantial among non-participating women in SHGs.

Table 2
Deprived Women's Personal Attainments

Indicator of Deprivation	*Respondent Woman's Contact with the Family*				*Participation in Women's SHGs*		*Level of Participation in Decision-Making*		
	Fre-quent & close (143)	*Mod-erate (29)*	*Infre quent (4)*	*Non-Existent (3)*	*'Yes' (46)*	*'No (133)*	*Non-Existen (102)*	*Pass-ive (41)*	*Act-ive (36)*
No access to medical care (92)	49.0 (70)	55.1 (16)	75.0 (3)	100.0 (3)	2.2 (1)	68.4 (91)	88.2 (90)	4.9 (2)	0.0 (0)
No access to food (105)	61.5 (88)	55.2 (16)	25.0 (1)	0.0 (0)	0.0 (0)	78.9 (105)	76.5 (78)	65.8 (27)	0.0 (0)
Holding no land title (149)	81.1 (116)	93.1 (27)	75.0 (3)	100.0 (3)	34.8 (16)	100. (133)	100.0 (102)	100.0 (41)	16.7 (6)
No control Over cash expenditur e of the family (143)	82.5 (118)	86.2 (25)	0.0 (0)	0.0 (0)	47.8 (22)	91.0 (121)	100.0 (102)	100.0 (41)	0.0 (0)

Source: Figures in the bracket Indicate absolute numbers.

Proportion of deprived women in terms of the indicators remained high among non-participating women in decision-making affairs on the family. However, women who could control cash expenditure of the family were also found to participate in decision-making process of the family actively. Thus, it is evident that control over cash expenditure of the family by a woman would empower her due to her access to the decision-making process of the family. It could be inferred from the table that control over cash expenditure of the family by a woman would enable her to participate in SHG even though she might not be holding any title to land. It is also evident from the Table 2 above that all those women who were found to participate actively in decision-making were non-deprived of basic needs.

In short, closeness of the respondent woman with her family, her participation in SHG as well as in decision-making activities of her family would enable her to be immune from deprivation of basic needs and resource controlling power.

Table 3
Caste-wise Deprivation Of Rural Agrarian Women

Socio-Economic & Socio-Cultural Status of rural agrarian women		Percentages of Cast-wise deprived women 1		2		3		4	
		SC.	*OTH*	*SC.*	*OTH*	*SC.*	*OTH*	*SC.*	*OTH*
II. Perceived economic Status	I.	69.1	30.9	78.2	21.8	84.5	15.5	89.1	10.9
	II.	45.5	54.5	57.7	42.3	65.1	34.9	40.0	60.0
	III.	50.0	50.1	0.0	100.0	33.3	66.7	85.7	14.3
III. Contribution of res. Woman to total cash income of the family	I.	80.0	20.0	97.8	2.2	71.3	25.7	78.2	21.8
	II.	42.9	57.1	28.6	71.4	30.8	69.2	47.4	52.6
IV. Level of education of the respondent woman	I.	70.9	29.1	74.0	26.0	85.6	14.4	67.0	33.0
	II.	83.3	16.7	66.7	33.3	36.2	63.8	57.1	42.9
	III.	0.0	0.0	0.0	0.0	100.0	0.0	0.0	100.0
V. Type of work of respondent woman	I.	0.0	0.0	0.0	0.0	68.8	31.2	72.2	27.8
	II.	68.5	31.5	77.1	22.9	65.4	34.6	73.6	26.4
VI. Command over agricultural inputs	I.	0.0	0.0	0.0	0.0	53.8	46.2	0.0	0.0
	II.	88.0	12.0	61.0	39.0	58.1	41.9	79.3	21.0
VII. Level of accessibility to agricultural extension training	I.	79.3	20.7	80.0	20.0	82.3	17.7	76.8	23.2
	II.	0.0	0.0	0.0	0.0	19.4	80.6	50.0	50.0
VIII. Access to credit	I.	84.8	15.2	83.5	16.5	74.6	25.4	83.5	16.5
	II.	0.0	0.0	21.4	78.6	84.2	15.8	37.5	62.5
IX. Respondent woman's contact with the family	I.	81.4	18.6	83.0	17.0	73.3	26.7	63.6	36.6
	II.	50.0	50.0	43.8	56.2	81.5	18.5	84.0	16.0

We shall now present deprivation caste-wise by sub-categorizing the women in terms of the existing status enjoyed by them in Table 3.

It could be observed from Table-3 that incidence of deprivation of women in respect of basic needs as well as control over resources in terms of perceived economic status at the bottom level was high among scheduled caste women. Similarly it remind relatively high for those scheduled caste women whose contribution to family cash income as well as level of education was low. Moreover, relatively large part of the deprived scheduled caste women were found engaged in arduous type of job. Among the deprived whose command over agricultural inputs as well as accountability to credit did not exist and who were found not to participate in agricultural extension training, the incidence of scheduled caste agrarian rural women was relatively high. It is also clearly visible that among the deprived women whose contact with the family was frequent, the incidence of deprivation among scheduled caste women was relatively high. Similarly, deprived women who were also found not to participate in women's SHGs, scheduled caste women had accounted for a larger proportion of deprived women. Moreover, the deprived women who were fond not to participate in decision-making affairs of the family, scheduled caste women constitute a substantial proportion of the deprived.

Our findings above would make it abundantly clear that among the deprived rural agricultural women, the incidence of deprivation such women in the scheduled caste community was relatively substantial, which in turn might call for taking a special attention to them for the amelioration of their socio-economic position.

Before we close this note it should be pointed out that there always remains a close interrelationship among the variables depicting the socio-economic and socio-cultural status of agrarian rural women. For example, level of education of the respondent might make her well conscious about the desirability of participation in a SHG. This participation in turn might allow her to contribute more to the family because of the income-generating effect of joining a SHG. Similarly, economically empowered woman might get freedom in respect of choosing a job conducive to her decent level of living as propounded by ILO in recent years. It is generally expected that a literate woman gets a larger scope for choosing job alternatives and her choice evidently would go for non-arduous type of work as referred to earlier. Similarly, frequent and close contact might help a woman to participate more actively in the decision-making.

The interrelationship existing among the variables to which we have referred to above points towards producing positive effects on each other. It should also be noted that a status showing poor level in terms of a particular index might be raised by another index elevating such status. Thus for a divorced women contact with the family might be non-existent, but she might participate in SHG which would eventually raise her level of income. She might be an illiterate, but could be quite articulate in speech and action. Eventually her access to credit, irrespective of the sources, would likely to be boosted up.

Taking into account of these interrelationships among the variables the differences existing in the deprivation of women in terms of each of the existing status enjoyed by the agrarian rural women are to be understood.

Another comment might be briefly added to this discussion. The variables which would likely to affect the status of agrarian rural women as well as their deprivation in respect of basic needs and control over resources would of course be depending on the socio-economic and socio-cultural factors for which some intervention of government as well non-governmental agencies might be called for. But the variables themselves could be controlled is the deprived women become more conscious about themselves. Thus a woman earner is taken as empowered, but in reality she may not be so if she is obliged to handover her entire earning to the male household. In this case what is required for the empowerment of such a woman is not simply her power to earn income. She should at the same time enjoy control over spending her income. The outside agency would fail to instill this willingness among the women until and unless the women themselves sincerely desire. This would necessarily call for an urgency for making agrarian women quite conscious about their deplorable socio-economic and socio-cultural status in their agrarian society. The urge to free oneself from the clutches of deprivation can be realized only when our agrarian rural women folk become well conscious through the spread of education among them. Will it be hard for a conscious woman then to become empowered ?

NOTES & REFERENCES

Agarwal, B. (1994), A Field of One's Own. *Gender and Land Rights in South Asia,* CUP, Cambridge.

Agarwal, Bina (2000), 'Gender Inequality– Some Critical Neglected Dimensions', presentation at the Symposium of the Governing Body of the ILO on *A Decent Work for Women,* Bureau for Gender Equality, ILO office, geneur, March 24.

Agarwal, Bina (2001), 'Land Rights and Gender Equity.' *Yojana,* Vol. -45

Banerjee, Nirmala, 'How Red is the Bogey of Feminisation?' *The Indian Journal of Labour Economics,* Vol. 40, No.1.

Rani, G.S. (2005), Micro credit for the Empowerment of Women' in *Economic Development Issues and Politics ed.* By *N. Narayan, Serials Publication,* New Delhi

Sharma, J.K. (2001), *"Rural Women," Rural Development in South Asia.*

Chakroborti, H.K. *et al* (2001), 'Impact of new Agricultural Technology on Economic Conditions of Agricultural Labourers. A Case Study of Two Villages of West Bengal; *Labour and Development,* Vol.8, No. 1 & 2 *Education, Employment and Empowerning Women,* ed. by A. Bhuimali.

Chakrabarti, H. K. (2002), " The Status of Rural Women".

Boserup, E. (1970), *Women's Role in Economic Development, Macmillan,* London.

Dyson and Moore (1983), 'On Kingship Structure, Female Autonomy and Demographic Behaviour in India', *Population and Development review,* Vol. 9(1).

Govt. of India (2000), 'Women and Entrepreneurship', *Yojana,* January.

Tisdell (2000), 'Asset- poor women in India and the relevance of Amartya Sen's Analysis', Artha Beekshamn: *Journal of the Bengal Economic Association,* Vol.8(2).

Tisdell, C. & R. Gopal (2005), "Economic, Social and Cultural Influences On The status and well being of Rural Women in India." *Economic Development Issues and Policies ed.* By N. Narayana.

Tisdell, C. and K.C. Roy (2000), The Socio-Economics, of and Gender Issues in Rural India, *Social Economics, Policy and Development,* No. 6, School of Economics, The University of Queensland.

Tisdell, C. *et.al* (2001), 'A critical Note on UNDP's Gender Inequality Indices', *Journal of Contemporary Asia,* Vol.31

4

INCOME INEQUALITY AND POVEPTY AMONG SCHEDULED CASTES AND SCHEDULED TRIBES IN SELECTED STATES IN INDIA

Maniklal Adhikary (Ph. D.)

INTRODUCTION

India being a large country-both by area and population, is the home of a very large number of communities. This accounts for India's diversity in ethnicity and culture. It is a common knowledge that some communities are still far behind other in various facets of life even by national standards. The human development indicators computed for different communities by NCAER (1999 and 2000) reveal notable disparity in quality of life among communities even after five decades of planning.

One of the major objectives of the government, reflected in various plan documents, has been to promote *economic growth with social justice* with a view to making the society more egalitarian. Both the central and state planning authorities have framed and implemented various policies for improvement of standards of living of Scheduled Castes (SC) and Scheduled Tribes (ST) who have historically been most backward classes. In order to evaluate the impact of National and State level development programmes, it is important that we obtain an accurate picture of standards of living of these less privileged social and ethnic groups. We believe that the development process for any society/ community is ultimately evaluated through its impact on quality of life and human well-being. Here we focus on the economic status of these backward communities using some standard measures of income inequality and poverty.

Conceivably, almost al types of deprivations initiate from lack of access to income necessary to maintain a minimum acceptable standard of living. UNDP would call this inadequate economic empowerment. However, the national and state average HDI, income inequality and poverty index figures mask much of the variations in empowerment across states and social groups. It is thus critical to observe the income inequality and poverty indices separately for SCs and STs to recognise the merits and limitations of planned development programmes aimed at improving the levels of living of these backward communities.

Apparently, household income is only an indispensable indicator of material well-being. An adequate household income is necessary though not sufficient to guarantee a reasonable quality of life. Higher the household income greater is the possibility of leading a decent life, implying a higher level of well-being. That is why a comparative analysis of earned income of households across communities is likely to unfold a few aspects of quality of life in relative terms.

The present study looks at the relative positions of SCs and STs *vis-a-vis* the rest of the population in terms poverty and income inequality. As we shall show in due course, the economic status of the said backward communities still remains miserably low in India even after 50 years of independence.

Some social scientists already have made rich contributions on the economic indicators of SCs and STs in India. Such works are generally based on data on consumption patterns for SCs and STs, collected and published by NSSO in its 28th and 32nd rounds. We mention three notable studies in this context. Kurien's (1982) study was entirely based on the findings of the 1971 Census. Occupation distribution/pattern of SCs *vis-a-vis* other segments of the population had been his principal focus. His observations on occupational distribution showed that 52 per cent of the working population among SCs comprise of agricultural labourers against only 26 per cent in the overall working population. It also reflected poor participation of SCs in specialised jobs both at the central and state levels. But his study does not deal with any of the poverty and inequality indicators. Nayak and Prasad (1984) examined the levels of living of SCs and STs *vis-a-vis* non-SCs/STs in Karnataka during 1973-78, based on the consumption data published by NSSO in its 28th and 32nd round. They also studied inequality in the levels of living of the SCs/STs and the non-SCs/STs over the same period without however computing the standard inequality measures. Disparities in education and occupational structure were also described.

Saggar and Pan (1994) computed the sophisticated inequality and poverty measures from NSS consumption data (38th round) for SCs, STs and others for four eastern states for the period 1982-83. Their study revealed that the eastern region as a whole suffered from economic backwardness and large incidences of poverty. This was more pronounced with SCs and STs. Interestingly, the inequality within SCs and STs was found to be lower than that observed within the non-SCs/STs.

Evidently, most of the studies conducted so far are generally based on secondary data. These studies have been conducted for different regions at different time points, which do not make the results comparable. Though important, the findings of these studies can be put only to some limited use. Moreover, none of these works are based on more recent post-liberalisation data.

Detailed and credible information on different aspects of human well-being are hard to obtain separately for SCs, STs and other social groups for the same point of time. The popular data sources like the National Population Census, the Sample Registration System, the National Simple Surveys, and the National Family Health Surveys among others, provide us with wide range of information that unfortunately are not always comparable. For instance, though the Census provides comprehensive information on demographic characteristics, it gives no information on income, asset holdings, and consumption patterns among other micro level economic indicators. Thus, the need was long felt for a multipurpose unified survey covering different facets of human well-being— standards of living, employment and wages, literacy and education, nutrition, fertility, morbidity and etc.

The National Council of Applied Economic Research (NCAER) took an extraordinary step in this direction. The NCAER (1999 and 2000) conducted a massive multipurpose survey covering 33,230 rural households in India between January and May 1994. This benchmark survey came to be popularly known as the

NCAER/HDI survey or simply the HDI survey. After five years of intensive data processing NCAER came up with a benchmark report in 1999 on India's human development related attainments and deprivation (NCAER, 1999).

The HDI survey was commissioned by the Planning Commission, Government of India and was funded, and supported by a consortium of United Nations and bilateral agencies like the United Nations Development Programme (UNDP), the United Nations Children's Fund (UNICEF), the United Nations Fund for Population Activities (UNFPA), the International Development Research Centre (IDRC), and the Canadian International Development Agency (CIDA). This overview is exclusively based on the findings of the 1994 HDI survey, published in benchmark survey report (NCAER, 2000).

Section 2 of this account describes objectives of the study, followed by methodology and data sources in section 3. Section 4 deals with results and discussions, and section 5 summarises the entire study.

OBJECTIVE

By and large, the objective of this production is to contrast the poverty and income inequality figures for SCs and STs *vis-a-vis* other groups in the population. We include some standard inequality and poverty measures computed from grouped income data for SC and ST households of nine major Indian states. The data for this study have been collected and compiled by NCAER (1999 and 2000) from its benchmark HDI survey of 1994. Comparisons are drawn between SCs, STs and other groups on the basis of the computed measures of poverty and inequality. Inter-state variations in poverty and inequality indices are also examined. We have not incorporated development indicators other than household income for this study. Admittedly, it makes this a very limited effort from the point of view of human well-being with all its variegated components. Had we incorporated other indicators of well-being – demographic, educational etc. and proceeded to compute the comprehensive HDI, we believe we would have lost much of the focus on poverty and income inequality in this presentation. Among the measures of inequality we include Gini coefficient or Gini measure, Theil's entropy measure and the squared coefficient of variation. Among the poverty indices we have considered the head count ratio, Sens index and Foster-Greer-Thorbeck index. The NCAER (1999 and 2000) results give us an opportunity for a credible comparative analysis of poverty and inequality among SCs, STs and others on more recent income rather than consumption data. All the results are based on grouped income data.

METHODOLOGY

1. Data Sources

This presentation is based on data collected from a rural sample of 33,230 households drawn from 16 states in a survey conducted between January and May 1994 by NCAER, better known as the benchmark NCAER/HDI survey. Out of the surveyed households, 7,943 were SC households and 4,220 were ST households. Based on an in-depth analysis of the data, NCAER (2000) published a comprehensive report covering the human development profile of SCs and STs in nine selected states out of those sixteen. These nine states together account for more than 75 per cent of India's SC/ST population. The nine selected states are Andhra Pradesh, Bihar, Gujarat, Madhya Pradesh, Maharashtra, Orissa, Tamil Nadu, Uttar Pradesh and West Bengal. The unit of the survey was household. Without going into the details of the sampling technique employed by NCAER we just mention that a stratified, multistage sampling procedure was adopted to identify the index household (NCAER, 1999). The report provides grouped income data for SCs and STs.

2. Measures of Inequality

Income inequalities in the nine selected states are calculated using three alternative measures of inequality, viz, Gini coefficient, Theil's entropy measure and the squared coefficient of variation. They satisfy the three desirable properties of a measure of inequality, viz., each measure is scale independent, population size independent and each follows the all important Pigou-Dalton condition— the inequality measure should rise if income transfer occurs from a poorer to a richer person, relative ranking remaining the same.

This study uses the geometric definition or the trapezoidal rule for grouped income data to compute the Gini coefficient. It can be derived from the general formula for grouped data given by,

$$G = \frac{1}{2}\sum_{i=1}^{n}\sum_{j=1}^{n} p_i p_j \left| \frac{y_i^{'}}{p_i} - \frac{y_j^{'}}{p_j} \right| \qquad (i)$$

where, $y_i^{'}$ is the income share of the ith income class only (not cumulative), p_i is the cumulative population proportion up to the ith income class, *i.e.*, proportion of persons with highest income of the ith class or less and *n* is the number of income classes. From formula (*i*), which uses the sum of weighted mutual differences, we can derive the trapezoidal rule (Kakwani, 1980) following some manipulation as under.

$$G = 1 - \sum_{i=1}^{n} p_i (Q_i + Q_{i-1}) \qquad (ii)$$

where, Q_i is the cumulative income share up to the ith income class, definition of P_i being the same. To compute *G*, using (*ii*), the data need to be arranged in ascending order of income classes. There are several alternative forms of computing *G* (Sen, 1973; Rao, 1981), but all these measures are equivalent to the geometric definition (Anand, 1980). By considering differences of all possible pairs of income proportions, the Gini coefficient avoids the total concentration on differences with respect to the mean, which the variance (*V*) and coefficient of variation (*C*) cannot. In avoiding the ad hoc *squaring* procedure of *C* and *V*, the Gini coefficient is a more direct measure of inequality taking note of differences between every income pair.

The term *entropy* is borrowed from thermodynamics. Entropy, in thermodynamics, implies increasing disorder. But here *entropy* is used to imply reduction in inequality rather than its converse. Theil goes on to define *entropy* as the expected information content in a particular situation. It implies the weighted average of information content of a situation where the weights are the respective probabilities. But apart from borrowing the term, Theil's entropy measure of inequality has hardly anything to do with the principle of thermodynamics. If *H*(*x*) denotes entropy, $h_i(x_i)$ the information content in the ith situation and X_i the probability that the ith situation will occur, then.

$$H(x) = \sum_{i=1}^{n} x_i h_i(x_i) \qquad (iii)$$

It has been assumed that $h_i(x_i) = \log \frac{1}{x_i}\cdot$ In other words, the more unlikely the event, the greater must be the information content in the situation. It implies that lower is the probability that the ith event will occur the higher the information content of the situation. Considering the ideal situation where probabilities of occurrence of all events are the same, *i.e.*, $x_i = \frac{1}{n}$, Theil's measure is expressed as $T = \text{Log } n - \text{H}(x)$

$$= \sum_{i=1}^{n} x_1 \log nx_i \qquad (iv)$$

Obviously, $\sum_{i=1}^{n} x_i = 1$. But for grouped income data, the following form is used to compute T.

$$T = \left\{\sum_{i=1}^{n}\left(\frac{Y_i}{Y}\right)T_i\right\} + \left\{\sum_{i=1}^{n}\left(\frac{Y_i}{Y}\right)\log(Y_i/Y)(n_i/n)\right\} \qquad (v)$$

where, Y_i denotes the mean income of the ith class, Y the mean of the entire population and T_i's are to be calculated for each class separately. The first term reflects the within group inequality, while the second term captures the between groups inequality. However, most studies use Theil's index to compute only the second term in (*v*).

The most rudimentary measure of inequality— variance, satisfies the Pigou-Dalton condition. But to get a clearer picture of relative variation we consider the squared coefficient of variation. It is simply $C^2 = \frac{V}{\mu^2}$, where V denotes the squared variance of grouped income data and μ is the mean income of the population. However, a major drawback of C^2 is that it attaches equal weights to income transfers from any level to all other income levels.

Both the coefficient of variation and the Gini coefficient satisfy the Pigou-Dalton condition, which requires that an income transfer from a richer person to a poorer person must reduce the value of the inequality measure. The coefficient of variation is equally sensitive at all income levels. But the sensitivity of Gini coefficient depends not on the size of income levels but on the number of people in between them. Sen (1973) provides a remarkable interpretation of the ungrouped variant of the Gini coefficient as presented in (i). He writes: "In any pair-wise comparison the man with the lower income can be thought to be suffering from some depression on finding his income to be lower. Let this depression be proportional to the difference in income. The sum total of all such depressions in all possible pair-wise comparisons takes us to the Gini coefficient."

3. Measures of Poverty

Among the standard measures of poverty we consider the Head Count Ratio (*H*), Sen's Poverty Index and the Foster-Greer-Thorbeck Index (*FGT*). We present a brief overview of these measures.

Let $y = (y_1, y_2, .., y_n)$ be a vector of incomes of *n* households arranged in increasing order, $z > 0$ the predetermined poverty line, $g_i = z - y_i$ the income shortfall of the ith household and *q* the number of poor households (having income less than or equal to *z*). It follows then that $H = \frac{q}{n}$ is the well-known head count ratio, which simply is the proportion of poor households. The Income-Gap ratio is $I = \frac{1}{qz}\sum_{1=1}^{q} g_i$. It merely expresses the total income gap (shortfall) of the poor as a proportion of the maximum total income of the poor. Sen's Poverty Index (1981) is given by $P = H\{I + 1 - I)\ G_p\}$, where G_p is the Gini coefficient among the poor. Sen's index, which is a ranked relative deprivation, satisfies both the monotonicity and weak-transfer axioms. According to Sen (*op cit*), these two axioms must be satisfied by any reasonable measure of poverty.

The monotonicity axiom states that other things unchanged a reduction in income of a household below the poverty line must raise the poverty measure. The weak transfer axiom says that a pure transfer of income to a poor household below the poverty line from a richer household, without making either cross the poverty line must reduce the poverty measure. Clearly, *H* violates both these axioms. I, on the other hand, satisfies the monotonicity axiom but violates the weak transfer axiom. But being a function of Gini coefficient among the poor, P is not additively decomposable across population sub-groups.

Following Sen (*op cit*), *FGT* index for ungrouped data expresses poverty as a normalized weighted sum of income shortfalls of poor.

For ungrouped data *FGT* index is written as $FGT = \frac{1}{nz^2}\sum_{i=1}^{q} g_i^2$. In contrast to P, which adopts a rank order weighted scheme, FGT takes the weights as the shortfalls themselves (Foster, Greer and Thorbeck, 1984). FGT index satisfies both the monotonicity and weak transfer axioms. In addition, it is additively decomposable over population subgroups. FGT index is associated with the squared coefficient of variation of income distribution among the poor. If the squared coefficient of variation among the poor is computed as $C_p^2 = \sum_{i=1}^{q}\left(\bar{y}_p - y_i\right)^2 /(q\bar{y}_p^2)$, where $\bar{y}_p = \sum_{i=1}^{q} y_i / q$ is the mean income of the poor, then the FGT index can be expressed as

$$FGT = H\,[I^2 + (1-I)^2 C_p^2\,] \qquad (v)$$

NCAER prefers (*v*) to compute the FGT index. These measures of poverty are consistent with Sen's (1973) focus axiom, which says that the poverty measure is entirely a characteristic of the poor and not of the general population. Specifically, if a poverty measure is invariant with respect to the incomes of the non-poor, then it is said to satisfy the focus axiom.

If asked, "How poor are the poor?" The head count ratio does not have an answer. The ratio merely gives the percentage of the population below the poverty line. It is thus a measure of the *incidence* of poverty showing just the number of poor rather than the intensity of their poverty. The answer is provided both by Sen and Foster-Greer-Thorbeck indices as both quantify the *intensity* of poverty among the poor. Stated differently, they denote the degree or the extent of poverty.

NCAER has estimated the mean income per person from the household survey data. They have also normalized the mean incomes of the poor (separately) by the state specific poverty lines to make these income figures comparable across states. For this purpose, the poverty line, estimated by the Planning Commission in 1973-74, has been updated using the state-specific Consumer Price Index for Agricultural Labourers. Mean income of the poor is normalized by simply dividing the mean income figures by the state specific poverty lines thus calculated. The mean income of the poor in normalized form indicates the proportion of the minimum basket of goods and services a typical poor can purchase if his income is equal to the mean income of the poor.

4. Results and Discussion

In Table 1 we present mean income per person (nominal per capita) in the entire sample as also the mean income (nominal as well as normalised) of the poor separately, across the nine selected states. The estimates for social groups – SCs, STs and others are also presented. Since the estimates relating to STs in Tamil Nadu are based on just six sample households they have been excluded (NCAER, op cit). STs in Tamil Nadu are not sizable – neither as a proportion of state population (1%), nor as a proportion of total ST population in the country (0.8%) [Population Census, 1991]. The reader may please note that the data for Bihar in this discourse refer to is for undivided Bihar where Jharkhand was a part of it. The creation of Jharkhand was based on the movement demanding a separate state for the indigenous tribal population (STs) of Chhotanagpur Plateau. This region, rich in mineral resources, contributed largely to erstwhile Bihar's state economy.

The per capita incomes of SCs and STs are lower *vis-a-vis* other social groups in all states. In particular, the gap in per capita income between SC/STs and non-SC/STs seems substantial for the richer states (in terms of per capita income) like Gujarat, Maharashtra, Andhra Pradesh and Tamil Nadu. Further, it is clear from Table 1. that the poorer states like Orissa, Bihar and West Bengal have a more egalitarian distribution of income; the reverse being true for all the richer states.

The general impression is that the per capita income of non-SC/STs is higher relative to SC/STs in all the states. Per capita income of STs is higher than that of SCs in Bihar, Gujarat, Maharashtra and UP; the SCs are ahead of STs in West Bengal,

Andhra Pradesh, Madhya Pradesh and Orissa (only marginally). STs dominate over SCs in per capita income in rural India, taken as a whole.

Table 1
Estimated Mean Income in Rural India by Social Groups Across States, 1994

States	*Nominal Mean Income of the Sample (Rs per person per annum)*			*Nominal Mean of the Poor (Rs per person per annum)*			*Normalised Mean Income of the Poor*[+]		
	SC	*ST*	*Others*	*SC*	*ST*	*Others*	*SC*	*ST*	*Others*
Andhra Pradesh	3756	3380	5552	1467	1440	1411	0.75	0.74	0.72
Bihar (undivided)	2773	3705	3971	1615	1535	1559	0.64	0.61	0.62
Gujarat	3534	3663	6371	1642	1522	1532	0.68	0.63	0.63
Maharashtra	3268	3560	6715	1607	1678	1729	0.69	0.72	0.74
Madhya Pradesh	3540	3212	4912	1643	1674	1717	0.71	0.72	0.74
Orissa	2520	2488	3444	1390	1370	1414	0.60	0.59	0.61
Tamil Nadu	3873	*	5772	1370	*	1646	0.58	*	0.69
Uttar Pradesh	3059	3293	4682	1459	1694	1520	0.57	0.66	0.59
West Bengal	3089	2166	3357	1656	1449	1708	0.63	0.55	0.65
Rural India	3298	3643	5088	1567	1600	1606	0.64	0.65	0.66

*Sample size is too small.
[+] Mean income is expressed as percentage of respective line.
Source: Compiled from 'Human Development Profile of Scheduled Castes and Scheduled Tribes in Rural India: A Benchmark Survey, NCAER (2000).

We now consider a state and community-wise ranking in terms of per capita income. In terms of per capita income of non-SC/STs, Maharashtra is at the top and West Bengal at the bottom. Among the SCs Andhra Pradesh tops the list in per capita income, Orissa is at the bottom. The STs of Bihar are far better off than the STs in any other state in per capita income. The STs of erstwhile Bihar, concentrated in Jharkhand area, are mostly engaged in mining and quarrying activities, providing them employment in the organized sector. Possibly the employers in these industries pay them in accordance with the norms set at the national level. The economic status of STs in West Bengal is most miserable. They, unlike their counterpart in Bihar, are engaged mostly in the unorganized sector, *viz.* landless agricultural labour, helpers in building and construction works and other labour intensive unskilled jobs. This perhaps explains their poor economic status in West Bengal.

Among the rural poor, income inequality appears marginal between all social groups across all states. This suggests that income inequality in India is more pronounced among those lying above the line of poverty than among those lying below the line. Further, normalised per capita incomes of the *poor* show smaller variation across social groups in all states, even though inter-state variations are obsrved. For instance, in rural Andhra Pradesh, a typical poor ST can afford to purchase only 74% of the minimum basket of goods and services necessary to keep him exactly on the line of poverty. The same figure is just 59% in Orissa and as low as 55% in West Bengal. In fact, the poor as a class are doing better in Andhra Pradesh than in most other states. A typical poor SC in West Bengal can however buy 63% of the minimum basket. Perhaps this shows substantial inequality between a typical poor SC and a ST with regard to standard of living or quality of life. In state and community-wise ranking, STs in West Bengal enjoying just 55% of the poverty income are at the bottom of the ladder, while SCs in Andhra Pradesh with 75% of the poverty income is ahead of others. Considering the nominal per capita income in the entire sample, rural West Bengal lies in the lowest income bracket.

Table 2
Estimated Income Inequality in Rural India by Social Groups Across States, 1994

	Gini Coefficient			*Theil's Entropy Measure*			C^2		
States	*SC*	*ST*	*Others*	*SC*	*ST*	*Others*	*SC*	*ST*	*Other*
Andhra Pradesh	0.3243	0.3030	0.4328	0.1728	0.1464	0.3222	0.3898	0.3051	0.7489
Bihar (undivided)	0.3418	0.4392	0.3832	0.1999	0.3464	0.2483	0.4903	0.9327	0.5827
Gujarat	0.3747	0.4748	0.4663	0.2291	0.4422	0.3787	0.5242	1.3890	0.8466
Maharashtra	0.3813	0.4079	1.4214	0.2611	0.3061	0.3060	0.6948	0.8448	0.6474
Madhya Pradesh	0.4064	0.3625	0.4121	0.3008	0.2325	0.2889	0.8227	0.5983	0.6734
Orissa	0.4240	0.3984	0.4265	0.3434	0.2663	0.3039	1.0519	0.6428	0.7231
Tamil Nadu	0.4200	*	0.4147	0.2896	*	0.2921	0.6387	*	0.6120
Uttar Pradesh	0.3930	0.3932	0.4269	0.2665	0.2782	0.3063	0.6605	0.6890	0.6939
West Bengal	0.3791	0.3385	0.3493	0.2723	0.1988	0.2068	0.7746	0.4675	0.4966
Rural India	0.3896	0.4191	0.4296	0.2619	0.3071	0.3136	0.6556	0.7856	0.7186

* Sample size is too small.
Source: Compiled from 'Human Development Profile of Scheduled Castes and Scheduled Tribes in Rural India :
A Benchmark Survey', NCAER (2000).

Table 2 presents the income inequality measures as estimated by NCAER (2000). A general pattern emerges from the inequality estimates. The distribution of income in the poorer states (West Bengal, Orissa, Bihar and U.P.) is more egalitarian in character than those in the richer states irrespective of the measure of inequality chosen. The non-SC/STs exhibit more unequal distribution of income the SC/STs in most states. Saggar and Pan (1994) also made a similar observation. Actually, those belonging to SCs and STs have a lower per capita income; while among others there are rich as well as poor households leading to a greater income inequality. Among SCs and STs, income distribution is more unequal among STs of Bihar, Gujarat and West Bengal and among SCs of Tamil Nadu, Orissa and Madhya Pradesh.

In the context of judging well-being on the basis of household income, the single most discussed issue is income poverty. India, it must be remembered, is the home of a very large number of the world's poor. Usually the income or consumption levels identify the poor. A variety of criteria suggested and used for such purposes have proved to be confusing and even controversial. Attempting to solve the problem, the Planning Commission appointed an expert committee, which submitted its report way back in 1993 (Govt. of India, 1993). Yet, the issue is still unresolved (NCAER, 1999 and 2000). All the poverty line estimates arrived at so far has its advantages as well as limitations making the choice a difficult one. NCAER has however opted for an easy way out. They have chosen the 1973-74 official rural poverty line (a per capita consumption of Rs 49.09 per month), estimated by the Planning Commission, for their HDI analysis. This figure was then updated using the state-wise Consumer Price Index for Agricultural Labourers (CPIAL). For the rural poor, consumption and income have a very close resemblance – the precise reason why NCAER has considered the poverty line based on poverty level consumption to identify the poor. This discussion uses the NCAER poverty estimates based on this measure of the poverty line. The choice of the poverty line is unlikely to change the estimates of poverty by any substantial amount provided the variation between the poverty lines selected is a small one.

The three different measures of poverty, computed from HDI survey data, are presented in Table 3. The head count ratio is about 50% both among SCs and STs in rural India. However, the ratio for non-SC/STs is 33%. In a broad sense, it implies that the incidence of poverty among SCs and STs is good deal higher compared to other social groups. Thus, every alternate person among SC/STs is a poor, while every third person, not belonging to SC/STs, is poor. By head count, the poorest state is Orissa where roughly 65% of SC/STs are poor. Next to Orissa, poverty is severe for all the three population subgroups in Madhya Pradesh and West Bengal. By head count, poverty among STs is most severe in West Bengal and least in Andhra Pradesh. The gap between SC/STs and others is strikingly high in the states of Maharashtra, Gujarat, Bihar, Madhya Pradesh and Uttar Pradesh. So, it can safely be inferred from the comparisons of head count ratio, both state-wise and rural India taken as a whole, that incidence of poverty among SC/STs is far greater *vis-a-vis* other social groups.

Table 3
Estimated Poverty Parameters in Rural India by Social Groups Across States, 1994@

States	*Head Count Ratio*			*Sen Index*			*FGT Index*		
	SC	*ST*	*Others*	*SC*	*ST*	*Others*	*SC*	*ST*	*Others*
Andhra Pradesh	0.2210	0.2872	0.2017	0.0769	0.0987	0.0765	0.0221	0.0217	0.0231
	(1)	(1)	(1)	(1)	(1)	(1)	(1)	(1)	(1)
Bihar (undivided)	0.5905	0.4908	0.3679	0.2790	0.2537	0.1862	0.1013	0.1002	0.0723
	(8)	(2)	(7)	(7)	(4)	(6)	(7)	(4)	(6)
Gujarat	0.4780	0.5366	0.2992	0.2049	0.2687	0.1484	0.0679	0.1030	0.0566
	(3)	(5)	(3)	(3)	(6)	(5)	(3)	(5)	(5)
Maharashtra	0.4991	0.5170	0.2519	0.2146	0.2017	0.0950	0.0716	0.0614	0.0287
	(4)	(4)	(2)	(4)	(3)	(2)	(4)	(2)	(2)
Madhya Pradesh	0.5003	0.5065	0.3250	0.2027	0.1993	0.1217	0.0641	0.0617	0.0364
	(5)	(3)	(5)	(2)	(2)	(3)	(2)	(3)	(3)
Orissa	0.6765	0.6449	0.4965	0.3652	0.3586	0.2636	0.1501	0.1516	0.1066
	(9)	(7)	(9)	(9)	(7)	(9)	(9)	(7)	(9)
Tamil Nadu	0.4103	*	0.3060	0.2303	*	0.1323	0.0982	*	0.0450
	(2)	(*)	(4)	(5)	(*)	(4)	(5)	(*)	(4)
Uttar Pradesh	0.5166	0.5545	0.3580	0.2899	0.2647	0.1901	0.1238	0.1038	0.0772
	(6)	(6)	(6)	(8)	(5)	(7)	(8)	(6)	(8)
West Bengal	0.5556	0.7193	0.4781	0.2676	0.4081	0.2163	0.0989	0.1782	0.0761
	(7)	(8)	(8)	(6)	(8)	(8)	(6)	(8)	(7)
Rural India	0.4994	0.4945	0.3322	0.2417	0.2314	0.1550	0.0897	0.0834	0.0558

@Figures in parentheses refer to the rank order of the states for each measure.
* Sample size is too small.
Source: Compiled from 'Human Development Profile of Scheduled Castes and Scheduled Tribes in Rural India : A Benchmark Survey', NCAER (2000)

From the state and community-wise comparison of poverty estimates using Sen index, it is clearly observed that the intensity of poverty among SC/STs is severe compared to that among other social groups. Intensity of poverty in Andhra Pradesh is minimum across all social groups both by Sen index; the intensity is highest in Orissa. The intensity of poverty among SCs (by Sen index) is alarmingly high in Orissa followed by U.P., Bihar and West Bengal. Somewhat different ranking of the states is observed for STs— West Bengal has the lowest rank preceded by Orissa, Gujarat and U.P. The pattern of ranking for non-SC/STs is similar to that observed for SCs. FGT index of poverty gives almost the same ranking of states across social groups as observed by using Sen index.

The general impression is that the lower the ranking of a state in terms of *incidence* of poverty, the lower is also its ranking in terms of *intensity* of poverty. That is, the three measures of poverty are closely related in the sense that the greater the *incidence* of poverty, the greater is its *intensity*.

SUMMARY AND CONCLUSIONS

This study focuses on the relative positions of SCs and STs *vis-a-vis* the rest of the population in terms poverty and income inequality. Some standard measures of poverty (head count ratio, Sen and FGT indices) and income inequality (Gini, Theil's entropy measure and the squared coefficient of variation) have been employed. The NCAER/HDI household survey conducted in 1994 covered 33,230 rural households in 16 different states. Among these, those nine states, which house more than 75 per cent of India's SC and ST population, have been selected for this study. We sum up our results below.

Income among SCs and STs is distributed around a lower mean and in a more egalitarian manner vis-a-vis income distribution among the non-SC/STs. Per capita income in rural India is clearly higher for non-SC/STs compared to that of SC/STs. But among the poor, mean income does not vary much across communities. Moreover it is generally seen that the income inequality is high in the richer states compared to that in the poorer ones. This is specifically true for the non-SC/STs.

In rural India, every alternate person among SCs and STs is poor while every third person not belonging to either SCs or STs is poor. Poverty is severe among all the three population groups in the states of Orissa, West Bengal, Bihar and Uttar Pradesh. The *incidence* and *intensity* of poverty are much higher among those belonging to the SCs and STs than that among others. The gap in terms of head count ratio between SC/STs and non-SC/STs is distinctly high in the states of Maharashtra, Gujarat, Bihar, Madhya Pradesh and Uttar Pradesh.

Finally, we observe that higher the incidence of poverty, the greater is its *intensity*. In other words, as the estimated indices show, the *incidence* and *intensity* of poverty are strongly positively correlated. This observation is based on sample data from only a few states, purposely selected to measure the incidence of poverty and its *intensity* among SCs and STs as against other social groups. Before claiming to call this relationship a general rule– *"the intensity of poverty rises as its incidence rises"*– we need to conduct similar studies on some of the other Indian states as well as on other poor nations.

REFERENCES

Anand, S. (1980), *Inequality and Poverty in Malaysia: Measurement and Decomposition*, Oxford University Press, London.

Chakrabarty, G. and P.K. Ghosh (2000), *Human Development Profile of Scheduled Castes and Scheduled Tribes in Rural India: A benchmark Survey*, NCAER, New Delhi.

Foster, J.,J. Green and E. Thorbeck (1984), 'A Class of Decomposable Poverty Measures.' *Econometrica*, Vol. 52, No. 3, pp 751-65.

Kakwani, N. (1980), *Income Inequality and Poverty— Methods of Estimation and Policy Applications*, Oxford University Press.

Kurien, C.T. (1982), 'Economic Conditions of Scheduled Castes', *Yojana*, October 16-31, pp 13-18.

Nayak, V. and S. Prased (1984), 'On levels of Living of Scheduled Castes and Scheduled Tribes', *Economic and Political Weekly*, July 28, pp 1205-1213.

Planning Commission (1993), *Report of the Expert Group on Estimation of Proportion and Number of Poor*, Perspective Planning Division, Govt. of India, New Delhi.

Rao, V.K.R.V. (1981), 'Measurement of Poverty', *Economic and Political Weekly*, Vol. XVI, No. 35, Aug 29, pp 1433-36.

Saggar, M and I. Pan (1994), 'SCs and STs in Eastern India, Inequality and Poverty Estimates' *Economic and Political Weekly*, March 5, pp 567-574.

Sen, A.K. (1973), *On Economic Inequality*, Oxford Clarendon Press.

Sen, A.K. (1981), *Poverty and Famines. An Essay on Entitlement and Deprivation*, Oxford University Press, New York.

Shariff, A (1999), *India Human Development Report*, NCAER, Oxford University Press, New Delhi.

5

GANDHI, JINNAH AND DR. BABA SAHEB AMBEDKAR: REFLECTIONS ON THEIR ROLE IN THE NATION-MAKING OF INDIA

Dr. I. Sarkar

India appears to be very much fortunate in producing at least three popular leaders namely, M.K. Gandhi, M.A. Jinnah and Dr. Baba Saheb Ambedkar. In fact, all these three sons of India faught against the British and various books and researches are at our disposal as to their contributions for our motherland. Gandhi made himself famous with his principle of Non-Violence while Jinnah not only organised the Indian Muslims against the British Raj but also took a vow to save the Indian Muslims from the tyranny of the upper caste Hindus. Incidentially, he has successful in his Two Nation Theory with the creation of Pakistan on the eve of Indian independence. The mission of Baba Saheb Ambedkar was not different from Gandhi and Jinnah in respect of fighting the british but in addition his excellency lies in his attempt to save the untouchables women and tribals from the age long exploitation and injustice prevailing in our Indian society. In this light, to quote a scholar, "Gandhi's struggle was one-fold, *i.e.* to fight the British; Jinnah's fight was two-fold, *i.e.,* to stand against the British and also to save the Muslims from the clutches of the upper caste Hindus. But Ambedkar's war which may be termed as crusade was manifold— he had to simutaneously fight the British, the caste system and the enemies with his own downtrodden community instigated by upper castes. Baba Saheb's revolution was thus socio-religions political one"[1]

It is not denying that India is now passing through a period of chasos and confusion and it seems that our country after more than 50 years of our independence is becoming ungovernable due to widespread terorism, violence and anarchy. But why this is happening and for what reason Indian people have become the loughing stock to the eyes of the world? It is perhaps a right moment to explore the forces behind such a situation and in this light to scan the contributions of these three national leaders viz. Gandhi, Jinnah and Ambedkar and to come to a conclusion as to what may be our duty to save our nation.

The first reaction that may hint one's mind is about Gandhi's won identity and how he wanted to change his social status in the Brahmamic dominated society. Although he all along stood for the interest of the *Banias* like Birlas the Tatas and the Gujrati mill owners,[2] still the Bania indentity was not acceptable to the Brahmin arthodoxy, because his own *Jati* indentity of *Vaisyas* or *Bania* was in the third grade in the so-called *Varna* ridden society of India. Naturally there was no chance of Gandhi to be recognised by the Brahmins. But the Brahmins had the calibre to utilise him to achieve their goal *i.e.* to free the country from the British and when Gandhi was successful in this objective he was brutally killed by a Brahmin in 1984. According to some: his death was due to his own misdeeds because he always tried to confound others.[3]

In this light it is pertinent to see what Gandhism as an ideology stands for? According to Ambedkar, "Gandhism is the philosophy of the well-to-do and the leisure class. It diluted people into accepting their misfortunes by presenting them as best of good fortunes, Gandhism seeks to perpetuate the system of scavenging as the noblest service to society. But these are evils that are deliberately imposed by one class over another."[4] If anybody tries to see the mission and design of Gandhi it appears that he was a man of different value where any man lest Ambedkar cannot comply with. Gandhi defended caste and his very name Gandhi was his Jati name. He not only stood for casteism but also strengthened the system and thereby defended the values of socalled caste ridden Hinduism. Gandhi could bear his Jati name and it is not a crime but the dangerous game he played was to include the non-Hindus, *i.e.* S.C./S.T. - B.C. of the Indian society comprising more than 65% of the Indian population into the fold of Hinduism. Over and above he gave them a lower status identifying them as the slaves of the upper castes. By doing this he wanted to serve two purposes (a) He enlarged the span of Hinduism from 15% to more than 80% of the population and thereby made Hinduism as the single largest religion of India. (b) He enslaved the 65% untouchables and pushed them to serve the upper caste Hindus as free servants. There is no example as such that a father of a nation might follow such a policy to enslave his countrymen. We do not know had Gandhi not come back from Africa and taken the leadership, there would have been a social revolution in India in respect of abolition of caste system. The policy of the British and the Western ideas that influenced the Indian society might have brought a natural death of this social stigma of India and this trend seems to have been checked by Gandhi because he not only stood on the way but all the more gave a new life to Hinduism based on caste system. Again he befooled the S.C./S.T./B.C. people by annexing them into the Hindu caste hierarchy and assigned them title like *Harijan* or *Sudra*. No matter he got it confirmed through the Puna Pact of 1932. As we know Dr. Ambedkar wanted a separate electorate which was accepted by the British Govt. and even Gandhi himself appreciated it at the Roundtable Conference. Having accepted it in London he went back on his word after returning back to India. Not only that he started a fast unto death" against the London agreement. Baba Saheb was forced to sign the pact which resulted in the enslavement of the dalits or the untouchables.[5]

At this juncture we may come down to the rise of Jinnah in Indian politics and what Congress and Gandhi had done behind such an occasion. In fact, Dr. Ambedkar was dead against partition and his point is clear from his lecture series at Wagle Hall Bombay in February, 1942. Here on his thoughts on Pakistan he wanted to explain "I have quarrelled with caste Hindus over some points but I take now before you that I shall lay down my life in defence of our land." Here we may recall that although he authored "Pakistan or the partition of India" with an intention to explain the scheme of Pakistan . On 26th October, 1946, he clarified his stand in London while he announced that "I am not in favour of partition in India, I think India should not be divided I try to say what I wanted to do in chapter." Must there be Pakistan But they take it as subordinate and give importance to other things. It is very bad. I am worried. It shows that Ambedkar gave a warning to all people concerned who were out for Pakistan or partition of India. But a common question arises who put Jinnah and his associates to stand for partition of India. It is curious that Jinnah who was an apostel of the Hindu-Muslim unity was turned into a staunch enemy of the Hindus. As a background it is said and quite rightly that, "It was imperialism of the upper caste people which forced him to give up secularism and seek solution in Muslim communalism".[6] How far this observation is correct is yet to decide but it appears to be convincing that Mahatma Gandhi stood for the rights and previlages of the *Banias* and the twice born and Jinnah apart from his mission of life worked for the Muslims. Babasaheb, on the otherhand, stood for all irrespective of caste, religion and faith. On this stand point he tried to convince Jinnah about the out come of partition and to solve problems of India by an united efforts of the Muslims and the lower classes of India. But it was of no use this difference with Gandhi was endless. For example, as he says." I admit I am opposed to Gandhi in politics. It is because I have no faith in Gandhi. I do not believe that Gandhi will do any good to the depressed classes. If Gandhi was sincere 'why should he not ask the premiers of central provinces and Bombay to include representatives of the depressed classes in their administration? The Congress Government of Bombay was not reducing the land revenue' nor was it prepared to tax the rich. The former government had recommended the grant of wastelands to the depressed classes for cultivation, recruitment of the depressed classes in the police services and a certain percentage of reservations in government departments for the depressed classes. But the Congress Government did not care for them.[7]

The insincerity of the Congress and Gandhi regarding the removal of untouchability was also a point of criticism by Dr. Ambedkar, Ambedkar condemned Gandhiji for his foul play to divide the Muslims and the untouchables. Dr. Ambedkar could realise this game and openly recorded how the Muslims refused to join Gandhi's comspiracy to cheat the dalits.[8] When Gandhi and his Congress were playing such an obnoxious game the fate of the Muslims of India was also to be determined. Ambedkar admits, "I do not think that demand for Pakistan is the result of mere political distemper, which will pass away with the effluse of time. As I read the situation, it seems to me that it is characteristic in the biological sense of the term, which the Muslim body politic has developed in the same manner as an organism develops a characteristic. Whether it will survive or not, in the process of natural selection, must depend upon the forces that may become operative in the struggle for existence between Hindus and Muslim. I am not staggered by Pakistan; I am not indignant about it, nor do I believe that it can be snatched by shooting into it, smiles and metaphors. I believe that it would be neither wise nor possible to reject summarily a scheme if it has behind it the sentiment, if not the passionate support of 90 per cent. Muslims of India. I have no doubt that the only proper attitude to Pakistan is to study it in all its aspects, to understand its implications and to form an intelligent judgement about it."[9]

How this statement was wise and practical can be testified by the then politics of India. What actually stands is that people like V.D. Savarkar or Gandhi did not try to study the real political situation of India. Nor did they try to study the Muslim sentiment of the then India.[10] It is said that V.D. Savarkar used to admit the Muslims as a separate nation but declined to comply with the claim of separate homeland for them. The Muslims demanded Pakistan with an excuse to create a monolitic state of the followers of Islam in order to escape from the tyranny of the Hindus and Central Government headed by them.[11] Ambedkar's view was that Hinduism was a menace to liberty, equality and fraternity, so it was dangerous for democracy. So, the crux of the question lies over there since a propaganda was made to establish a democracy in India after the British. But what would have been the nature of that democracy was not at all clear. Since in a democratic set up all category of people may have equal voice and rights. It should not be distorted by a *Hinduraj*. So Ambedkar had a clear point that *Hinduraj* should be prevented and on this cause the lower orders of the Hindu society would be ready to make common cause with the Muslims for achieving common ends. It should be directed against the high caste Hindus who have deprived them even ordinary human rights over the centuries.[12]

But the subsequent trend of Indian politics was such that nobody was ready to abide by the principles an advise for the interest of the country. The result was tension and Hindu Muslim riots and if properly scrutinised the situation was not better than a civil war between these two communities. Curiously enough Gandhiji, amidts all these, was advocating Hindu-Muslim unity. India got her independence but partition could not be avoided.

Jinnah achieved his desired goal with the formation of Pakistan. Gandhiji was fully utilised by the caste Hindus to the destination of India's independence. But what next? Gandhi was murdered in 1948 and he was an utter failure being victim of those who once became his friends and advisors. According to Ambedkar, "He (Gandhiji) was a man who had no mision, no knowledge, no judgement. He was a man who had been failure all his life in public life. There was no important occasion when India was about to succeed when Mr. Gandhi had brought anything good. When Jinnah raised his Pakistan issue, two or three years ago, Mr. Gandhi called it a sin and turned a deaf ear. Ultimately the Frankestein grew, Mr. Gandhi got frightened. He was grappling with it now making a complete somesault. Yet he continued to be the leader in this country, because the Congress did not put its leader in trial."[13]

The ultimate fate of Jinnah was not different from that of Gandhi. He achieved Pakistan but he could not ensure the protection and safeguard to the people of his own community. The emergence of Bangladesh fairly indicates the mistake he committed for the cause of saving the lot of Muslims from injustice. The condition of present day Pakistan is also not better being a country with having series of civil strifes. What may be the possible factors? What led the Pushtuns and the Baluch to organise separatist movement. These are, however, all termed as ethnonational movements which can be defined as ideological movements based on shared meanings of common descent. Real or imagined, that elite within the appropriate group formulate in order to mobilise political support for a variety of objectives ranging from autonomy to secession to staehood.[14] What kind of India we have got sofar,? Is it different from Pakistan? The ruling class of India has run out of all idea. And today not only its members are busy stabbing each other in the back but all of them are collectively suffering from a siege mentality. Who are responsible for these condition of these allegedly peaceful region of the world? Neither Gandhi and his followers nor Jinnah and his flatterers have been able to ensure peace and stability of these South-Asian countries. Once Dr. Ambedkar was out to formulate a process of Hindu-Muslim unity to save this country but it was foiled in the 1940s by the clique of the Brahmins.[15] Under this situation if India is to be saved there should be a repeatation of the call for Dalit Muslim unity which may be a powerful mechanism of political and social change.

Ambedkar believed without social and economic equality, political democracy will colapse.[16] Hindu religion, Ambedkar admits being based on caste system, is against democracy and fraternity. He also believed Brahmanism must die if democracy has to live. But it will be in no way against a Brahmin because the principle will be a crusade or a war against Brahminism— a socio-cultural system which is more dangerous than the Brahmins.[17] History has the record that for any social movement in India there was an organised effort to fight against or the system therefrom Brahminism and not the Brahmins as individuals in Indian Society. Vasavanna, Mahatma Phule, Sri Narayan Guru, Dr. B.R. Ambedkar, E.V.R. Lohia and so no.[18]

Dr. Ambedkar all along fought for this. His temperament is fairly reflected in the framing of our Constitution. We cannot forget how he donated the Constitution to knit all races of this country as a federation of general nations/races on the basis of equality and fraternity. In fact, this country, may be treated as a country as long as the constitution guides it. In other words, this country, may stand for its constitution. Dr. Ambedkar thus, can claim to be the Father of India as he happens to be the promoter of such a constitution. He is the saviour of Indian races called SC/ST/BCS, Dalit Muslim, Punjabis and Dalit Christians. In this sense, he is an international leader, and liberator much above all other pigmis. He being a, 'free man' formulated the universal principle of justice and emancipation of all nations or races in the world.

NOTES AND REFERENCES

An article entitled Gandhi, Jinnah and Dr. Ambedkar their role in History by Shankarananda Shastri, New Delhi, in Delhi, Voice (D.V) Vol. 7, July-16-31, 1988 No. 17, P.8

Did Gandhi fight the British and the Big business? in D.V. Vol. 8 May 1-15, 1989 No.12, PP. 3-5

V.T. Rajeshekar, why Godse Killed Gandhi? Dalit Sahitya Akademy.

Dr. B.R. Ambedkar, Congress and Gandhi PP. 280.

Dr. B.R. Ambedkar-Writing and Speeches Vol. XII, PP 737 – 38

Shankarananda Shastri, D.V. Vol. 7, July 16-31, 1988, No. 17 P8

D.r. B.R. Ambedkar, Gandhi and Gandhism. (Bhim Patrika Prakashan Nakodar Road, Jalandhar, Punjab) P. 14.

Dr. Babasaheb Ambedkar-Writings and Speeches Vol. V. 1989 P 323; Also see S.K. Biswas, Hindusraj, Today, Yesterday and Tomorrow, New Delhi 1996, P. 67

Ibid Vol. VIII, 1990 P.8

Dr. B.R. Ambedkar, Pakistan or Partition of India P. 133.

V.N. Kuber, Ambedkar: A critical Study, New Delhi 1991 P. 188

B.R. Ambedkar Pakistan or Partition of India P.358

B.R. Ambedkar Gandhi and Gandhism P. 24

For details see Tahir Amin, Ethno-National Movements of Pakistan (Domestic and International factors) Institute of policy studies Islamabad, 1988.

S.K. Biswas, The Hindu Raj Today Yesterday and Tomorrow. PP. 22 –24.

Dr. B.R. Ambedkar-Writings and Speeches Vol. X PP. 108

V.T. Rajshankar, "Why everybody attacks only Brahmins in D.V. March 16-13, 1995 No.9 P. 3

Ibid.

6

DEVELOPMENT AND EMPOWERMENT OF DISADVANTAGED PEOPLE OF INDIA

Dr. Anil Bhuimali

INTRODUCTION

Inequality among men, as Rousseau considered, is of two types. One type of inequality is established by nature. People have no control over this. This is called physical inequality. The other type is called political or moral inequality. Men solely create this. This is imposed by a group of people on the other group. The Indian society is based on the institution of caste with massive inequalities in social, economic and political spheres. This practice started for more than 3,000 years ago. The caste system is, in fact, a two-tier construction. We have upper caste (advantaged group) consisting of Brahmin, Kshatriya and Vaishya and lower caste (disadvantaged group) consisting of Sudra and Outcaste. The institution of caste had framed some laws and regulations, which in effect, alienated a vast section of the society from the mainstream. Social relationship was mostly governed by the divine superstition of rights. This is the root cause of social exploitation. The advantaged group enjoys rights and privileges more than its contributions to the society while the disadvantaged group has been denied these equal to its contributions. The Indian society was never in harmony and always experienced conflict of interests between different groups. The disadvantaged group wants to get more while the advantaged group prevents then from taking what is available.

The disadvantaged group was not allowed to follow the activities other than those prescribed by the institution of caste.

The status of this group in the society was very low the it had to perform activities that were servile in nature. It had no right to land, property, education and religious rituals. Naturally it was subjected to social, economic and cultural suppression and oppression. This has been continuing even today in one form or other. The division of the society, according to privileges enjoyed by the people, paints carefully the picture of social exploitation of disadvantaged group of people by the advantaged group of people.

The untouchable castes were listed in 1931 Census of India which was officially defined as deprived castes in 1932. The Simon Commission first created the expression "Scheduled Castes and Scheduled Tribes" and it was incorporated in the Government of India Act of 1935. Before 1935 they were known as untouchables depressed classes or exterior castes. The Government of India published a list of scheduled castes under the Government of India (Scheduled Caste) Order, 1936.

Since independence, the Government of India has been providing some constitutional safeguard to the people who are economically, socially and culturally backward. The objective of such a policy is to benefit the weaker sections of the society. The Central and the State Governments have administered this benefit. The policy package consists of a set of goals. In the first place, it tries to remove social and religious inabilities of the lower caste. Secondly, it provides facilities in education, employment, parliament, state legislators and local bodies and finally, the policy safeguards the deprived class from all sorts of social injustice and exploitation.

Some benefits are provided to the lower caste (especially the scheduled castes and scheduled tribes) in the fields of education and occupation. As a result, many deprived people have enjoyed educational, administrative and other benefits and sought employment opportunities. A section of them has been in a position to seek entry in urban occupation. Naturally a change in the life pattern has been noticed. This section in particular has been enjoying benefits for about fifty-five years since independence and a legislation extending reservation for a further ten-year period beyond 2001, has been enacted. The people at the lowest, strata *i.e.* people living below the poverty line are not in position to avail the opportunity provided by the Central and State Governments through reservation package. Most of them live in the rural areas and slums. They are not only poor but they suffer from a number of socio-economic bottlenecks. It is obvious that the course of economic development will not reach to them unless the institutional barriers and handicaps from which they suffer are removed. For the development of the tribal people the Government of India formulated and implemented Tribal Sub. Plan approach in the fifth five-year plan (1974-1979). The main objective of such a policy was the opening of the inaccessible forest areas in which tribal people live and bring them in contact with mainstream of national life. On the other hand, the Government adopted Special Component Plan for the development of the scheduled castes in sixth five-year plan (1980-85). These programmes are meant for their socio-economic development.

OBJECTIVE OF THE STUDY

In the past the upper cast was given right to education, assets, weapon and so on. These accumulated capital over a period of time and improved the volume of every individual's human capital. This was denied to the lower caste. Accumulation of capital and hence the development of human capital by the advantaged group empowered every member of this group. This group played the role of arbiter and enjoyed the patronage of pre-British and British rulers. After independence the upper caste with educated and skilled manpower controlled the activities of the economy. Jatirao Phooley, A.B. Latthe, B.R. Ambedkar and some other benevolent social reformers started organising the people of the disadvantaged group. They thought that development and empowerment largely depended on the involvement of every member in education, employment and representation in political bodies.

The main purpose of this paper is to investigate the development and empowerment of the disadvantaged group especially the scheduled castes and scheduled tribes who, at present, constitute for about 25 per cent of the total population, on the basis of their performance in education, employment and representation in political bodies. The prospects of their development and empowerment will also be studied in the context of liberalisation policy of the Government. We will also make a comment on the existing reservation policy at the end. For this purpose data from secondary sources such as books, journals, Government reports and documents have been gathered.

ATTAINMENT OF EDUCATION

Education is a first step in developing human capital and capability. The lower caste people had no right to education for centuries. The British rulers introduced the present form of education. The purpose of spreading education among the Indians was very limited. The upper caste, with the help of its resource-base, adopted Western education. Naturally a new educated class came up in the Indian society.

Moved by the Western education some benevolent personalities like Ram Mohân Roy, Iswer Chandra Vidyasagar and some Christian missionaries came forward for spreading up of education. Two eminent lower caste social reformers, among others, dedicated their lives to the cause of the depressed caste. They were Jotirao Phooley and B.R. Ambedkar. Phooley was a man of Mali caste. The people under this category traditionally engage in gardening occupation. He was a man of determination. He realised the necessity of educating the disadvantaged people. He set up schools for lower caste boys and girls in the late forties and early fifties of the last century. Poona was birthplace. He formed "Satya Shodhak Samaj". The main purpose of such an association was to assert the worth of man of any caste.

After Phooley, B.R. Ambedkar was a dynamic and well educated leader of the depressed caste people who fought throughout his life for the development of the untrodden people. He belonged to Mahar community. He had a belief that upward mobility of the lower caste people largely depended on education. He thus founded educational institutions in Bombay and Aurangabad in mid forties of the last century especially for the under-privileged sections of the society under the patronage of People's Education Society.

The Constitution of India provides some educational benefits to the lower caste people especially the scheduled castes and scheduled tribes for upward mobility in the society. We have completed fifty three years of Indian republic. But our Government intentionally neglected the vital issue for providing free and compulsory education to all children up to the age of 14 years. According to recent estimate by a group of experts, for about 10 crore children in the age group of 5 to 14 years do not attend school and major percentage of them work as child labour. We can expect actual development of a child only when he or she is educated. It is education that is capable of providing every child with the right to grow up with dignity. Without right to education, the right to equality and hence the attainment of an egalitarian society is a farce. Mere legal provisions will not ensure complete literacy unless there is proper implementation of schemes with active participation of all sections of the society. The education development can be discussed with the help of literacy rate, gap between rest of the population and scheduled castes and schedule tribes and enrolment at various levels.

The literacy rates of scheduled castes and scheduled tribes and the rest of the population is shown in terms of table1.

Table 1
Literacy Rate of Scheduled Castes and Scheduled Tribes

Year	*Scheduled Castes*	*Scheduled Tribes*	*Rest of the population*
1961	10.27	8.53	27.86
1971	14.67	11.30	33.80
1981	21.38	16.35	41.22
1991	37.41	29.60	52.21

Source: Censusis of India 1961, 1971, 1981, 1991.

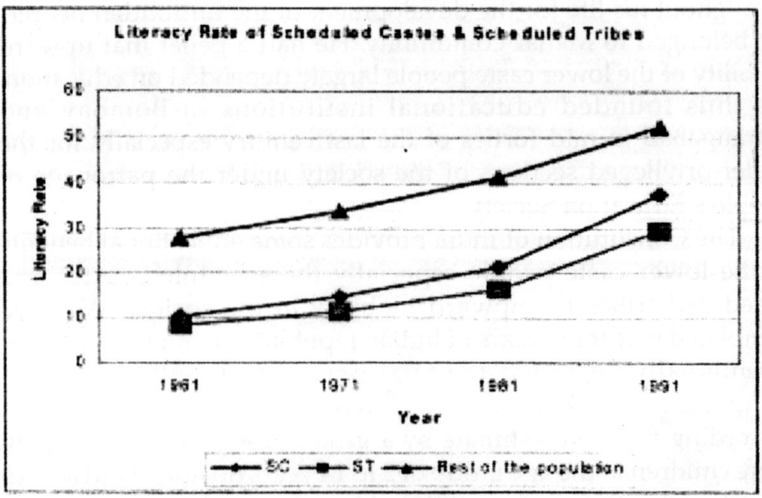

Table 1 shows that scheduled castes and scheduled tribes are far behind compared to the rest of the population in respect of literacy rate. The 2001 Census [provisional] does not have separate accounts of scheduled castes and scheduled tribes and for that we cannot make a comparison of literacy rate between the scheduled castes and tribes and the rest of the population. Difference in literacy rates between the rest of the population and scheduled castes and scheduled tribes is shown in Table 2.

Table 2
Difference in Literacy Rates between Rest of the Population and Scheduled Castes and Scheduled Tribes

Year	*Difference*	
	Scheduled Castes	*Scheduled Tribes*
1961	17.59	19.33
1971	19.13	22.50
1981	19.84	24.87
1991	17.20	25.01

Source: Censuses of India 1961, 1971, 1981, 1991.

From Tables 1 and 2 it is clear that some developments have been noticed in the literacy rate of scheduled castes and scheduled tribes. But the fact is that their relative backwardness in education still remains. Table 2 shows that the difference in literacy rate between scheduled castes and the rest of the population was 17.59 per cent in 1961. It rose to 19.13 and 19.84 per cent in 1971 and 1981 respectively but went down to 17.20 per cent in 1991. This difference between scheduled tribes and the rest of the population increased in thirty years. It was 19.33 per cent in 1961. In 1991 it rose to 25.01 per cent. The data presented here show a dismal picture of the improvement in literacy among the disadvantaged people.

The literacy rate of some states of India has been presented in table 3 to grasp the educational development pattern of scheduled castes and scheduled tribes people and total population in general.

From Table 3 it is clear that some states have made stride in literacy rate. Among them are Mizoram, Kerala, Goa, Himachal Pradesh, Gujarat, Manipur, Assam and Arunachal Pradesh. Bihar's position is the worst. Literacy rate among the scheduled castes and scheduled tribes is not good in states like Uttar Pradesh, Madhya Pradesh, Rajasthan and West Bengal. Male literacy is worst in Bihar and female literacy is worst in Rajasthan.

We notice another interesting variation in educational development among scheduled castes people in urban and rural areas. Table 4 shows that scheduled caste people living in the urban areas are able to avail better education facilities. This is reflected in the development of literacy rate. This mainly is due to the fact that those employed in white collar jobs settle in the urban areas to take benefits of infrastructural and other facilities for development. On the other hand, a section of the scheduled castes people living in the rural areas are not in a position to take advantage from modern amenities like education, health, communication, information and other facilities. Table 4 also shows that literacy rate among women in general and scheduled castes women in particular are lower than the male literacy rate. Also there are wide variations across regions, states, castes, classes and sexes. The female literacy rate among scheduled castes community is higher both in urban and rural areas in Kerala and Mizoram. In Kerala-Urban and rural women literacy rate is 79.60 and 73.09 per cent respectively and in Mizoram it is 75 and 85 per cent respectively. This is deplorable in Rajasthan, Bihar and Uttar Pradesh. Madhya Pradesh is also lagging behind.

Table 3

Literacy Rate of Some States of India

States	*Literacy Rate in General*			*Literacy Rate Among Scheduled Castes and Schedule Tribes*	
	Persons	*Males*	*Females*	*Scheduled Castes*	*Scheduled Tribes*
Kerala	89.8	93.6	86.2	80.0	57.0
Mizoram	82.3	85.6	78.6	78.0	83.0
Goa	75.5	83.6	67.1	59.0	43.0
Maharashtra	64.9	76.6	52.3	56.0	37.0
Himachal Pradesh	63.9	75.4	52.1	53.0	47.0
Tamil Nadu	62.7	73.7	51.3	47.0	28.0
Gujarat	61.3	73.1	48.6	61.0	36.0
Tripura	60.4	70.6	49.6	57.0	40.0
Manipur	59.9	71.6	47.6	56.0	54.0
West Bengal	57.7	67.8	46.6	42.0	28.0
Assam	52.9	61.9	43.0	54.0	49.0
Meghalaya	49.1	53.1	44.9	44.0	47.0
Madhya Pradesh	44.2	58.4	28.8	35.0	22.0
Arunachal Pradesh	41.6	51.5	29.7	57.0	34.0
Uttar Pradesh	41.6	55.7	25.3	27.0	36.0
Rajasthan	38.6	55.0	20.4	26.0	19.0
Bihar	38.5	52.5	22.9	20.0	27.0

Source: Completed from Census of India, 1991.

Tables 5 and 6 represent enrolment of scheduled caste students from standards 1 to 12 and at various levels of higher education at an all-India level. Table-5 shows that enrolment of scheduled castes students is very poor. Enrolment decreases with the increase in the educational level.

Table 4

Literacy Rate among the Scheduled Castes Population in the Urban and Rural Areas of Some States

States	*Among the Total Scheduled Castes Population*			*Among the Urban Scheduled Castes Population*			*Among the Rural Scheduled Castes Population*		
	Persons	*Male*	*Female*	*Persons*	*Male*	*Female*	*Persons*	*Male*	*Female*
Kerala	79.66	85.22	74.31	84.47	89.56	79.60	78.55	84.22	73.09
Mizoram	77.92	77.54	81.25	82.30	83.24	75.00	75.76	74.81	85.00
Goa	58.73	69.55	47.51	61.76	71.69	51.53	56.05	67.67	43.94
Maharashtra	56.46	70.45	41.59	67.07	78.17	54.94	50.27	65.86	33.99
Himachal Pradesh	53.20	64.98	41.02	70.32	78.87	60.16	52.00	63.95	39.78
Tamil Nadu	46.74	58.36	34.89	62.24	72.58	51.68	42.50	54.47	30.30
Gujarat	61.07	75.47	45.54	70.06	82.35	56.53	55.59	71.21	38.96
Tripura	56.66	67.25	45.45	64.06	73.43	54.40	55.24	66.07	43.69
Manipur	56.44	65.28	47.41	56.22	65.14	47.32	56.69	65.43	47.52
West Bengal	42.21	54.55	28.87	53.98	63.90	42.71	39.98	52.72	26.32
Assam	53.94	63.88	42.99	65.71	73.72	56.66	51.95	62.19	40.72
Meghalaya	44.27	54.56	31.19	53.05	63.34	39.70	37.11	47.28	24.35
Madhya Pradesh	35.08	50.51	18.11	52.26	67.29	35.38	30.22	45.70	13.30
Arunachal Pradesh	57.27	66.25	41.42	61.99	69.39	50.40	55.29	65.02	37.25
Uttar Pradesh	26.85	40.80	10.69	42.30	54.79	27.36	24.76	38.87	8.47
Rajasthan	26.29	42.38	8.31	43.35	61.37	22.88	22.06	37.63	4.73
Bihar	19.49	30.64	7.07	39.23	52.74	22.90	17.49	28.30	5.54
India Total	37.41	49.91	23.76	55.11	66.60	42.29	33.25	45.93	19.46

Source: Compiled from Census of India 1991

Table 5

Enrolment of Total and Scheduled Castes Students for 1985-86

Standard	*Total Students (Number)*	*Total Scheduled Castes Students (Number)*	*Castes (Scheduled) Students in %*
1 – 5	8,64,65,189	1,39,21,021	16.10
6 – 8	2,81,24,756	36,18,840	12.87
9 – 10	1,16,17,262	1,96,712	1.69
11 – 12	34,88,672	64,192	1.84

Source: India, 1984-86

Literacy Rate of Some States of India

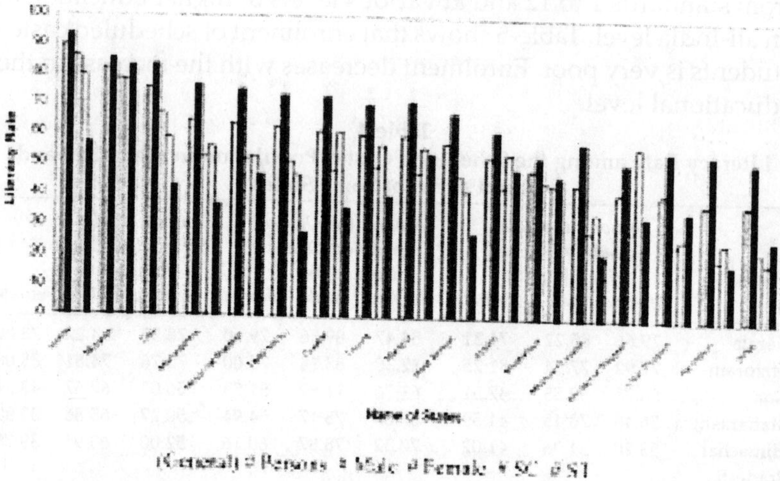

Table 6

Enrolment of Scheduled Castes Students at Various Levels of Higher Education at an All India Level (as on March 1, 1992)

Course	*Boys*	*Percentage*	*Girls*	*Percentage*	*Total*	*Percentage*
Ph.D./D.Sc./D.Phil.	724	0.0001	208	0.28	932	0.28
Post-Graduation (MA, M.Sc. M.Com.)	27341	10.59	6,494	8.87	33,835	10.20
Undergraduation (General)	2,07,799	80.46	60,943	80.30	2,68,742	81.09
Undegraduation (Enginering, Medicine & Education)	22,371	8.66	5,515	7.53	27.886	8.41
Total	2,58,235	100	73,160	100.00	3,31,395	100.00

Source: India, 1993.

Table 6 shows that only a very small percentage of scheduled caste students pursue doctoral, post-Graduation and professional studies.

Enrolment of students by institutions, gender and scheduled castes and scheduled tribes in West Bengal is shown in terms of Table 7.

Table 8 shows post-Matric scholarships for scheduled castes during 1994-95. This shows that some states have enjoyed post-Matric scholarships in excess of their percentage in the scheduled caste population of India. As a result of this some states like Kerala, Maharashtra and Gujarat have enjoyed privileges over some states like Bihar, Orissa and Rajasthan.

Table 7
Enrolment of Students by Institutions, Gender and Scheduled Castes and Scheduled Tribes for 1998-99
(Data Received for 279 out of 390 Institutions)

	Boys				*Girls*				
Institutions	*General*	*S.C*	*S.T.*	*Total*	*General*	*S.C.*	*S.T.*	*Total*	*Total*
University	1784	326	29	2139	1280	173	3	1456	3595
General Degree College	188395	36677	4439	229511	137388	19316	2596	15930	388811
Educational College	1429	521	116	2066	769	92	65	926	2992
Technical College	2321	357	56	2734	169	30	5	204	2935
Law College	17	0	0	17	17	0	0	17	34
Music & Fine Arts college	401	76	6	483	320	33	0	353	836
Physical Education College	44	32	2	78	36	30	1	67	145
Other Institute /college	53	0	0	53	22	0	0	22	75
Total	194816	38096	4649	237561	140032	19687	2670	162389	399950

Source: Annual Report of the Department of Higher Education, Government of West Bengal,1998-99.

EMPLOYMENT

In the pre-British period lower castes people comprising of Sudra and out-caste were prevented from acquiring education, non-polluted work and were excluded from temples, bathing ghats, wells and public places. Naturally, the process of upward mobility among them was slow and gradual. During the British period the country was in a transition stage. It was passing from the laws of custom to the rule of competition. The Britishers, for the first time, introduced the principle of equality before the law. Thus restrictions previously imposed on the lower castes people had been removed.

Since independence a section of the lower castes people have benefited from welfare programmes and education. They are able to utilize the benefit of improved technology. Employment generates income and income is an important means that is used to enhance well-being of the individual. Modern white-collar job is based on the development of education and knowledge. Disadvantaged group of people has employment opportunities because of the special constitutional provisions. Like education, employment empowers and through empowerment education and hence employment affect larger social processes. Employment of lower caste people (scheduled castes and scheduled tribes) in Central Government services and public sector undertakings is shown in term of tables 9 and 10.

Table 8
Post-Matric Scholarships for Scheduled Castes during 1994-95

State	*No. of Beneficiaries*	*Percentage to Total Awardees*	*Percentage of Scheduled Castes to Total Population*
Kerala	45090	3.36	2.40
Mizoram	Not available	Not available	Not available
Goa	130	0.01	0.02
Maharashtra	187708	14.02	4.30
Himachal Pradesh	2678	0.22	1.00
Tamil Nadu	118250	8.83	8.40
Gujarat	66871	4.99	2.30
Tripura	3174	0.38	0.30
Manipur	755	0.05	0.02
West Bengal	85610	6.39	11.50
Assam	41453	3.09	Not available
Meghalaya	124	0.01	0.01
Madhya Pradesh	77097	5.76	7.00
Arunachal Pradesh	132380	9.89	7.60
Uttar Pradesh	243826	18.21	22.40
Rajasthan	32744	2.44	5.60

Source: Compiled form Annual Report of the Ministry of Social Welfare, Government of India, 1994-95.

Table 9
Employment of Scheduled Castes and Scheduled Tribes in Central Government Services

Category	Scheduled Castes (%) 1971	1991	Scheduled Tribe (%) 1971	1991
Class-I	2.58	9.09	0.41	2.53
Class-II	4.06	11.82	0.43	2.35
Class-III	9.59	15.65	1.70	4.98
Class-IV (Excluding sweepers)	10.37	21.24	3.65	6.82

Source: Eighth Five Year Plan, 1990.

The employment of scheduled castes and scheduled tribes in Central Government services and public sector undertakings is not in line with their percentage in the total population. Their employment in Group-A and Group-B services is not satisfactory at all. This is shown in Table 11.

Table 10
Employment of Scheduled Castes and Scheduled Tribes in Public Sector Undertaking (%)

Category	Scheduled Castes 1971	1989	Scheduled Tribes 1971	1989
Class I	0.52	5.76	0.17	1.29
Class-II	1.54	8.41	0.16	2.31
All categories	8.17	20.36	2.24	9.68

Source: Eighth Five Year Plan, 1990.

Table 11
State-wise Representation of Scheduled Castes and Scheduled Tribes in Group A and Group B Services, 1986-87.

State	Reservation Prescribed (%)		Actual Employment (%) Group A		Group B	
	SC	ST	SC	ST	SC	ST
Himachal Pradesh	15	7.5	5.40	3.90	7.80	3.70
Madhya Pradesh	15	18	2.13	1.94	5.31	2.44
Orissa	15	23	1.41	0.88	2.87	1.56
West Bengal	15	05	4.63	0.92	6.01	0.82
Maharashtra	13	07	6.90	2.29	7.91	2.28
Gujarat	07	14	9.64	5.91	11.49	4.00
Karnataka	15	03	12.23	1.79	8.06	1.49
Andhra Pradesh	15	06	3.99	0.70	5.52	0.80

Source: Complied from the Report of the Commissioner for Scheduled Castes and Scheduled Tribes, 1986-87.

Employment of Scheduled Castes in academic and ministerial posts in universities is shown in Table 12.

Table 12
Scheduled Castes Representation in 41 Indian Universities and Ministerial Posts

Categories *Teaching Posts*	*Total*	*Scheduled Castes*	*Percentage*
Professors	2133	13	0.61
Readers/Associate Professors	3261	34	1.04
Lecturers	5341	169	3.16
Research Associates	674	71	10.53
Ministerial Posts			
Group – A	3525	118	3.35
Group – B	4833	221	4.57
Group – C	14811	1686	8.51
Group – D	17607	2628	14.93

Source: India, 1985-86

As per table 12 the representation of scheduled castes people in Universities (both teaching and non-teaching) is discouraging. Many reasons can be offered for this marginal representation. In the first place, Universities are autonomous and not under the direct control of State and Central Governments. University authorities thus do not always obey Government rules and regulation. Secondly, the selection committees very often do not favour the scheduled caste candidates considering that the quality of teaching may go down as most of them lack skills. Recent experience shows that reserved category candidates are not selected if they are not at per with the general category candidates. As a result many reserved posts are lying vacant for a long period of time (in some cases 10 years or more). This is particularly noticed in services in schools, colleges, universities and research institutes. The same is true for Central Government jobs. It might be the fact that students from disadvantaged group (Scheduled Castes, Scheduled Tribes and Other Backward. It is difficult for them to be at par with general category students.

We have liberalised our economy and the process of liberalisation began in 1991. The new economic policy believes in the laissez faire policy. The new economic policy advocates that there should be no control from the part of the Government. A section of the society who is out of the reservation basket is of the opinion that at this age of liberalisation, privatisation and globalisation there should be no special protection to the lower caste people especially the scheduled castes, scheduled tribes and other backward castes in education, employment and political bodies. They also argue that reservation policy may not improve the social, economic and political development of disadvantaged group of people and would maintain their backwardness by taking away the entire urge for competition. The fruit of the new economic policy will not reach to the disadvantaged group especially the least-privileged people living in the rural and slum areas. This policy will not create opportunities in public and private sector for the disadvantaged group of people. We apprehend the new economic policy will only benefit people living in the metropolis and urban areas. The disadvantaged group of people cannot influence market forces. Therefore, they cannot be the gainers of the globalisation, liberalisation and privatisation. They are, in fact, the worst sufferers in respect of obtaining employment in the context of reformed regime.

REPRESENTATION IN POLITICAL BODIES

Upto the mid-thirties of the last century the disadvantaged group of people could not share political power. It was Ambedkar who demanded separate electorate for scheduled castes in the local self-government. But this was strongly opposed by the Congress and M.K. Gandhi. Due to Gandhiji's interference, communal award was withdrawn. As against this, reservation of seats was made for scheduled castes in Parliament and State Legislatures. Reservation of seats was made in Parliament, state legislatures and local bodies like municipalities and village panchayats. As a result, underprivileged group of people would be able to improve their socio-economic status in the society. According to this provision, in a reserved constituency only reserved category candidates can contest but every adult individual, irrespective of his/her caste or class, can cast his/her vote. If the majority people accept the reserved category candidate he will be voted to power. On the other hand, if the lower caste people cast to their favourite candidate he may not be elected if the upper caste voters think otherwise. This is due to the fact that the voters representing lower castes will represent not more than one-fifth of the total voters. Naturally, elected members are bound to act according to the wishes of the upper caste politicians. Therefore, the act of the elected members from the reserved seats shows that they are not the representative of the disadvantaged group. This is why the lower caste elected members of Parliament of members of legislative assemblies or members of local bodies cannot voice the problems of disadvantaged group even if they want to do so.

According to 1991 Census data, there are 22 dominant scheduled castes, which constitute more than 50 per cent of the total scheduled caste population. The rest is being represented by about 1000 small sub-castes. The dominant scheduled castes take the upper hand in representing themselves in political bodies. Least-privileged people represented from small sub-castes cannot enjoy the benefits offered by the Constitution. The ruling political parties at the center and at different states always encourage leaders from dominant scheduled castes for electoral politics. Ultimately, the basic problems of small sub-castes remain unfulfilled. The policies framed by the Central and State Governments cannot reduce the specific problems faced by several small sub-castes spreading across different regions of the country.

COMMENT ON THE RESERVATION POLICY

The reservation policy aims at reducing inequality in society by giving some social, economic and political benefits to the disadvantaged group of people. The history of the reservation policy dates back to the first decade of the last century. The existing policy package derives the legal status from our Constitution since 1950. There are, at present, three groups of people who are in the basket of reservation packages. They are scheduled castes, scheduled tribes and other backward castes. It is very often argued that the reservation policy cannot improve the social, economic and cultural status of the really disadvantaged group. By really disadvantaged group of people, we mean those who live below the poverty line. According to a rough estimate, of the 30 crore people living at present below the poverty line, 75 per cent belong to reserved category people *i.e.*, S.C., S.T. and OBC Reservation in Government, semi-Government and educational institutions for OBC is a recent phenomenon is some states. But the states of North India, Gujarat and Maharashtra have reservation policy for the OBC since the mid-seventies of the last century. In the North Indian states especially Kerala, Andhra Pradesh, Karnataka and Tamil Nadu there exist reservation for the OBC for more than 60 years. For proper implementation, the extent of reservation has entered nearly to the optimal point. In those states no further extension of reservation is necessary to those who have taken advantages for two or more generations. The policy should continue with proper implementation to those states which still are lagging behind due to administrative, bureaucratic and some other bottlenecks.

The implementation of the reservation policy should be flawless. In that context, the existing policy needs thorough revision. More emphasis should be given at the grassroot level. The children of the least-privileged people will be provided food, shelter, clothing, education, nutrition and health care facilities in an integrated manner.

We clearly observe two distinct divisions of the lower caste people on the basis of economic capability. Relatively economically developed people can derive reservation benefit. The least-privileged section is far from sharing effective social, economic and political powers. Even after fifty-three years of Indian republic only negligible portion of this section can be found in professional and white-collar jobs. The actual rate of utilisation of reservation in Government, semi-Government, and educational institutions is much more less than the allocation really made. For an all round development of the society the weaker section needs to be brought at par with others by equipping them with talent and tool. To attain this, the NGOs, the Government and the society as a whole should play a dominant role.

CONCLUSIONS

If we want equitable and all round development of society, stress should be given for the uplift of 30 crore people living below the poverty line. They are so poor that the many infrastructural and other facilities for development lie beyond their imagination. The problem of poverty renders them helpless despite improvement taking place in so many areas of the society. The goods and services produced do not reach to them in the present competitive economic system. Poverty is, now-a-days, discussed in terms of relative deprivation. In our case, poverty means denial of the right to survive to 30 crore people who are really in need of bare minimum necessaries. Poverty is a social product, which clings to families over generations. This strikes not only the lower caste people but also a sizeable section of the upper caste people as well. Reservation benefits for those unfortunate sections of people should also be extended.

In conclusion, we would like to make some important comments for better implementation and greater coverage of reservation policy. We propose that the reservation policy should continue with better implementation and without any leakage. Secondly, the objective of the policy should be more social rather than political. Thirdly, there should be reservation for the people living below the poverty line in upper caste category too. Fourthly, more opportunities need to provide to the lowest strata of the lower caste category. Finally, no reservation would be provided to those who have taken reservation benefit for two generations. If the present from of reservation policy continues it would further deteriorate the socio-economic position of the lowest strata of the lower caste. This is because the social benefits received are much less than the social cost incurred. Therefore, the policy should be more 'social benefit maximising' and 'social cost reducing'.

REFERENCES

Abbasayalu, Y.B. (1972), Scheduled Caste Elite, Hyderabed. Departement of Sociology, Osmania University.

Aikarra, J. (1980), Scheduled Caste and Higher Education. A Study of College Students in Bombay, Poona : Distance.

Beteille, A. (1983), *The Idea of Natural and Other Essays,* Delhi, Oxford University Press.

Beteille, A. (1991), "Distributive Justice and Institutional Well-Being," Economic and Political Weekly, (Annual Number), March.

Beteille, A. (1992), *Society and Politics in India,* Essays in a Comparative Perspective, Delhi, Oxford University Press.

Bhuimali, A (2000), "In Search of an Appropriate Reservation Policy for the Under-Privileged People of India", Lecture delivered at the UGC National Seminar on "Development, Deprivation and the

Roots of Inequality" at University of North Bengal on 29-30 January.

Chalam, K.S. (1998), "Caste and Economic Reforms", Seminar 471 – November, New Delhi.

Choudhary, K. (1998), "The Policy of Reservation. Need to Continue and Transcend."

Social Action, Vol. 48

Dreze, J. (1998), "Squaring the Circle", Seminar, 464

Dave, M. (1985). 'Backward Classes and Reservation' in Haroobhi Mehta and Hasmudh Patel (eds.), *Dynamics of Reservation Policy,* New Delhi.

Eighth Five-Year Plan (1992), *Planning Commission, Government of India,* Vol.II.

Government of India (1990), *B.R. Ambedkar, Castes in India,* Speeches and Writings of Dr. Babasaheb Ambedkar, Vol. I.

Ghurye, G.S. (1994), *Caste and Race in India, Popular Prakashan,* Bombay.

Government of India (1980), *Reports of the Backward Classes Commission,* First Part (Vols. 1 & 2).

Government of West Bengal (1999), *Annual Report of the Development of Higher Education,* 1998-99.

Gupta, D. (1998), " A Question of Quotas", *Seminar 471,* November.

Kabra, G.D. (1984), *Development of Weaker Sections. Organisational Alternatives,* Inter-India Publications, New Delhi.

Kamble, R. (1998), "Dalit Interpretations of Society, Seminar 471, November.

Narayan, S.S. (1998). Gender Equality Through Reservation in Decision-Making Bodies, *Social Action,* Vol.48 April.

Panini, M.N. (1999), "M.N. Srinivas and Sociology", *Economic and Political Weekly,* January 22.

Patil, S. (1979), Dialectics of Caste and Conflicts, *Economic and Political Weekly,* Annual Number, February.

Sau, R. (1999), "Human Development Index in View of Caste, Census 2001", *Economic and Political Weekly,* December 18.

Shah, G. (1987), "Middle Class Politics, Case of Anti-Reservation Agitation in Gujarat", *Economic and Political Weekly,* (Annual Number), May.

Ray, A. (1979), "Caste and Class: An Inter-linked View". *Economic and Political Weekly,* Annual Number, February.

Sen, A. (1987), Commodities and Capabilities, Oxford University Press.

Sheth, D.L. (1987), "Reservations Policy Revisited", Economic and Political Weekly.

Srinivas, M.N. (1966), Social Change in Modern India, *Allied Publishers,* Bombay.

Srinivas, M.N., S. Seshaiah (1977), *Dimensions of Social Change in India, Allied Publishers,* New Delhi.

Sudarshan, R.M. (1998), "Where Are We At?", *Seminar 464.*

Swaminathan, M.& Vikas Rawal (1999), "Primary Education for all in India Development Report, 1999-2000 (Eds.), Kirit S. Paridh, IGIDR, Mumbai.

Wankhede, G.S. (1999), "Social and Educational Problems of Scheduled Castes: Some Critical Insights", *The Indian Journal of Social Work,* Volume 60, Issue 3.

7

DISADVANTAGED MIGRANT PEOPLE ON BALASAN RIVER BED

Sri. Samar Kumar Biswas and Mr. Somenath Bhattacharjee

INTRODUCTION

Our motherhood motherland India is made up of varied landscape. Each landscape and region has its own climatic and environmental scenario. With the variability of landscape there occurs the variation of existing population from one region to another. Thus, India is a multiethnic and multi-religious country with different cultural practices and different norms, values and customs. Indian society is old and it is extremely complex. According to a popular estimate it has covered a span of 5000 years since the period of its first known civilization. During this long period, several waves of immigrants, representing different ethnic strains and linguistic families have merged into its population to contribute to its diversity, richness and vitality. Conceptually the Hindu regards the scheduled castes as the Aryans, literally without castes they are outside society. Beyond the pole of Hinduism with all over absence of elementary rights they were considered as untouchables because of their unlearned occupations like cremating dead bodies or sweeping human excreta. They are residentially segregated in the villages and forbidding access to village temple, the homes of touchable villagers and the water sources like wells, tanks etc. They were the poorest of the villagers poor. They were deprived of education and other basic needs thus leading a miserable life. They constituted the Majority of India's disposest and dehumanized population; their disabilities were often forced by traditional sanctions. The institutionalized inequality in the caste system manifests its extreme form in the group of completely segregated set of caste called untouchable caste, the scheduled castes that comprise the bulk untouchables are technically outside the four-fold Varna system. The scheduled castes did not constitute a homogeneous stratum. Before being scheduled in 1935 the scheduled castes were classified as exterior castes, or depressed castes, out castes etc. Mahatma Gandhi designated them as Harizans. In 1931 census, some social criteria were used for identifying the castes as exterior; on the same basis the castes were listed as "scheduled caste" in 1935. Some of those criteria were whether they are served by Brahmins or by *purohits,* whether they are served by barbers, tailors etc., whether they can serve water to caste Hindus, whether they can enter into Hindu temples, whether they can use public conveniences like road, wells etc.

After independence the term scheduled castes have been defined in a specific manner in the constitution. They come from communities which was listed by Central Government Notification. The list can be revised by only Presidential authority. According to Article 336(24) of Indian Constitution-scheduled castes mean such castes, races or tribes or parts or group within such castes, races or tribes as are deemed under Article 341 to be schedule scheduled castes. For the purpose of this Government of India had accepted the following criteria of the social groups to label as "scheduled castes" as recommended by L.M. Srikant "the groups being within the Hindu fold suffer from economic, social, educational backwardness and social segregation, may be termed as scheduled castes."

The North-Eastern Himalayan Range of India is provided with a number of scheduled castes and scheduled tribes communities. Among them the Bodos are an important group of North East India as well as of Assam. It does not refer to a tribe, but to a large number of communities speaking Bodo language of Tibeto Burman Family. The Kacharis, once a powerful people with their own kingdom belong to this group. So are the Rabhas. Now both are being rapidly hinduized; in fact one section identifies itself as Hindu. These people of diverse origin, after their absorption into Hinduism, have given themselves a new identity as Rajbansis. This group also includes the koch, now a Hindu jati who ruled over substantial part of Assam, too have discarded their traditional name and call themselves as Rajbansis and now they belong to scheduled caste. In 1991 census, the total population of West Bengal was 68077965, where the total scheduled caste population was 1,60,80,611. And in it, the Rajbansis are 2839481 (17.65 percent). The district-wise total Rajbansi population is given below______

Distribution of Rajbansi Population

Name of The District	*Total Rajbansi Population % to total*
Koch Bihar	865622
Jalpaiguri	656073
Darjeeling	96745
West Dinajpur	489642
Maldah	114697
Murshidabad	53285
Nadia	59377
North 24 Parganas	99245
South 24 Parganas	137732
Calcutta	16390
Howrah	58900
Hooghly	45772
Midnapur	117338
Bankura	984
Purulia	389
Burdwan	13914
Birbhum	13376

Source: Census of India, 1991.

In census 2001 census, the scheduled castes are 16.2 per cent among the country's total population. In West Bengal scheduled castes are 23.02 per cent in its total population. In case of North Bengal, the feature is given below:

Scheduled Caste Population of North Bengal

Name of The District	*Total Population 2001*	*Schedule castes Population 2001*	*Percentage of S.C. Population to Total Population*
Darjeeling	1609172	258881	16.09
Jalpaiguri	3401173	1248577	36.71
Koch Bihar	2479155	1242374	50.11
Uttar Dinajpur	2441794	676582	27.71
Dakshin Dinajpur	1503178	432660	28.78
Maldah	3290468	554165	16.84

Source: Census of India, 2001

The studied area, North Bengal is situated in the north eastern Himalayan belt. It is a region of varied landscape, terrain morphology, economic and socio-cultural characteristics. It is broadly divided into hills, sub-Himalayan foothills and barinth plain. The entire region is provided with a number of castes, tribes and occupational groups. The varied landscape and varied people give a number of cultural traits and trait complexes. Nuturally with the changing environment the concept of basic needs and the ways to acquire those needs are variable too. The Rajbansis are one of the early settlers of North Bengal and primarily depended on agriculture. They were villagers and far from urban attractions. Their way of life and mode of behaviour ware totally based on folk culture with a very simple mind.

Their existences were totally enmeshed with their land and their beloved neighbours. Their enjoyments were shared commonly and their recreations too related with each other. But the dimension of time is always changing. During the decade of 70's (1970), there took place a number of political changes in this region. The Naxalbari Peasant Movement was launched in March-April, 1967. The idiom of the movement was that power come from the barrel of total annihilation of the big farmers, land lords and *Jaigirdars* and nothing sort of it would change the structure of society. The Rajbansis are the preponderant community of this region. Earlier this community was a tribal group known as Koch. In the purpose of political development which took place in the terai region the Rajbansis acquired large proportion of land and come to be known as *jotdars.* They leased out land to tenants who paid annual rents to them. The landlords used to take larger shares out of the produce made by the share croppers. They have no power with them and helplessly they were under the bondage of big landholders. The movement turned out as a class war between big farmers and ordinary peasants. In 1971, there occurred a severe political unrest in Bangladesh. As a result, a huge number of migrants took shelter in Siliguri and other suburban areas. On the other hand, the socio-political unrest in Nepal's Royal Monarchy and other north eastern states of India also resulted a severe land pressure and the concept of need of the people rapidly changed.

Census 2001 gives the feature that nearly 27 per cent of our country's populations are the urban dwellers and simultaneously

North Bengal is not exceptional from this trend. The followings table shows this.

Distribution of Urban Population in North Bengal

State/District	*Percentage of Urban Population in Total Population* 1991	2001
West Bengal	27.48	28.03
Darjeeling	30.47	32.44
Jalpaiguri	16.36	17.74
Koch Bihar	7.81	9.10
North Dinajpur	13.34	12.06
South Dinajpur	13.35	13.09
Maldah	7.07	7.37

Source: Census of India, 2001

The Decennial Growth Rate for Rural and Urban Areas

State/District	*Percentage of Urban Population in Total Population* Total	Rural	Urban
West Bengal	17.84	16.94	20.20
Darjeeling	23.54	20.4	31.51
Jalpaiguri	21.52	19.51	31.77
Koch Bihar	14.15	12.55	33.04
North Dinajpur	28.72	30.61	16.40
South Dinajpur	22.11	2.47	19.74
Maldah	24.77	24.43	29.15

Source: Census of India, 2001

Siliguri is the most important urban center of North Bengal. Its importance line in its role as a commercial center at the gateway between Duars, Sikkim, Darjeeling, Kalimpong, Koch Bihar with other north eastern states of India like Assam. Arunachal Pradesh, and Bihar as well as with International Borders like Nepal, Bhutan, Bangladesh, China, Myanmar. The network has a direct contact with other metropolitan cities of India. Still it is a developing urban center. Many rivers like Mahananda, Balasan, pass through the heart of the Siliguri town and natural resources like boulder, stone, sand come downward from the high hilly areas. To fulfil the huge demand of these raw materials for urban construction the foremost important tyhing is the huge amount of manual labour. Question of daily existence was a prime factor for the migrated and landless people who were devoid of any source of income. Thus the land pressure and the lack of purchasing capacity forced on them to search for a permanent occupation to give a backbone regarding their establishment as early as possible. The stone field of Balasan River Bed thus becomes unquestionably the best option for them as it does not need any kind of capital investment. The Balasan River Bed provided them the land to establish a new residence. The roofless, resource less migrated Rajbansis started to live in the balasan River Bed by forming a colony named as "Tarijot Colony" since 35 years which have been discussed. The study has been done on 100 families of this colony who are primarily engage with stone based economy. The stone collection, stone crushing and the related socio-economic scenario has a direct impact on their livelihoods. These have been discussed here one after another.

THE SOCIO-ECONOMIC SCENARIO OF THE STONE CRUSHERS

Among the studied 100 families (having 503 people 252 males and 251 females) 85 per cent are migrant and 15 per cent are non-migrant. Maximum number of migration took place during the decade of 1970 from Bangladesh due to severe political unrest. Migration from other districts of West Bengal is due to loss of economical holds because of natural calamities and other factors.

The migrated people have started living in the Balasan River Bed ever since 35 years ago. They are totally undocumented migrants and even now most of them are devoid of any kind of rationing system and voting. They have started to live by forming Tarijot Colony without any governmental influence or rule and it is totally made on local adjustments and by means of other influential capabilities. Simultaneously with migration, people were in search of new way of income. The parental generations were totally agriculture based, while the ego's have a 90 per cent engagement with the stone based economy. Even the present generations (ego's child) have an engagement of 84.21 per cent in the stone based work.

At present (Table-1) near about 81 per cent people are either primarily or secondarily engaged with stone based economy. Only 3.52 per cent are engaged with other source of income which is indicating that this occupation is unable to provide the daily necessities of the stone crushers, and so they are searching for an alternative way. In this table, the children who are mainly school going and upto 14 years having no hard working schedule are exempted. The interesting feature in that due to acute poverty only 20 per cent women could give prime importance to their family. It is to be mentioned here that the school-going children and women engaged in household works use to do stone crushing secondarily at their home or in the stone field for shorter time schedule scheduled everyday. Without any gender bias all of the members of the families do this hard working job for their livelihood. They had to work in dusty, polluted, unhygienic stone field from dawn to dusk devoid of climatic factors. They had a mere moment to spend in leisure throughout their daily busy schedule. Both the male and female worked even upto more than 8 hours (Table-2). With other daily activities the prolonged working schedule was compulsory for them. The whole family worked here as a production unit to give the financial support for their whole family.

Table 1
Distribution of People on the basis of Primary occupation

Category	*Stone Crash*	*Day Labour*	*Mason*	*House Hold*	*Total*
Male	114 (77.55)	22 (14.96)	10 (6.80)	1 (0.68)	147 (51.76)
Female	103 (75.18)	6 (4.37)	-	28 (20.44)	137 (48.24)
Total	217 (76.40)	28 (9.85)	10 (3.52)	29 (10.21)	284 (100.00)

Source: Field Study, 2004 (Excluding 0-4 years).

Table 2
Daily Working schedule of the People Engaged in Stone Based Economy (Primarily or Secondarily)

SEX	*Daily Working Schedule In Hours (No. & Percentage)*					*Total (No. & %)*
	1-2	2-4	4-6	6-8	8+	
Male	30 (17.86)	24 (14.29)	10 (5.95)	31 (18.45)	73 (43.45)	168 (100)
Female	25 (16.34)	25 (16.34)	8 (5.23)	26 (16.99)	69 (45.10)	153 (100)

Source: Field Study, 2004.

The workers are not at all paid proper remuneration against their hard work. The monthly incomes of the families are in a very poor condition. The stone based workers worked under *sardars*.

The *sardars* paid them either on daily or weekly basis. Among the families of the colony 13 per cent earned below Rs. 1000/- per month, 77 per cent earned Rs. 10001- to Rs. 2000– per month and only 10 per cent have the monthly income Rs. 2001 to Rs. 3000/-.With this poor level of income they could manage their basic needs anyhow. Poverty and misery were an integrated part of their life. These factors had raised other serious problems simultaneously.

The people are keenly interested to make their children literate. They made themselves engaged to the school in the primary level. But the guardians are unable to give proper care to their children because neither they have time nor proper educational backbone. After returning from the school the children cannot see their parents at their houses so, they rush to the stone field for their search. In this way, they gradually get enmeshed with the stone based work. They are forced by the poverty and need of the family to start the same occupation simultaneously with their elders. The tender mind of a child faces a critical situation. Poverty, malnutrition and hard working have a direct impact on the stone crushers. These factors tell upon their physical and mental fitness and they have to face an early aging. So, to give the familiars a financial backbone the child are forced to join the work. The immature children thus have to face the competitive working environment in the colony and it has a great psychological impact on them. Moreover, they are debarred from proper schooling as well as education. Due to their lack of knowledge development they are acing many problems. Their socialization is improper too from their early childhood both from family and society. Their struggle for survival forces them to engage in the work at a very early age. So why the basic personality formation has been seriously effected from their early adolescent period. It is seriously affecting on their socio cultural life as well as development of society.

In census 2001, it is known that the scheduled castes population of West Bengal has a literacy rate of 59.04 per cent where male literacy is 70/54 per cent and 46.90 per cent is female literacy. Particularly in Darjeeling district the literacy rate of Scheduled Castes population is 62.43 per cent among this, 73.91 per cent males are literate and 50.31 per cent females are literate. At the Tarijot Balasan colony considering the level of primary education, the enrollment rate is very high and it is cent per cent upto 14 years.

But as they gradually grow up the cases of drop out increase and it is a very common phenomenon to them (Table – 3). It is more acute in caśe of females. Thus, in V—VIII standard there are only 12.35 per cent females and in the secondary level there is not a single female student. In Tarijot Colony, the literacy rate of male is 64.68 per cent and the literacy rate of female is 52.99 per cent. The 25.25 per cent population is confined within primary level and 14.46 per cent only has secondary level of education. Dropout is the major and common feature of these families.

Table 3
Distribution of Population on the Basis of Education

Category	*Illiterate*	*Literate*	*If Literate*						
			Without Standard	*I-IV*	*V-VIII*	*IX-X*	*XI-XII*	*Graduate & Post Graduates*	*Total Population*
Male	51	163	31	55	66	11	—		214
	(23.83)	(76.17)	(19.01)	(33.74)	(40.49)	(6.75)			(100.00)
Female	77	133	30	72	31		—		210
	(36.67)	(63.33)	(22.56)	(54.14)	(23.61)	-	—		(100.00)
Total	128	296	61	127	97	11	—		424
	(30.19)	(69.81)	(20.61)	(42.91)	(32.77)	(3.72)	—		(100.00)

Source: Field Study, 2004 (Excluding 0-6 years).

Due to poor economical infrastructure the physical setting of the houses are in their worst ever condition and most of those are devoid of basic amenities of sufficient room and drainage systems. As a result, the houses are the key birth place of germ and are generating a number of diseases. The families mostly depend on cheapest fuel like wood dust and cowdung cake. The emitted smoke from them might have an adverse effect on children and women health, as the houses are too small and smoke passes out throughout the room. Besides, women give their child birth at home, thus, it is both dangerous from child and mother health perspectives.

The physical workloads of the stone crushers are heavy and it is their daily phenomenon. Simultaneously, the living conditions and immense poverty are also telling upon their normal livelihood. These factors are the main causes of their physical and mental depression. As a result, they find an alternative way to forget for sometime about their misery in the mode of addictions. People from their early teenage were in the web of number of addictions including alcohol, tobacco etc. and the females are not exceptional too. As a result it is telling upon their health in the form of a number of chronic diseases.

Normally, the addicted natures of males were not accepted by females in their houses. As a result problem regarding familial affairs is very common here. Wife battering and separations are often seen. Thus after some kind of temporary and permanent separation, illegal sexual relations between males and females naturally become quite common. The women get married at an early age. Though the females are also an earning member but they have no right over their earned wealth and it concentrates in their husband's hand. Thus, they have to accept silently all the situations forcefully implied by the males. The habitats kept the feature of illegal relations and problem with neighbourhood very much hushed up and often temporary solutions were done behind the closed doors. Overall, it is noteworthy to mention that the social life at the colony is disturbed very much interiorly.

Now, the whole scenario can be analyzed from another dimension. The role of environment is very much related with the psychological development of the child. Societal environments, guidance of family members and interaction among the kin members have a great influence regarding socialization and personality formation of a child. The study of Japanese National Character by Ruth Benedict in his book *"Chrysanthemum and The Sword (1946)"* gives the feature that how the tender and soft mind of Japanese Child gradually changes into an aggressive and violent as their parents imposed strict discipline on them and forced them to face the harsh reality of life. Naturally, the social environment of Tarijot Colony also has a serious impact on their child. From the early childhood the children are debarred from their formal education and start to work in the field. Their socialization is improper from early childhood. So why their basic personality formation has been seriously effected from early adolescent period. It is telling upon the socio-cultural life as well as development of society. The illegal affairs of their seniors and elders greatly affect on their psychology and mind. Thus their simple thoughts and behaviours in the context of the exposed surrounding environment starts to become more and more complex. They make enmesh themselves in a number of addictions. The relationship between male and female in the colony are based on offensive adultery practices and this make the child an improper application of kinship bonds. Thus the norms, prohibitions and customs of kinship bonds are in front of a serious threat in the colony. The kinship ties are the fundamental aspect for the formation of a society, so, if it gradually breaks up in the colony then there would be a severe challenge regarding the future existence of the colony.

Let us now consider the other factors. Poverty has a direct impact on the nutritional quality of the people. Lack of purchasing capacity forces them to concentrate on lunch and dinner with vegetarian diet. The poor level of income is making the animal protein as a mere dream to them. Women are the nurserers of a child. The working schedule of the mothers is so busy that they have to nourish their child at the stone field and they also take their food in the dusty and polluted environment of the river bed. As a result, it may tell upon them in the form of a number of physical disorders. Even the pregnant women are lacking proper nutritious food. During their pregnancy period, they are given simple vegetarian diet and only 30 per cent can afford to manage animal protein once weekly in this stage. Females get married at an early age, so, they start to bear child too from an early age. Thus, their malnourished pregnancy period is common to them from an early age. Thus the malnourished mothers are giving birth to the malnourished children. In the context of civilization and its continuation, the foremost essential thing is the healthy society. In society the fundamental unit is family and in family the prime one is child. So, the prime requirement of a healthy and civilized society is a healthy child. In the Tarijot Colony it is in a worst ever condition. From the early embryonic development the children here are in malnourished unhealthy environment. By birth they are facing malnutrition and ill health. Not only the physical health but their mental health is too facing a serious challenge. Poverty, educational hindrance, unhealthy societal atmosphere are all playing inconvenient role towards their development. Thus it is simply impossible to think about the future development of the colony until young and coming generations are well protected from unhealthy circumstances. Taking Body Mass Index of 100 children in the colony the feature of malnutrition is well proved. It shows that 83 per cent are in the feature of improper growth thus malnourished and only 17 per cent have proper growth.

The conditions of the people are so much hand to mouth that the pregnant mothers are unable to take any rest in this stage. Even they work for 7 hours and 8 hours in 14.93 per cent and 4.54 per cent cases respectively with facing labour pain. Meanwhile, most of the child birth takes place at home (60.15%) because they are reluctant to go to medical clinic or hospital as they think that their valuable time would be lost. As a result, child death and foetal loss is a common phenomenon. Among 132 ever pregnant women 22 (16.67%) have faced the foetal loss in 3-4 month, 4-5 month of conceiving period in 22.73 per cent, 45-45 per cent and 31.82 per cent respectively. Total 45-child death in the colony is due to diarrhoea, malnutrition and fever in 42.22 per cent, 35.55 per cent and 22.22 per cent respectively. This creates a psychological frustration to the mothers.

As a result of poor income, unhygienic livelihood, and lack of nutrition the stone crushers are suffering from a number of diseases. Some of those are seen just after their engagement to the occupation and some of those are observed due to their prolonged engagement in the occupation, which are categorized as short-term and long term diseases. There is not a single stone crusher avoiding physical injuries or fever cold and cough. The people are also suffering from tuberculosis, asthma, serous body injuries, and skin diseases as shown (Table-4). But according to the employee of the Colony Health Centre 100 per cent of the stone crushers of the colony are suffering from tuberculosis and other respiratory problem. The X-Ray report of the stone crushers reveals that they are suffering from silicosis about which they were completely unknown.

Table 4

Distribution of Total Population on the basis of Long-Term Diseases

Category	*Asthma*	*T.B*	*Hand Injury*	*Hand +Eye Injury*	*T.B. & Asthma*	*Skin Diseases*	*Anemia*	*Total*
Male	19 (7.53)	22 (8.73)	23 (9.12)	1 (0.39)	9 (3.57)	29 (11.50)	11 (4.31)	252 (50.10)
Female	11 (4.38)	-	37 (14.74)	22 (8.76)	-	20 (7.97)	17 (6.77)	251 (49.90)
Total	30 (5.96)	22 (4.73)	60 (11.92)	23 (4.57)	9 (1.78)	49 (9.74)	28 (5.56)	503 (100)

Source: Field Study, 2004.

The poor and distress economic condition as well as the socio-cultural circumstances have given the people a setback to accept modern medical treatments (Table-5). Besides their indigenous treatment they took *allopathic* medicine from the Colony Health Centre without properly seeking doctor's advice. But when the conditions become critical then they go to the doctors and hospitals.

Table 5
Distribution of Families on the basis of Medical Practices

Total Family	*Modern Medical Treatment*		*Indigenous Method*		*Only Quack Method*		*Quack + Indigenous Method*		*Modern + Indigenous Method*		*Healer + Indigenous Method*	
100	No.	%	No.	%	No.	%	No.	%	No.	%	No.	%
(100.00)	30	(30)	-	-	-	-	14	(14.0)	49	(49.0)	7	(7.0)

Source: Field Study, 2004.

OBSERVATION

Migration is an ongoing phenomenon in the colony. The migrants are mostly undocumented and are devoid of any kind of governmental support. So, they arrange their livelihood in their own fashion. From the above all discussion, it has come in front that the fundamental right of human life in the form of education, health and nutrition are violated strongly in the colony. Both male and female participated in the earning but the financial powers are confined into the hand of males and females are often deprived from their status. The males are often involved in illegal sexual affairs which are variable in number. So the kinship relations are not well protected in the colony. Another dimension of problem comes in front if the cases of children are considered. From their early childhood they achieve a psychological pressured mind to develop a competitive attitude and probable findings to survive in the struggle for existence. After taking birth with a malnourished physique and ill health they gradually came in the web of acute poverty. So, from early childhood they were debarred from formal and proper education and this lack of knowledge is a hindrance for their socialization and personality development. This is making them incompatible in the outer world competition. Due to migration there occurred a huge number of contacts among different types of people in the colony. Meanwhile from the NACO Report 2004 in India 96978 people are HIV/AIDS patients and according to the report of UNAIDS/WHO 2003, 51 lakh people have HIV virus in their body. According to their report migration and admixture of population is one of its primary factor. So, in the Tarijot Colony the prediction comes for various sexually transmitted diseases as all the factors fit here with the internationally accepted causes. The women here were suffering from psychological disorder regarding their menstrual cycle (16.73%), and it should not be ignored, because it is feared that sexually transmitted diseases may outburst in the colony. The prime unit of society is family and where the child is the prime one. In the colony, the generations one after another *i.e.* from father to child and so on, are facing the same scenario of hard working, improper remuneration, poverty, malnutrition, illiteracy, ill health and other problems.

CONCLUSION

The dilemma of political unrest forced the people to expose in a new environmental and occupational background. This new type of occupation provided them the way to earn money. But unfortunately it could not provide them a strong economic backbone. At present, though the problem of untouchability is being reduced but the problem of the scheduled castes in the Tarijot colony are multifarious. Problem is present in each and every sector of the society. There is lack of educational knowledge, there is acute malnutrition, and there is poverty. All these factors are creating the problem of early aging, unhealthy atmosphere, household's problems, illegal affairs and severe diseases. Physical and mental ill health of the women are creating a frustration among them because they have to accept silently all the hindrance regarding their livelihood. The overall socio-economic scenario makes a serious impact on their daily livelihood. But they cannot alter this situation and it is creating a depression on their mind. At least the working atmosphere can be altered. The foremost essential thing is to understand the real problem and their root causes. The problems could not be solve only by giving them economical support. But the government has to come beside them from humanitarian ground. They have to observe whether their measures are appropriately getting implemented or not. Their working schedule can be minimized and they may use some protective measures during their work to avoid injuries. The government has to take initiative to aware the people about hygienic practices and way to lead a disciplined life. These may bring a new and developed dimension in the socio-economic and working infrastructure at the colony.

REFERENCES

Ahuja, R. 2001. Social Problem in India, Rawat Publications, Jaipur and New Delhi.

Ahuja, R. 2003. Violence Against Women, Rawat Publications, Jaipur and New Delhi.

Banerjee, D. 1986. Social Science and Health Service Development in India, Lok Prakash, New Delhi.

Bose, A. 1979. Indias Urbanisation, 1901-2001, New Delhi.

Bose, A. 1996. Meeting Indias Best Needs. The Human Development Index, Delhi.

Census of India. 2001. Govt. of India, New Delhi.

Census of India. 2001. Govt. of India, New Delhi.

Chaudhuri, B. 1990. Culture and Environmental dimension on Health, Inter India Publication, New Delhi.

Datta, P. 2005. "Undocumented Migration from Bangladesh to West Bengal" in Vijoy S. Sahay, Pradip K.Singh, Gautam K. Bera (ed). Dimension of research in Indian Anthropology (147-159), Serials Publications, New Delhi.

Doshi, S. L. and P.C. Jain. 1999. Rural Sociology, Rawat Publications, Jaipur

Gated, P. 1984. Direct Attacks on Rural Poverty, Concept Publications, New Delhi.

Gil, D. 1970. Violence Against Children. Physical Child Abuse in the United State, Harvard University Press, Cambridge.

Gore, M.S., 1968. Urbanization and Family Change, Popular Prakashan, Bombay.

Hand book of Social Welfare Statistics, 1981. Ministry of Social Welfare, New Delhi.

Jain, A. K. and P. Visavia, 1998. Infant Mortality in India, Sage publication New Delhi.

Kewalramani, C.S. 1992. Child Abuse, Rawat Publication, Jaipur.

Khatu, K.K. 1983. Working Children in India, Rawat Publication, Jaipur.

Landis, Paul. H. 1959. Social Problems, J. B. Lippincott Co. Chicago.

Leonard, E.B. 1982. Women, Crime and Society, Longman, New York.

Pagelow, M.D. 1984. Family Violence, Praeger Scientific, New York.

Sanyal, C.C. 2002. The Rajbansis of North Bengal, The Asiatic Society, Kolkata.

The Indian Child A Profile, 2002. Ministry of Human Resource Development, Govt. of India, New Delhi.

Vargashree, K.V. 1985. Economic Problem of Modern India, Ashish Publishing House, New Delhi.

Waskin, R. (ed)1964. Social Problems, Mc. Graw Hill and Co., New York.

WHO, 1997. The World Health Report, World Health Organizations, Geneva.

Wolfe, D.A. 1987. Child Abuse, Sage Publication, Beverly Hills.

8

DEVELOPMENT OF PRIMARY EDUCATION AMONG SCHEDULED CASTES IN ANDHRA PRADESH

Dr. D. Pulla Rao

INTRODUCTION

In the traditional caste system (Varna vyavastha), the Indian society has been divided into four groups, known as castes, on the basis of occupations. But, in the modern Indian social system there are two more marginalized caste groups namely, Scheduled Castes (SCs) and Scheduled Tribes (STs).

The term SC has a long historical origin. Prior to the year 1935, when the Government of India Act was enacted, the communities suffering from the stigma of untouchability were being referred to as 'untouchables' or 'exterior' or 'depressed' classes or by various caste names most of which were derogatory. As a part of the social and political changes sought to be introduced in 1935 the various castes, which suffered social disabilities, were listed in a Schedule and from that time onwards they came to be described as SCs. After the Constitution of India was enacted, the list of scheduled castes was notified by the President of India in accordance with the provisions of Article 341 of the Constitution. The SCs, thus, represent constitutionally declared groups of castes or communities with the characteristic of being suffering from 'untouchability'. In terms of the provisions in Article 341, they have been specified separately in relation to each of the States and Union Territories.

The SCs live mostly in rural areas, with only about 14 per cent of them living in urban agglomerations. The habitations of the SCs are scattered all over the Country generally in parts of villages or small villages. While some of them are small and marginal farmers, most of the SC families in rural areas work largely as agricultural labour. Almost all primary workers in the leather industry are from these castes. Fishermen belonging to SCs are found in the eastern region of the Country. There is a large concentration of weavers belonging to this category in the western parts of India. In the urban areas, a large proportion of unorganized workers belong to the SC category. The scavengers and sweepers constitute one of the most vulnerable sections among the SCs. They suffer from the inhuman practice of untouchability, which is the most extreme form of the denial of human dignity and social oppression. The proportion of the SCs among the poverty groups is high and they are among the poorest of those below the poverty line. Two thirds of the bonded labourers identified in the country are SCs and STs. The observations of the Working Group on the Development of the Scheduled Castes (1980-85) are worth recalling. Notwithstanding this extremely adverse situation, they contribute significantly to the sustenance and growth of the production systems of the Country and the national economy. The largest single group among the agricultural labourers in the Country is SCs. Footwear and other leather products, a variety of handicraft and handloom products are mostly made by them. They have a considerable share in the fishing activity of the country. Moreover, they are the people who keep the country clean and tidy. They constitute the bedrock on which the society and economy rest. Rarely has any section of a nation contributed so much for so long in return for little. Indian society owes to the SCs a heavy moral and material debt yet to be discharged.

The caste-based stratification of society adversely affected the equality of educational opportunities to the disadvantage of these groups as they were engaged in traditional family occupations, which did not require any kind of education or special training. This situation persisted through the ages and the depressed classes continue to be deprived of educational opportunities, which were cornered by the upper castes.

POLICIES AND PROGRAMMES

The founding fathers of our Constitution desired to secure justice, social, economic and political, for all citizens. To them "all citizens" obviously included scheduled castes, socially, economically and educationally very backward. The State has been enjoined to secure equality of status and opportunities for all. Article 46 of the Constitution goes of further to state that "the State shall promote with special care the educational and economic interests of the weaker sections of the people, and in particular, of the scheduled castes and scheduled tribes, and shall protect them from social injustice and all forms of exploitation". A new clause 15 (4) to the effect that "nothing in this Article or in clause (2) of Article 29 shall prevent the State from making any special provision for the advancement of any socially and educationally backward classes of citizens or for the scheduled castes and the scheduled tribes" was added in 1951. The object of this clause was to bring Article 15 and 29 in line with Articles 16(4), 46 and 340 and to make it constitutional for the State to reserve seats for the backward classes of citizens, scheduled castes and scheduled tribes in the public educational institutions as well as to make other special provisions as may be necessary for their advancement. The most important problem identified was untouchability. Article 17 abolished this outright. The Protection of Civil Rights (PCR) Act followed in 1955. Later, in 1989, the Scheduled Castes and the Scheduled Tribes (Prevention of Atrocities) Act came into force. As a means of achieving the objectives enshrined in the Constitution, the provision for reservation of seats in legislatures and services was made in favour of both the scheduled castes and scheduled tribes.

Concerning the provision of education to the disadvantaged sections, the Draft National Policy on Education 1979 expressed its grave concern over the dismal educational conditions of certain disadvantaged sections of the society including Scheduled Castes and Scheduled Tribes. It stated:

"While there has been considerable expansion in all sectors of education in our country, imbalances and inequalities still persist. Girls, Scheduled Castes and Tribes, landless labourers, backward classes and urban slum poor generally continue to lag behind in education. Special effort must be made to identify the problems in these cases and to bring all such people into the fold of education."

The Government of India reviewed the progress of education in 1985 and published a discussion document, and subsequently, formulated the National Policy on Education (NPE). A Programme of Action (PoA) too was chalked out in 1986. In these documents, the detailed proposals (NPE-1986) and schemes (PoA-1992) to be pursued for the improvement of educational status of Scheduled Tribes was given. The relevant statements of the NPE-1986 are given below:

The following measures are initiated to bring the SCs on per with others.

The central focus in SCs' educational development is their equalization with the non-SC population at all stages and levels of education, in all areas and in all the four dimensions— rural male, rural female, urban male and urban female. The measures contemplated for this purpose include:

- Incentives to indigent families to send their children to school regularly till they reach the age of 14;
- Pre-matric scholarship scheme for children of those families engaged in occupations such as scavenging, flaying and tanning to be made applicable from class I onwards. All children of such families, regardless of income, will be covered by this Scheme and time-bound programmes targeted on them will be undertaken;
- Constant micro-planning and verification to ensure that the enrollment, retention and successful completion of courses by SC students do not fall at any stage, and provision of remedial courses to improve their prospects for further education and employment;
- Recruitment of teachers from Scheduled Castes;
- Provision of facilities for SC students in students' hostels at district headquarters, according to a phased programme;
- Location of school buildings, balwadis and adult education centers in such a way as to facilitate full participation of SCs;
- Utilization of NREP and RLEGP resources so as to make substantial educational facilities available to SCs; and

- Constant innovation in finding new methods to increase the participation of SCs in the educational process.

Recently the United Progressive Alliance (UPA) Government at the center in its Common Minimum Programme (CMP) promises, among other things, to provide for full equality of opportunity in education and employment for the SCs and concrete action to put these lofty ideals is yet to be undertaken, however.

Any programme of action needs to be based on the present status of education among this disadvantaged group. Since SCs lack of primary education this paper focused its attention on several variants with special reference to Andhra Pradesh.

The Government of Andhra Pradesh has taken up several projects to promote primary education in the State. These include Operation Black Board (OBB), Andhra Pradesh Primary Education Project (APPEP), District Primary Education Programme (DPEP), Chaduvala Panduga (CP), Akshara Sankranti (AS), Sarva Shiksha Abhiyan (SSA), Vidya-Volunteer Scheme (VVS), Mid-day Meal Scheme, etc. These Programmes may have had some impact on enrollment of all children including SCs, recruitment of teachers including SC teachers, and student-teacher ratios. The present Study examined their impact on primary education of SC children. In the process, it also analysed the trends in primary education in Andhra Pradesh, for the period 1959-60 to 1999-2000.

OBJECTIVES

The present study aims at :

1. To compare SC literacy rates with the overall literacy rates.
2. To estimate and compare the rates of growth of enrollment of SCs and all children.
3. To examine the district-wise enrollment ratios of SC children and all children.
4. To analyse the proportion of SC teachers to the total, district wise, and
5. To estimate the student teacher ratio at the district level in the state.

While pursuing these objectives it was also provided a gender-dimension to the study-literacy rates and enrollment rates of boys and those of girls and the relative significance of male and female teachers are highlighted.

THE DATA

The secondary data relating to the number of children enrolled and the number of teachers working in primary schools by caste group are obtained from the office of the Bureau of Economics and Statistics, Government of Andhra Pradesh and the Commissioner and Director of School Education, Government of Andhra Pradesh. It was, however, found that there are some discrepancies in the data supplied by these offices. Therefore, it is important to throw in some caveats at the very beginning, that the data are to be analysed cautiously. First, there is a difference between enrollment in primary school and enrollment of primary stage. The former excludes the enrollment in primary sections of the upper primary schools, whereas the latter, includes such enrollment. Only the latter definition was considered in the analysis of the enrollment of primary stage. But, in the case of teachers, the number of teachers working only in primary schools, as per the data provided by the offices of the Bureau of Economics and Statistics; and Commissioner and Director of School Education were considered.

DISPARITIES IN LITERACY RATES BETWEEN SCHEDULED CASTES AND ALL COMMUNITIES

Literacy plays a vital role of all the social factors. As per the figures based on 2001 census, SCs constitute 16.19 per cent of the total population of Andhra Pradesh. In the field of literacy, the disparities between males and females are still large. Table-1 shows the gap between the literacy rates of all males and SC males, all females and SC females and total literacy (total males + total females) and SC literacy rate. It shows how the gap has been persisting since 1961. In 1961 SC males literacy rate was 13.4 per cent as against 30.2 per cent among all males. The disparity index (ratio of all male literacy rate to SC male literacy rate) in 1961 was 2.2. The literacy rate of SC males rose to 63.5 per cent in 2001 even as the rate for all males increased to 70.8 per cent. The disparity index in 2001 was 1.1. It shows the disparity in literacy rate between SC males and all males has come down from 2.2 in 1961 to 1.1 in 2001.

In the case of females, the literacy rate of SCs as recorded in 1961 was 3.4 per cent as against 12.0 per cent among all females. The disparity index in 1961 was 3.5. The literacy rate was 43.3 per cent among SC females in 2001 as against 51.2 per cent among all females. The disparity index has decreased from 3.5 in 1961 to 1.2

in 2001. Understandably the female literacy rates at all points of time are lower than those for males. This is true irrespective of whether one considers SCs or all persons. Also, the disparity in literacy rates between all persons and SCs is higher among females than among males.

The total literacy rate of SCs was 8.5 per cent as against the overall rate of 21.2 per cent in 1961. The disparity index in 1961 was 2.5. The total literacy rate was 53.5 per cent among SCs in 2001 as against overall rate of 61.1 per cent. The disparity index decreased from 2.5 in 1961 to 1.1 in 2001.

Table 1
Gender-Wise Literacy Rates Among All Persons And SCs In Andhra Pradesh

Year	*Male literacy rates*			*Female literacy rates*			*Total*		
	All	*SC*	*Disparity Index**	*All*	*SC*	*Disparity Index**	*All*	*SC*	*Disparity Index**
1961	30.2	13.4	2.2	12.0	3.4	3.5	21.2	8.5	2.5
1971	33.2	15.9	2.1	15.8	5.3	3.0	24.6	10.7	2.3
1981	39.3	24.8	1.6	20.4	10.3	2.0	29.9	17.7	1.7
1991	55.1	41.9	1.3	32.7	20.9	1.6	44.1	31.6	1.4
2001	70.8	63.5	1.1	51.2	43.3	1.2	61.1	53.5	1.1

**Disparity Index:* Ratio of literacy rate among all persons to that among SCs
Source: Census of India, different periods.

ENROLLMENT OF SC CHILDREN VERSUS ALL CHILDREN IN PRIMARY STAGE

Literacy rate is but one dimension of the progress of education of a community. Another dimension of the progress is the enrollment ratio of children at the Primary stage.

Table-2 shows that the number of children enrolled in primary stage in 1959-60 was 28.06 lakhs. of this, 62.12 per cent were boys and 37.88 per cent were girls. Enrollment of students in general increased to 91.12 lakhs by 1999-2000 recording a 52 per cent boys and 48 per cent increase among girls. An interesting trend which can be observed is that enrollment of girls has grown at a higher rate than that of boys during the period of study. The annual compound growth rate of enrollment of girls was 3.62 per cent as against 2.51 per cent among boys.

In the case of SCs, the total enrollment in 1959-60 was 3.91 lakhs. Of those enrolled, 64 per cent were boys and 36 per cent were girls and the proportion of the enrollment of SC children to all children was 14 per cent. The enrollment of SC children reached 18.83 lakhs by 1999-2000. Of this 52 per cent were boys and 48 per cent were girls. In 1999-2000, the proportion of the enrollment of SC children to all children was 21 per cent. The trend growth rate shows that the enrollment of SC girls has been higher at 4.79 per cent than that of SC boys at 3.45 per cent during the period of our study. This is a welcoming feature. The fact that the special programmes and initiatives taken to motivate SCs to enroll their children in ever-larger numbers in primary schools are bearing fruit and it is evident from the data presented in Table-2. The annual compound growth rate of enrollment during the period 1959-1960 to 1999-2000 was 2.51 per cent and 3.45 per cent for all boys and SC boys and 3.62 per cent and 4.79 per cent for all girls and SC girls.

DISTRICT-WISE ENROLLMENT OF SC CHILDREN VERSUS ALL CHILDREN IN PRIMARY STAGE

The analysis on the enrollment ratios given above is based on the state-level data. In as much as there are wide variations in the economic development of different districts of the State, there could also be wide divergencies between districts in the enrollment ratio. In order to reflect upon these differences, we now take up an analysis of inter-district variations in enrollment ratios was taken up. Because the question of development of the three traditional regions of the State—Coastal Andhra, Rayalaseema, and Telangana—has always occupied the center stage in state politics, it is also useful to identify which region is in the forefront in respect of enrollment and which is in the back seat.

Table-3 shows the percentage of enrollment of boys and girls among all and SC children. The enrollment of all children in the primary stage in Andhra Pradesh during the academic year 1999-2000 was 91.12 lakhs of which 52 per cent were boys and 48 per cent were girls. The highest percentage of enrollment of all boys was recorded in Mahabubnagar District (in Telangana) *viz.,* 56 per cent. It was around 50 per cent in the remaining districts of the State.

Enrollment of girl children in the Districts of East Godavari, West Godavari and Hyderabad are higher compared to the boys among the districts of the State. Kurnool district recorded only 46.28 per cent enrollment, the lowest rate among the districts of the State.

Table 2
Enrollment of all and SC students by sex in Primary Stage in Andhra Pradesh: 1959-60 to 1999-2000

Year	Overall enrollment			SC enrollment						
	Boys	Girls	Total	Boys	Proportion of SC boys to all boys	Girls	Proportion of SC girls to all girls	Total	Proportion of SCs to all children
1959-60	174336	1062965	2806451	251760	14.44	139567	13.13	391327	13.94
	(62.12)	(37.83)	(100.00)	(64.33)		(35.67)		(100)	
1969-70	2331634	1572320	3903954	293483	12.59	200605	12.76	494088	12.66
	(59.72)	(40.23)	(100.00)	(59.40)		(40.60)		(100)	
1979-80	3024697	2130618	5155315	580572	19.19	392992	18.44	973564	18.88
	(58.67)	(41.33)	(100.00)	(59.63)		(40.37)		(100)	
1989-90	4205423	3115165	7320588	819177	19.48	609325	19.56	1428502	19.51
	(57.45)	(42.55)	(100.00)	(57.35)		(42.65)		(100)	
1999-00	4702696	4409365	9112061	977601	20.79	905790	20.54	1883391	20.67
	(51.61)	(48.39)	(100.00)	(51.91)		(48.09)		(100)	
% Growth rate in 1999-00 over 1959-60	169.73	314.82	224.68	288.31		549.00		381.28	
Annual compound growth rate	2.51	3.62	2.99	3.45		4.79		4.01	

Note: Figures in brackets indicate percentage to the total.

Sources: 1. Commissioner and Director of School Education, Government of Andhra Pradesh, Hyderabad.

2. Statistical Abstracts of Andhra Pradesh for various years, Government of Andhra Pradesh, Hyderabad.

Table 3

Number of all and SC students enrolled by sex in Primary Stage at District level in Andhra Pradesh (1999-2000)

Sl. No.	Name of the District	All enrollment (I-V) Boys Percentage	Girls Percentage	Total Percentage	SC enrollment (I-V) Boys Percentage	Proportion of SC boys to all boys	Girls Percentage	Proportion of SC girls to all girls	Total Percentage	Proportion of total SCs to over all enrollment
1	2	3	4	5	6	7	8	9	10	11
1	Srikakulam	50.64	49.36	100.00	49.60	9.68	50.40	10.09	100	9.88
2	Vizianagaram	50.57	49.43	100.00	49.92	11.81	50.08	12.12	100	11.96
3	Visakhapatnam	51.39	48.61	100.00	50.69	9.30	49.31	9.57	100	9.42
4	East Godavari	49.70	50.30	100.00	49.88	22.68	50.12	22.52	100	22.60
5	West Godavari	49.70	50.30	100.00	49.93	27.64	50.07	27.39	100	17.52
6	Krishna	50.06	49.94	100.00	50.79	29.82	49.21	28.96	100	19.39
7	Guntur	50.69	49.31	100.00	51.82	29.00	48.18	27.71	100	28.36
8	Prakasam	51.92	48.08	100.00	52.75	30.02	47.25	229.03	100	29.55
9	Nellore	50.81	49.19	100.00	50.98	28.41	49.02	28.22	100	28.31
	Coastal Andhra	50.57	49.43	100.00	50.92	22.52	49.08	22.30	100	22.46
10	Chittoor	51.07	48.93	100.00	51.24	21.40	48.76	21.26	100	21.33
11	Cuddapah	51.41	48.59	100.00	52.88	19.92	47.12	18.79	100	19.37
12	Anantapur	51.27	48.73	100.00	52.00	17.77	48.00	17.26	100	17.52

Contd....

13	Kurnool	53.72	46.28	100.00	54.78	22.09	45.22	21.16	100	21.66
	Rayalaseema	*51.99*	*48.01*	*100.00*	*52.88*	*20.35*	*47.12*	*19.63*	*100*	*20.01*
14	Mahabubnagar	55.55	44.45	100.00	56.82	19.01	43.18	18.05	100	18.58
15	Ranaga Reddy	52.60	47.40	100.00	52.27	19.75	47.73	20.01	100	19.87
16	Hyderabad	49.53	50.47	100.00	49.10	10.38	50.90	10.57	100	10.48
17	Medak	52.62	47.38	100.00	52.40	20.88	47.60	21.06	100	20.96
18	Nizamabad	52.66	47.34	100.00	53.24	16.87	46.76	16.49	100	16.69
19	Adilabad	51.76	48.24	100.00	51.95	21.32	48.05	21.16	100	21.24
20	Karimnagar	51.69	48.31	100.00	51.72	21.83	48.28	21.80	100	21.82
21	Warangal	52.06	47.94	100.00	51.90	20.40	48.10	20.53	100	20.46
22	Khammam	51.95	48.05	100.00	51.64	20.58	48.36	20.84	100	20.70
23	Nalgonda	52.93	47.07	100.00	52.35	21.36	47.65	21.86	100	21.59
	Telangana	*52.40*	*47.60*	*100.00*	*52.51*	*19.34*	*47.49*	*19.26*	*100*	*19.30*
	Andhra Pradesh	*51.61*	*48.39*	*100.00*	*51.91*	*20.79*	*48.09*	*20.54*	*100*	*20.67*
	Gross enrolment ratio of primary stage in AP	87.70	84.83	86.28	107.91		103.36		105.67	

Source: Commissioner and Director of School Education, Government of Andhra Pradesh, Hyderabad.

The gross enrollment ratio at the primary stage in the State was 86.28 per cent, 87.70 per cent among boys and 84.83 per cent among girls during the academic year 1999-2000. Barring a couple of exceptions, enrollment ratio was uniformly lower, albeit marginally, among girls than among boys.

The ratio was the highest among boys in the Telangana region– which is often claimed to be economically most backward of the three regions of the State– and the lowest in the Coastal Andhra– the most developed of the three regions. In respect of girls, however, the enrollment ratio was the highest in Coastal Andhra and the lowest in Telangana.

In the case of SCs, the enrollment ratio of boys was the highest at 57 per cent in Mahabubnagar district and the lowest at 49 per cent in Hyderabad district. The gross enrollment ratio at the primary stage in the State among the SCs was 108 per cent for boys and 103 per cent for girls. As in the case of the enrollment ratio of all boys was the highest in Telangana and it was the lowest in Coastal Andhra. The ratio of SC boys was the highest in Rayalaseema and the lowest in Coastal Andhra. This is in contrast to the case of girls, where the enrollment ratio was the highest in Coastal Andhra and the lowest in Rayalaseema.

The enrollment among SC boys as a percentage of all boys and SC girls as a percentage of all girls was calculated using the district-wise and region-wise data. The following points emerge from this exercise (Table-3). (1) Barring five, enrollment ratio was relatively more among SC boys than among SC girls in all districts, (2) Enrollment ratio was the highest in the Coastal Andhra, for boys as also for girls (3) The highest proportion of the enrollment of SC boys to all boys was 30 per cent in Prakasam District and it was the lowest (9.30 per cent) in Visakhapatnam District, and (4) In the case of SC girls, the highest proportion of enrollment (29.03 per cent) was recorded in Prakasam District and the lowest proportion (9.57 per cent) in Visakhapatnam District. It is unfortunate that the proportion of enrollment of SC boys to all boys and SC girls to all girls was the lowest in the district of Visakhapatnam even though it is one of the fast developing cities in the country. The gross-enrollment ratio at the primary stage in Andhra Pradesh among SC children was 105.67-107.91 among SC boys and 103.36 among SC girls.

CLASS-WISE ENROLLMENT AT PRIMARY STAGE IN THE STATE

Table-4 shows that the enrollment of boys and girls from I to V standards during the academic year 1999-2000. One interesting aspect of the Table is that the enrollment ratio is higher for SC boys than for all boys except in I and II standards. One expects this to be because of the existence of social welfare hostels and Ashram schools. As food and clothes are provided freely, SCs are prompted to enroll their children here. In respect of the enrollment of girls, SCs, however, lag behind. In recent years, a number of steps have been taken up by the Government of Andhra Pradesh to strengthen the educational base of SCs. Ideally, the enrollment of SCs in educational process should be as per their proportion in the total population of the State. Though, overall progress in this direction is satisfactory, yet much work is to be done to bridge the educational disparities in enrollment.

Table-4 also shows the dropout rates of children at the primary stage, and it may be concluded that (1) it is slightly higher for a girls (41.23%) than boys (39.42%) in general, but much higher for girls (50.45%) than boys (45.73%) among SCs(2) between all children and SC children, it is much higher for the latter (47.96%) compared to the former (40.28%).

TEACHERS WORKING IN PRIMARY SCHOOLS

So far, only the student enrollment at primary stage was examined. But, it does not really indicate the quality of education. One indicator of quality education is the student-teacher ratio. As such it was examined here the data on number of teachers working in primary schools in each district in the State. In Table-5 data on the number of teachers working in primary schools by sex in each district in the State during the academic year 1999-2000 were presented. The total number of teachers working in primary schools in 1999-2000 was 1.37 lakhs, comprising of 65 per cent males and 35 per cent females. The following points emerge from Table-5 (1) Barring in Hyderabad (77.29%) and Krishna (52.07%) districts, the proportion of female teachers in the total is lower than male teachers, (2) the proportion of female teachers was the highest, though not by a large degree, in Coastal Andhra, among the three regions, (3) understandably enough, the female teachers' proportion among

Table 4

Class– Wise Enrollment of SC students and all students by sex at Primary Stage in Andhra Pradesh (1999-2000)

Classes	*All Enrollment*			*SC Enrollment*					
	Boys percentage	*Girls percentage*	*Total percentage*	*Boys percentage*	*Proportion of SC boys to All boys*	*Girls percentage*	*Proportion of SC girls to All girls*	*Total percentage*	*Proportion of SC enrollment to all enrollment*
I	51.00	49.00	100.00	50.80	20.87	49.50	21.04	100	20.95
II	50.97	49.03	100.00	50.85	20.79	49.15	20.89	100	20.84
III	51.43	48.57	100.00	51.55	20.87	48.45	20.76	100	20.82
IV	52.09	47.91	100.00	52.92	20.97	47.08	20.28	100	20.64
V	53.39	46.61	100.00	55.06	20.33	44.94	19.01	100	19.72
I to V	51.61	48.39	100.00	51.91	20.79	48.09	20.54	100	20.67
Gross enrollment ratio of Primary stage in Andhra Pradesh	87.70	84.83	86.28	107.91		103.06		105.67	
Dropout rate	39.42	41.23	40.28	45.73		50.45		47.96	

Source: Commissioner and Director of School Education, Government of Andhra Pradesh, Hyderabad.

SC teachers is much lower than that of their male counterparts in most of the districts, (4) nevertheless, in the districts of Visakhapatnam, Krishna, Guntur and Hyderabad females among SC teachers constitute more than their counter parts, (5) It is in Coastal Andhra that females' proportion among SC teachers is the highest, (6) Krishna is the district where SCs' from the largest proportion of all teachers among males (21.33%) and East Godavari is the district where SCs from the largest proportion of all teachers among females (24.66%).

STUDENT-TEACHER RATIO

The student-teacher ratio in the primary schools in Andhra Pradesh during the academic year 1999-2000 was recorded at 66.58. In Coastal Andhra it was 54.07, in Rayalaseema region 59.76 and in Telangana 90.73. It is interesting that in the case of student-teacher ratio it was the lowest (36.52) in Nellore District and it was the highest (206.85) in Hyderabad District. Though, the student-teacher ratio of 40 students per teacher for aided schools is the norm, it has never been possible for the government to achieve this objective. The data presented in Table-5 indicate only the districts' average figures and it is much less than 40 in several schools. The Table also shows that the average student-teacher ratio was more than 100 in the districts of Hyderabed and Rangareddy. Low student-teacher ratio affects the quality of education at the primary level, because the school teacher does not find any motivation to teach if the ratio is low, let alone paying the much needed individual attention, which is so essential at the primary stage of education.

CONCLUSIONS

The study sought to place SCs vis-a-vis total population in respect of literacy rates, and enrollment ratio at the primary education stage. Besides, it also tried to focus on the relative significance of SC school teachers compared to all teachers.While gender dimension is provided in the study throughout, the inter-temporal data were also in the analysis of literacy rates and enrollment ratios. For the reason that Andhra Pradesh exhibits wide regional variations district/regional level variation in the variables taken into consideration.

Table 5

Number of ST teachers and all teachers by sex working in primary schools at district-wise in Andhra Pradesh (1999-2000)

Sl. No.	Name of The District	*All teachers* Male %	Female %	Total	Student Teacher ratio	*SC teachers* Male %	Proportion of SC to all teachers-males	Female %	Proportion of SC to all teacher-females	Total	Proportion of total SC teachers to All teachers
1	2	3	4	5	6	7	3	9	10	11	12
1	Srikakulam	78.79	21.21	6006	56.27	78.64	9.81	21.36	9.89	590	9.82
2	Vizianagaram	74.03	25.97	5875	48.25	67.17	9.13	32.83	12.71	591	10.06
3	Visakhapatnam	60.90	39.10	6616	59.20	43.73	6.40	56.27	12.83	590	8.92
4	East Godavari	61.48	38.52	9256	59.59	52.18	16.85	47.82	24.66	1838	19.86
5	West Godavari	56.83	43.17	7531	54.30	55.89	20.61	44.11	21.41	1578	20.95
6	Krishna	47.93	52.07	6800	60.41	45.37	21.33	54.63	23.64	1532	22.53
7	Guntur	52.77	47.23	8058	55.70	47.20	17.26	52.80	21.57	1555	19.30
8	Prakasam	67.85	32.15	7319	56.98	52.96	12.99	47.04	24.35	1218	16.64
9	Nellore	59.80	40.20	8159	36.52	51.51	14.35	48.49	20.09	1359	16.66
	Coastal Andhra	*61.62*	*38.38*	*65620*	*54.07*	*52.84*	*14.18*	*47.16*	*20.32*	*10851*	*16.54*
10	Chittor	63.14	36.86	8742	46.03	80.61	14.91	19.39	6.15	1021	11.68
11	Cuddapah	65.38	34.62	6708	50.71	63.91	14.30	36.09	15.25	981	14.62
12	Anantapur	66.67	33.33	7263	65.07	69.10	7.81	30.90	6.98	547	7.53
13	Kurnool	57.96	42.04	6325	82.24	52.31	16.04	47.69	20.16	1124	17.77

	Rayalaseema	*63.41*	*36.59*	*29038*	*59.76*	*65.78*	*13.12*	*34.22*	*11.83*	*3673*	*12.65*
14	Mahabubnagar	73.69	26.31	5203	87.38	84.49	13.93	15.51	7.16	632	12.15
15	Ranaga Reddy	60.32	39.68	3130	149.83	55.00	9.90	45.00	12.32	340	10.86
16	Hyderabad	22.71	77.29	1836	206.85	17.91	5.76	82.09	7.75	134	7.30
17	Medak	77.24	22.76	3572	91.84	64.29	9.13	35.71	17.22	392	10.97
18	Nizamabad	73.64	26.36	2879	95.52	76.62	7.26	23.38	6.19	201	6.98
19	Adilabad	82.55	17.45	4950	68.44	86.27	10.92	13.73	8.22	517	10.44
20	Karimnagar	74.34	25.66	4727	84.41	69.70	9.82	30.30	12.37	495	10.47
21	Warangal	76.35	23.65	5255	82.97	69.66	10.07	30.34	14.16	580	11.04
22	Khammam	64.36	35.64	4983	62.45	55.56	15.59	44.44	22.52	900	18.06
23	Nalgonda	72.39	27.61	5660	77.22	71.47	12.84	28.53	13.44	736	13.00
	Telangana	70.94	29.6	42195	90.73	68.44	11.26	31.56	12.68	4927	11.68
	Andhra Pradesh	64.88	35.12	136853	66.58	59.24	12.98	40.76	16.50	19451	14.21

Source: Commissioner and Director of School Education, Government of Andhra Pradesh, Hyderabad.

The major conclusions, as they energy from the Study are as follows: (1) While females generally lag behind males in literacy rates, the disparity in the rate between all persons and SCs is higher among females than among males, (2) Government's initiatives aimed at motivating the SCs to enroll their children in increasing numbers are bearing fruit especially in respect of enrollment of boys, (3) Enrollment ratio does not seem to be related to the development of a region. In fact, the backward Telangana is found to have recorded high enrollment is respect of boys, (4) The dropout rate among SC girls is much higher than that of SC boy s and, between all children and SC children, it is much higher for the latter. The opportunity cost of sending SC children to primary school, notwithstanding the incentives provided by the government to them, seems to be very higher, (5) Student-teacher ratio, as seen from the district-level averages, seems to be promising. However, wide variations between schools, with some schools reporting an extremely adverse ratio could be noticed, and (6) Females are yet to gain considerable foothold as teachers in schools and this is much more so in respect of SC females.

REFERENCES

Chalam, K.S. (1985), Educational Development of the Scheduled Castes in the Districts of Andhra Pradesh, (Mimeo), School of Economics, Andhra University, Visakhapatnam.

Chalam, K.S, (1988), Education and Weaker Sections, Inter India Publication, New Delhi.

Chauhan, B.R. and others (1975), Scheduled Castes and Education, Anu Publications, Meerut.

Gopinathan Nair, P.R. (1981), Primary Education, Population Growth and Socio-Economic Change, Allied Publishers, New Delhi.

Government of India (1986), National Policy on Education 1986: Programme of Action, New Delhi.

Kabra, G.D. (1984), Development of Weaker Sections, Inter-India Publications, New Delhi.

Naik, J.P (1975), Elementary Education is India– a Promise to Keep, Allied Publishers, Bombay.

Rajaiah, B (1987), Economics of Education, Mittal Publication, New Delhi.

9

RIGHTS AND PRIVILEGES OF THE SCHEDULED CASTES COMMUNITY OF INDIA

Tapan Kumar Ghosh

INTRODUCTION

The term 'Scheduled Castes' was first introduced in the Government of the India Act, 1935 to mean such castes, races, or tribes, which correspond to the classes of persons formerly known as the 'Depressed classes'. The Scheduled Castes have been specified by 15 Presidential orders issued under the provisions of Article 341 of the Constitution. According to the 2001 census, about 16.20 per cent of the country's population comprised the Scheduled Castes. The term Scheduled Castes is both a legal and social concept. The term 'Scheduled Castes' to connote depressed classes was coined by Government of India Act, 1935.

The Scheduled Castes-the Harijans— who are considered by caste-Hindus to be those ordained by God to serve the higher castes in unpleasant, disgraceful and menial task comprise about 15 per cent of India's total population. About 90 per cent of these castes live in rural India and most of them are illiterate (Report of the Backward Classes Commission, 1956, p.3). More than 75 per cent of the Scheduled Caste population is engaged in agriculture and a majority of them are landless labourers.

Marc Galanter argued long ago long ago that "there is no indication in the Constitution that executive action, even in pursuance of expressly granted and exclusive constitutional powers, is immune from judicial review for conformity with constitutional guarantees of fundamental rights" (Galanter, p.351).

Wollheim and Berlin both have emphasized the concept of equality in the context of nature by asserting the dual assumption in respect of equality: "(a) men are all makes of one species, of a simple class of objects, i.e., human being, and (b) that all members of a class should be treated uniformly, unless there is good and sufficient reason not to do so" (Wollheim and Berlin, p.281).

To escape the stigma and scourge of the age-old malady, thousands of Scheduled Castes became converted to other religions, but even this could not wipe off the scar of untouchability. Even after 57 years of independence, various steps taken to eradicate this evil appear to have achieved negligible success; on the other hand these have led to social tensions, suppression of overt reactions, and putting a false veil on caste prejudices. The masses in general have on wisdom to adopt a rational approach to this evil, and thus untouchability has corroded the solidarity, prosperity and emotional integration of our nation and plagued the principles of secularism, democratic socialism and social justice to which we are committed (Upadhyay, p.5).

The Constitution of India has not only abolished and forbidden the practice of untouchability, but it has also made it an offence punishable by law. Accordingly, the Parliament has passed "The Untouchability (Offence) Act, 1955 and Civil Rights Protection Act, 1976" to prescribe punishment for various offences of untouchability. Thus, the supreme law of the land, i.e. the Constitution has provided for its abolition and punishment for its practice in any from (Upadhyay, pp. 14-15).

Article 46 envisages that the State shall promote with special care the educational and economic interest of the weaker sections of the people and, in particular, of the Scheduled Castes and the Scheduled Tribes (STs) and shall protect them from social injustice and all froms of exploitation. In addition, there are other provisions, *inter-alia,* for representation in Parliament (Article 330) and the State legislation (Article 332), representation in the Central and State services (Article 335), abolition of the practice of Untouchability (Article 17), throwing open of Hindu religious institutions, admission into educational institutions (Articles 25 and 29), banning of traffic in human beings, and beggars, and similar forms of forced labour, appointment of a special officer to investigate all matters relating to safeguards provided to the Scheduled Castes and Scheduled Tribes (Article 338). Prohibition of discrimination on grounds of religion, race, caste, sex or place of birth, special provision for Scheduled Castes and Scheduled Tribes (Article 15), protection of certain rights regarding freedom of speech, etc. (Article 19), prohibition of traffic in human beings and forced labour (Article 23), legislation to give effect to the provisions relating to Fundamental Rights (Article 35), state to secure a social order for the promation of welfare of people (Article 38), equal justice and free legal aid (Article 39), other provisions as to Ministers (Article 164), administration of Scheduled Areas and Tribal Areas (Article 224), functions of Public Service commissions [Article 320(4)], control of the union over the administration of Scheduled Areas and the welfare of Scheduled Tribes (Article 339), appointment of a Commission to investigate the conditions of Backward Classes (Article 340), list of Scheduled Castes (Article 341), and special provision with respect to the State of Nagaland, Assam and Manipur (Article 371A, 37B and 371C (Upadhyay, pp.19-20).

As noted above and as it will be clear from the following discussion that theoretically Scheduled Castes have been given more constitutional safeguards. But the questions are: What is the condition of the Scheduled Castes? What do they feel about themselves in relation to others? What distance do others maintain with them at the village through the existence of caste system? A through investigation into this matter is necessary.

The present paper makes an attempt to find answers to the above questions alongwith some other relevant questions, which have contemporary as well as long lasting relevance and implications for future socio-economic development of Scheduled Castes. For our purpose we have mainly used secondary data and literature from various sources. The paper is divided into five sections. The first section deals with the introduction, definition and genesis of SCs. The second section deals with the present status of Scheduled Castes in India since 1931. In the third section we have discussed the constitutional safeguards and laws, relating to Scheduled Castes. In the fourth section— we have discussed a comment on the reservation policy. Section five concludes the discussion.

Who are the Scheduled Castes?

Those people belonging to the last '*Varna*' (Caste) namely the '*Shudra*' and '*Avarnas*' (people outside the caste system) include many caste groups, which have suffered social and economic inequity since the ages. Particularly those people who were outside the '*Varna*' system were known as '*Avarnas*' or '*Panchmas*' or '*Antyajas*'. They were external in the sense that they were required to stay outside the village settlement. The concept of pollution was attached to them and they were treated as untouchable castes. These castes were systematically listed in the 1931 census of India. These untouchable castes in India were officially defined as depressed castes in 1932 (Harold, p.36). Gandhiji named them Harijans where 'Hari' means God, 'Jan' means people and thus "Harijan" means people of God. This word in Marathi, Gujarathi, Hindi, and other languages means a child whose father's identity is unknown, and hence a bastard progeny. Therefore, the name Harijan was not only disliked but was hated and opposed by the untouchables. Surprisingly enough, their reaction to the word Scheduled Caste or even to the word untouchable is not that sharp. As a result there was a wild cry, an agitation and a strong opposition to the Bill using the word Harijan in the Bombay Legislative Assembly. It was duly replaced by the term Scheduled Castes in 1938 and it is continuously used as Scheduled Castes in government records and circulars even today.

The expression Scheduled Castes was first coined by the Simon Commission and embodied in the Government of India Act of 1935. While the castes were listed systematically in the 1931 census of India, the terms Scheduled Castes was applied to these castes for the first time in the Government of India Act of 1935. Until then they were known as untouchables, depressed classes or exterior castes. Then the Government of India published a list of Scheduled Castes under the Government of India (Scheduled Castes) Order, 1936 (Yadav, p.237)(See Appendix).

Genesis of Scheduled Castes

With the coming into force of the Constitution of India, the Scheduled Castes have assumed certain essential rights and privileges. The Constitution has attempted to give a definition of the Scheduled Castes in Article 341 and has refrained from defining the other groups. Article 341, as amended says:

(1) The President may with respect to any State or Union territory, and where it is a State, after consultation with the Governor there of, by public notification, specify the castes, races or tribes or parts of or groups within castes, races or tribes which shall for the purposes of this Constitution be deemed to be Scheduled Castes in relation to that State or Union territory, as the case may be.

(2) Parliament may by law include in or exclude from the list of Scheduled Castes specified in a notification issued under (1) any caste, race or tribe or part of or group within any caste, race or tribe, but save as aforesaid a notification issued under the said clause shall not be varied by any subsequent notification (Bakshi, p.285).

Article 341 closely resembles Section 26(1) of the first Scheduled of the Government of India Act, 1935, which defines Scheduled Castes as follows: The 'Scheduled Castes' means such castes, races or tribes or parts of or groups within castes, races, or tribes, being castes, races, tribes, parts or groups which appear to His Majesty in Council to correspond to the classes of persons formerly known as "the depressed classes", as His Majesty in Council may specify.

The term 'Scheduled Castes' as we have already mentioned was used for the first time in the 1935 Act and in pursuance of the provisions in the 1st, 5th and 6th Schedules of the Act, the Government of India (Scheduled Castes) Order, 1936 was issued delineating the castes and tribes to be treated as the 'Scheduled Castes' for the purposes of the Act in the respective provinces. The Constitutional Adviser in his Draft Constitution, prepared in October 1947, adhered to this 1936 Order of the Government of India and put these castes in the Eleventh Schedule of the Draft Constitution, Provincewise. The Drafting Committee, however, simplified the procedure and instead of enumerating all the Scheduled Castes in a Schedule of the Constitution, simply stipulated that the expression Scheduled Castes should mean those as were specified in the Government of India (Scheduled Castes) Order, 1936 in relation to the corresponding provinces (Chatterjee, p.962).

But towards the fag end of the Constituent Assembly sessions, on September 17, 1949, on a motion moved by Dr. Ambedkar, the Chairman of the Drafting Committee, a new Article (Article 341) was inserted empowering the President to issue a general notification, in consultation, with the Governor or Ruler of the State, specifying the castes, races or tribes which should be deemed to be Scheduled Castes for purposes of the Constitution.

PRESENT STATUS OF SCHEDULED CASTES

Table-1 gives the total population as well as the Scheduled Caste population in India as enumerated in the censuses since 1931. The 1931 figure has been calculated according to the 1936 Order. Both the 1931 and 1941 figures pertain to undivided India. In 1981, census could not be held in Assam because of the disturbed condition prevailing there at the time of census operations. The projected population of Assam has, however, been given in the census report of 1981.

In 1991, census could not be conducted in Jammu and Kashmir due to the disturbed condition in that state.

Table 1

Total Population as Well as the Scheduled Caste Population Since 1931.

Censuses	*Total Population*	*Total Scheduled Caste Population*	*Percentage of Scheduled Caste Population to Total Population*
1931	256757818*	39912634*@	15.54
1941	295808722*	39920807*	13.49
1951	356700000	51343898	14.40
1961	439234771	64449275	14.67
1971	548159652	80005398	14.60
1981	685184692**	10602707**	15.47
1991	846302688***	138864477***	16.41
2001	1028610328#	166635700#	16.20

* Only British Indian Provinces in Undivided Indian.

* * Includes Projected Population of Assam.

* * * Includes Projected Population of Jammu and Kashmir.

@ Approximately,

\# Excludes Mao-Maram, Paomata and Purul sub-divisions of Senapati district of Manipur.

Sources:

Census of India, 1931, Vol. XVIII, Part I, pp.634-638.

Census of India, 1941, Vol. I, Pt. I (Tables), Table XIII, p.98.

Census of India, 1951, Paper 4 of 1953, p.3.

Census of India, 1961, Vol. I, Part V A (1), P. xiviii.

Census of India, 1971, Series I, Paper 1 of 1975, pp.2-4.

Census of India, 1981, Series I, Paper 2 of 1984, p. 6 and pp.14-16.

Census of India, 1991, Series I, Paper 2 of 1992, ,p.86.

Census of India, 2001, Primary Census Abstract.

It will appear from Table-1 that the Scheduled Caste population declined appreciably in the 1941 census, *i.e.*, immediately after the 1936 Order listing the castes as 'Scheduled' was issued. It registered a steady in ready increase since 1951, with the exception in 1971 when it decreased marginally compared to that of 1961.

Table-2 shows the total population, population of Scheduled Castes and their proportions to the total population in 2001. According to the 2001 census the population of the Scheduled Castes stands at 166635700, which constitutes 16.20 per cent of the country's total. Of the total Scheduled Caste population, more than 90 per cent live in rural areas; only less than 10 per cent live in urban areas. The largest population of the Scheduled Castes to the total population of the State is found in Punjab, *i.e.*, 28.9 per cent, followed by 24.7 per cent in Himachal Pradesh, 23.0 per cent in West Bengal 21.4 per cent in Uttar Pradesh, 19.3 per cent in Haryana, 19.0 per cent in Tamil Nadu, 17.9 per cent in Uttaranchal, 17.4 per cent in Tripura, 17.2 per cent in Rajasthan and 16.5 per cent in Orissa.

In the States of Andhra Pradesh, Kanataka and Pandicherry, their proportion is the same of the national level i.e., 16.2 per cent. In the remaining States their proportion is less than the national average of 16.2 per cent. Among the union territories Chandigarh stands first (eighth at the all-India level), with 17.5 per cent of its total population returned as the Scheduled Castes, followed by Delhi (eleventh at the all-India level) with 16.9 per cent and pandicherry (thirteenth at the all-India level) with 16.2 per cent.

The smallest concentration of the Scheduled Castes is in the tribal States, such as Manipur (2.8 per cent of Scheduled Castes to the total state population), followed by Arunachal Pradesh (0.6 per cent), Meghalaya (0.5 per cent) and so on. The States Nagaland and Mizoram and the union territory of Lakshadweep and Andaman and Nicobbar Islands have no Scheduled Caste population.

CONSTITUTIONAL SAFEGUARDS AND LAWS

There was already a general feeling in the country that the two most disadvantaged groups of society, *i.e.*, Scheduled Castes and the Scheduled Tribes needed a fair generous treatment at the hands of the society so as to bring them up socially, economically and politically to the same level as the rest of the nation by providing them permanent safeguards. So the founding father of the Indian

Constitution thought it fit to make special provision in the Constitution for the Scheduled Castes, Scheduled Tribes and other Backward Classes (Dutta, p.1 and Pandey, p.457).

Table 2
Total Population, Population of Scheduled Castes and Their Proportions to Total Population 2001.

State Code	India/ State/ Union Territory	Total Population of the State/Union Territory	SC Population of the State/UT	Prop. of SC Pop. to total Pop. of the State
01	Jammu and Kashmir	10143700	770155	7.6
02	Himachal Pradesh	6077900	1502170	24.7
03	Punjab	24358999	7028723	28.9
04	Chandigarh	900635	157597	17.5
05	Uttaranchal	8489349	1517186	17.9
06	Haryana	21144564	4091110	19.3
07	Delhi	13850507	2343255	16.9
08	Rajasthan	56507188	9694462	17.2
09	Uttar Pradesh	166197921	35148377	21.1
10	Bihar	82998509	13048608	15.7
11	Sikkim	540851	27165	5.0
12	Arunachal Pradesh	1097968	6188	0.6
13	Nagaland	1990036	0	0.0
14	Manipur @	2166788	60037	2.8
15	Mizoram	888573	272	0.0
16	Tripura	3199203	555724	17.4
17	Meghalaya	2318822	11139	0.5
18	Assam	26655528	1825949	6.9
19	West Bengal	80176197	18452555	23.0
20	Jharkhand	26945829	3189320	11.8
21	Orissa	36804660	6082063	16.5
22	Chhattisgarh	20833803	2418722	11.6
23	Madhya Pradesh	60348023	9155177	15.2
24	Gujarat	50671017	3592715	7.1
25	Daman and Diu	158204	4838	3.1
26	Dadra and Nagar Haveli	220490	4104	1.9
27	Maharashtra	96878627	9881656	10.2
28	Andhra Pradesh	76210007	12339496	16.2
29	Karnataka	52850562	8563930	16.2
30	Goa	1347668	23791	1.8
31	Lakshadweep	60650	0	0.0
32	Kerala	31841374	3123941	9.8
33	Tamil Nadu	62405679	11857504	19.0
34	Pondicherry	974345	157771	16.2
35	Andaman and Nicobar Islands	356152	0	0.0
	India @	1028610328	166635700	16.2

Source: Primary Census Abstract: Census of India 2001.

Note: @ - Excludes Mao-Maram, Paomata and Pural sub-divisions of Senapati district of Manipur.

The positive preferential treatment of these depressed classes of the society is called by different names like Protective Discrimination, Reverse Discrimination, Compensatory Discrimination, Special Treatment, Concession, Privilege Special Provisions and Preferential Treatment. But scholars have inclined touse either Protective Discrimination or Compensatory Discrimination (Galanter 1984, Prasad 1991).

Galanter (1984, p.43) mentions that preferences are of three basic types.

These are as under:

(1) Reservation facilities access to valid position such as reserved seats in legislature, reservation of posts in government service, and reservation of places in academic institutions. Reservation device is also used in the distribution of land allotment, housing and other scarce resources.

(2) There are programming involving expenditure or provision of services e.g. scholarship, grants, loans, land allotments, health care, legal aid etc.

(3) There are efforts to protect the Backward Classes from being exploited and victimized. Forced labour is prohibited and victims of debt bondage are released to protect the Scheduled Castes and Scheduled Tribes. From the economic oppressions they are to be protected by legislations regulating the money lending and providing the debt relief and restricting land transfer. The protection of Civil Rights Act attempts to relieve the untouchables from the social disabilities.

The need for providing adequate safeguards to Scheduled Castes and Scheduled Tribes was recognized by the framers of the Indian Constitution. For this purpose, special provisions were made in the Constitution to promote social, educational, economic and service interests of these weaker sections of the society. The Constitution of India also provided for appointment of a Special Officer under Article 338 for investigation of all matters relating to the safeguards provided for the Scheduled Castes and Scheduled Tribes.

PROVISIONS MADE IN THE VARIOUS ARTICLES OF THE CONSTITUTION ARE AS FOLLOWS;

(A) Development and Protective Safeguards

These safeguards are contained in the Directive Principles of State Policy of the Constitution and a specific provision in Article 46 which is a comprehensive provision comprising both the developmental and regulatory aspects. It reads as follows:

Article 46: "The State shall promote with special care the educational and ecomomic interests of the weaker sections of the people, and in particular, of the Scheduled Castes and the Scheduled Tribes, and Shall protect them for social injustice and all form of exploitation." (Bakshi, p.90)

(B) Social Safeguards

These safeguards are contained in Article 17, Article 23, Article 24 and Article 25(2)(b). It reads as follows:

Article 17: "Untouchability" is abolished and its practice in any from is forbidden. The enforcement of any disability arising out of "Untouchability" shall be an offence punishable in accordance with law.

To give effect to this Article, Parliament made an enactment viz., Untouchability (Offences) Act, 1955. To make the provisions of this Act more stringent, the Act was amended in 1976 and was also renamed as the Protection of Civil Rights Act, 1955.

Article 23:

(1) Traffic in human beings and beggar and other similar forms of forced labour are prohibited and any contravention of this provision shall be an offence punishable in accordance with law.

(2) Nothing in this Article shall prevent the State from imposing compulsory service for public purposes, and in imposing such service the State shall not make any discrimination on grounds only of religion, race, caste or class or any of them.

It does not specifically mention Scheduled Castes and Scheduled Tribes but since majority of bonded labour belong to SCs/STs this Article has a special significance for these communities. In pursuance of this Article, Parliament has enacted the Bonded Lobour System (Abolition) Act, 1976. For effective implementation of this Act, the Ministry of Labour is running a Centrally Sponsored Scheme for identification, liberation and rehabilitation of bonded labour (Bakshi, pp.60-61).

Article 24: No child below the age of fourteen years shall be employed to work in any factory or mine or engaged in any other hazardous employment.

There are Centrally and State laws to prevent child labour. This Article is also significant for Scheduled Castes and Scheduled Tribes as a substantial portion of child labour engaged in hazardous jobs belong to these groups.

Article 25(2) (b): Providing for social welfare and reform or the throwing open of Hindu religious institutions of a public character to all classes and sections of Hindus.

This provision is relevant as some sects of Hindus used to claim that only members of the concerned sects had a right to enter their temples. This was only a subterfuge to prevent entry of Scheduled Caste persons in such temples. For the purpose of this provision the term Hindu includes Sikh, jain and Budddhist.

(C) Economic Safeguards

The provisions of Articles 23, 24 and 46 mentioned above also form part of the economic safeguards for Scheduled Castes and Scheduled Tribes. The specific safeguards provided for the Scheduled Tribes are mentioned below:

Article 244:

(1) The provisions of the Fifth Schedule shall apply to the administration and control of the Scheduled Areas and Scheduled Tribes in any State other than the States of Assam, Meghalaya, Tripura and Mizoram.

(2) The provisions of the Sixth Schedule shall apply to the administration of the tribal areas in the States of Assam, Meghalaya, Tripura and Mizoram (Bakshi, pp.217-218).

(D) Educational and Cultural Safeguards

These safeguards are contained in Article 15(4), Article 29(1) and Article 350(A). These are mentioned below:

Article 15(4) empowers the State to make any special provision for the advancement of any socially and educationally backward classes of citizens or for SCs and STs. This provision has enabled the State to reserve seats for SCs and STs in educational institutions including technical, engineering and medical colleges and in scientific and Specialized courses (Bakshi, p.26).

Article 29(1) provides "Any section of the citizens residing in the territory of India or any part there of having a distinct language, script or culture of its own shall have the right to conserve the same." This Article has special significance for all the Scheduled Tribes.

Article 350(A): "It shall be the endeavour of every State and of every local authority within the State to provide adequate facilities for instruction in the mother-tongue at the primary stage of education to children belonging o linguistic minority groups; and the President may issue such directions to any State as he considers necessary or proper for securing the provisions of such facilities." (Bakshi, p.289)

Most of the Tribal communities have their own languages or dialects, which usually belong to a different family of languages than the one to which the State's official language belongs.

(E) Political Safeguards

These safeguards are contained in Article 330, Article 332 and Article 334. These can be mentioned below:

Article 330 provides for reservation of seats for the Scheduled Castes and Scheduled Tribes in the house of people (Lok Sabha).

Article 332 Provides for reservation of seats for the Scheduled Castes and the Scheduled Tribes in Legislative Assemblies of the States (Vidhan Sabhas).

Article 334 originally laid down that the provisions relating to the reservation of seats for SCs/STs in the Lok Sabha and State Vidhan Sabhas (and the representation of the Anglo-Indian community in the Lok Sabha and the State Vidhan Sabhas by nomination) would cease to be effective on the expiration of a period of ten years from the commencement of the Constitution. This Article has been amended five times, extending the said period by ten years on each occasion. This provision will now expire in January 2010 (National Commission for Scheduled Castes and Scheduled Tribes).

(F) Service Safeguards

These safeguards are contained in Article 16(4), Article 335 and Article 320(4). The specific safeguards are mentioned below:

Article 16(4) empowers the State to make "any provisions for the reservation of appointments or posts in favour of any backward class of citizens which in the opinion of the State, is not adequately represented in the services under the State" (Bakshi, pp.28-29).

Provided that nothing in this Article shall prevent in making of any provision in favour of the members of the SCs and STs for relaxation in qualifying marks in any examination or lowering the standards of evaluation, for reservation in matters of promotion to any class or classes of services or posts in connection with the affairs of the Union or of a State.

Article 320(4) provides that nothing in Clause (3) shall require a Public Service Commission to be consulted as respects the manner in which any provision under Article 16(4A) may be made or the manner in which effect may be given to the provisions of Article 335.

Enforcement of the Protection of Civil Rights Act

Ever since the Untouchability (Offences) Act, 1955 came into force, there has been criticism both inside and outside Parliament that the Act is not serving the purpose for which it was enacted. It was pointed out that the punishments awarded under the Act were too few and inadequate. In view of this criticism, the Government of India tried to enlarge the scope of the Act and the amended Act, now known as the Protection of Civil Rights Act, aimed at plugging the loopholes of the principal Act. It came into force with effect from 19th November 1976. Some of the features of the amended Act are given below:

(1) Punishment for untouchability offences has been considerably enhanced, and both imprisonment and fine are simultaneously awarded for such offences.

(2) Untouchability offences have been made non-compoundable.

(3) Every offence, except where it is punishable with imprisonment for a minimum term exceeding three months, may be tried summarily.

(4) Direct or indirect preaching of untouchability or its justification on historical, philosophical, religious or traditional grounds has been made an offence punishable under the Act.

(5) State Government have been empowered to impose collective fines on the inhabitants of any area where such inhabitants are concerned in or abetting the Commission of untouchability offences.

(6) A public Servant, who willfully neglects the investigation of any offence punishable under this Act, shall be deemed to have abetted an offence punishable under the Act.

(7) State Governments are required to take up necessary measures to ensure that the rights accruing from the abolition of 'Untouchability' are made available to, and are availed of by the persons subjected to any disability arising out of 'Untouchability'.

In sub-section (2) of section 15A of the Act, the State Government have been directed to undertake inter-alia the following measures:

(1) Provision of adequate facilities, including legal aid, to the persons subjected to any disability arising out of 'Untouchability' to enable them to avail themselves of such rights.

(2) Appointment of officers for initiating or exercising supervision over prosecutions for the contravention of the provisions of the Act.

(3) Setting up the special courts for the trial of offences under the Act.

(4) Setting up of Committees at such appropriate levels as the State Government may think fit to assist the State Government, in formulating and implementing such measures.

(5) Provision for a periodic survey of the working of the provisions of the Act with a view to suggesting measures for the better implementation of the provisions of the Act.

(6) Identification of the areas where persons are under any disability arising out of 'Untouchability' and adoption of such measures as could ensure the removal of such disability from such areas.

Working of the 1955 Act

It appears that the passing of the Untouchability (Offences) Act, 1955 was a small reform in the direction of abolition of untouchability, because there was no special machinery provided for the implementation of the Act. The Committee on Untouchability urged, "a genuine need for the formulation of an effective machinery for the enforcement of the provisions of the Untouchability (Offences) Act, 1955 cannot be denied" (Report of the Committee on Untouchability, Economic and Educational Development of the Scheduled Castes and Connected Documents, p.55). The fact that the said Act not properly and effectively working is clear from the reports of the Commissioner for SCs and STs and also from the information collected by the Committee.

The incidence of untouchability prevailing in the country is quite high. The cases registered under the Untouchability (Offences) Act, 1955, show a rising trend. This shows that legislative enactment against untouchability has not proved very effective and could not eradicate it completely. Untouchability has struck its roots deep in the Indian soil, resisting all attempts to unearth it. More than legislative measures, what is needed today is a change of heart. People should realize that untouchability is not only a social problem but also a national necessity.

Thus the Untouchability (Offences) Act, 1955 was not found effective in the eradication of untouchability and was therefore, amended in 1976 and is now knows as the Protection of Civil Rights Act.

Protection of Civil Rights – The Amended Act, 1976

The salient features of 1976 Amended Act are as under:

(1) Imprisonment of not less than one month and not more than six months and also a fine ranging from rupees 100 to rupees 500 for all offences under the Act except for the unlawful compulsory labour where the imprisonment shall be from three to six months and also fine ranging from rupees 100 to 500.

(2) Employment of any job cannot be refused on grounds of untouchability.

(3) No persons shall be compelled on grounds of untouchability to do any scavenging or sweeping or remove carcass or to flay any assimal or to remove the umbilical cord or to do any job of a similar nature.

(4) No public officer shall willfully neglect the investigation of any offence punishable under the Act.

(5) There shall be enhanced penalty for subsequent conviction, for example, for a second offence the imprisonment may run from six months to one year and also a fine of rupees 200 to 500; for a third or subsequent to the third offence, the imprisonment would be form one year to two years and also a fine of rupees 500 to rupees 1000.

(6) Imposition of collective fine.

(7) No application of the probation of Offenders Act, 1958 shall be available against conviction under this Act.

(8) Duties of State Government: The Act enjoins on the State Governments certain duties relating to the enforcement and effectiveness of the Act.

The duties may be summarized as follows:

(a) Provision of adequate facilities including legal aid to the persons subjected to any disability arising out of untouchability.

(b) Appointment of officers for initiating or exercising supervision over prosecution for the contravention of the provisions of the Act.

(c) Setting up of committees at appropriate levels to assist the State Governments in formulating and implementing such measures as are for furtherance of the Act.

(d) Setting up of special courts for the trial of offences under the Act.

(e) Periodic survey of the working of the Act.

(f) Identification of the areas, localities, and habitants where persons are under such disabilities as are mentioned in the Act.

(g) Adoption of such measures as would ensure the removal of disabilities mentioned in the Act.

(9) The offence, which was compounded under the 1955 Act, shall no more be compoundable after the 1976 amended Act. Where the minimum imprisonment is less than three months, the offence shall be summarily triable.

(10) Insulting or attempting to insult a member of a Scheduled Caste on the ground of untouchability.

(11) Commission of any offence against the person or property of any individual as a reprisal or revenge for his having exercised any right accruing to him by reason of the abolition of "Untouchability" (Upadhyay, pp.158-160).

A COMMENT ON THE RESERVATION POLICY

Historical Background of Reservation

Realising the inequitable distribution of posts in the administration between different castes and communities, the rulers of some of the then Princely States, who were genuinely interested in the upliftment of disadvantageous sections of the society, took initiatives and introduced reservations in the administrative posts in favour of the backward castes and communities in their States as early as in the first quarter of the 20th century. Mysore and Kolahpur were amongst the first to do so. Because of the movement for social justice and equity started by the justice party, the then Presidency of Madras initiated the reservation in Government employment in 1921 (Committee on the Welfare of Scheduled Castes and Scheduled Tribes, 2001-2002). It was followed by Bombay Presidency comprising the major portion of present States of Maharashtra, Karnataka and Gujarat. Thus, the first quarter of the 20th century saw reservations in Government jobs in almost whole of Southern India. These reservations were not only in favour of the depressed classes which were rechristined as Scheduled Castes in the Government of India Act, 1935, but also in favour of other backward castes and classes including what were then known as intermediate castes.

Before the Poona Pact 1932 the representation of depressed classes in public service was negligible except for a few packets of old presidency of Madras and Princely State of Mysore. In the Poona Pact under Clause (6) a provision was made under which government was to make every endeavour to secure fair representation of the depressed classes in elections to local bodies and appointments to public services.

Reservation Prior to 1947 – British India

For the first time, instructions were issued in 1934, without providing a formal reservation that candidates belonging to depressed classes and possessing the requisite qualifications should not be deprived of fair opportunities of appointment merely because they could not succeed in open competition. The term Scheduled Castes was used for the first time in the Government of India Act, 1935. In August 1943, Government of India provided reservation at the rate of 8 1/3 per cent for the Scheduled Castes in the vacancies filled up by direct recruitment through open competition. The relaxation in the upper-age limit and concessions in examination fee prescribed for appointment to a service or post were announced in favour of the Scheduled Caste Candidates.

Reservation after Independence

Soon after independence, orders were issued by the Government on 21.09.1947 providing for reservations in services for Scheduled Castes at the rate of 12.5 per cent of vacancies in respect of direct recruitment through open competition. In the case of recruitment otherwise than by open competition separate reservation at the rate of 16 2/3 per cent was provided in favour of Scheduled Castes.

Constitutional Provisions for Reservation

The framers of the Constitution felt that unless special provisions were made for the protection of the right of Scheduled Castes and Scheduled Tribes to secure fair representation in public employment in proportion to their population, it would never be possible to catch up and complete successfully for securing public employment. Therefore, to secure fair representation of SCs and STs in service and posts under the State, special provisions of reservation under Article 16(4), Article 46 and Article 335 of the Constitution were made.

The Constitution prescribes protection and safeguards for Scheduled Castes and Scheduled Tribes, either specifically or by way of general rights of Citizens, with the object of promoting their educational and economic interests and of removing certain social disabilities the Scheduled Castes were subjected to. These are as follows:

(1) The abolition of 'Untouchability' and the forbidding of its practice in any form (Article 17);

(2) The promotion of their educational and economic interests and their protection from social injustice and all form of exploitation (Article 46);

(3) The throwing open of Hindu religious institutions of a public character to all classes and sections of Hindus (Article 25);

(4) The removal of any disability, liability, restriction or condition with regard to access to shops, public restaurants, hotels and places of public entertainment, the

use of wells tanks, bathing ghats, roads and places of public resort maintained wholly or partly out of State funds or dedicated to the use of the general public (Article 15);

(5) The right to practice any profession or carry on any occupation, trade or business (Article 19);

(6) The forbidding of any denial of admission to educational institutions maintained by the States or receiving aid out of State funds (Article 29);

(7) The obligation of the State to consider their claims in the making of appointments to public services and reservation for them in case of inadequate representation (Articles 16 and 335);

(8) Special representation in Parliament and the State Legislation for a period of twenty years (Articles 330, 332 and 334);

(9) The setting up of advisory councils and separate departments in the State and the appointment of a special Official at the Centre to promote their welfare and safeguard their interests (Articles 164, 338 and Fifth Schedule); and

(10) Special provision for the administration and control of schedule and tribal areas (Article 244 and Fifth and Sixth Schedules).

CONCLUSIONS

The Scheduled Castes have passed a long way to reach the present condition. They have long suffered from innumerable disabilities as stated above. Reformers thought about it and finally the Scheduled Castes have been protected through providing constitutional and juridical measures. Although the commissioner for Scheduled Castes and Scheduled Tribes from time to time has been suggesting various remedies, it has to be made clear that instead of suggesting ideological remedies it may prove more beneficial if the suggestions are based on rational thinking and the principles of social equilibrium. At present, we require a well consistent plan for the socio-economic upliftment of the Scheduled Castes keeping in view their present attitudes and emerging trends of relationships with other castes. With this objective in mind, the following suggestions may prove more useful and constructive to improve the conditions of Scheduled Castes suitable to the total structure of our society.

1. To abolish the virus of untouchability in India, it is felt necessary to modify the provisions of Untouchability (Offence) Act in order to control and minimized quite effectively the deprivation of and the incidence of atrocities on Scheduled Castes. Incidentally it should be noted that the incidence of bonded labours amongst them is quite high. Virtually speaking the problem arising out of bonded labour is largely social and cultural then economic in nature. And as such, the removal of such practice requires a change of mindset of those who employ them.
2. It is observed that untouchability is inherent in some section of the community and as such it should be eradicated completely and not partially. Although the public places like well, temple, school, hospital, shops, streets, etc., are covered by the Act, the private places like house and private premises including well or tap, temple or place of worship are not similarly covered by the protection of Civil Right Act.
3. Much controversies and arguments for the against have been raised in connection with reservation issues. It is strongly felt that in order to minimize the frustrations of Scheduled Caste community, heavy backlog of reserved vacancies existing in the public sector and autonomous bodies needs urgent attention of the Government and at the same time arrangements should be made for filling up the quota of reserved vacancies in such a way that the Scheduled Castes communities are adequately represented in all categories of sevices. Unless a strict vigilance by the constitutional authority is ensured, there is perhaps no likelihood of the reservation rules being implemented effectively. But it should be noted that reservation as is existing in the field of some kind of promotions, for example, may not be justified, as it is expected to tell upon efficiency heavily.
4. In spite of the constitutional safeguards and socio-economic protection, the problems of Scheduled Castes

are continuing in our society especially in rural and interior areas. They are infact the worst victims of the sorry state of affairs. Hence it might be suggested that sincere efforts would be necessary towards the formulation of a uniform policy applicable throughout the entire rural areas of India as a whole. It is only with the uniformity of laws and their effectiveness that the unequal treatment in respect of Scheduled Castes in rural areas can be wiped out to our satisfaction. This would at the same time call for a proper identification of the areas where discrimination among castes is largely visible. Under such circumstances an organized effort could go a long way towards the complete eradication of the discriminatory treatment received by the Scheduled Castes at the hands of the upper castes of the society, which is believed to foster cooperation among people of the society irrespective of castes in a congenial social atmosphere.

5. It is generally accepted that improvement in the levels of living is intimitately connected with economic upliftment. Hence, it is apparent that any economic improvement in Scheduled Caste community is bound to improve their levels of living too. Granting this, it may be recommended that proper financial assistance to be provided to them for ensuring their economic upliftment. It may also be suggested that special measures to increase employment opportunities should be created which in turn would enable them to secure an equal footing in the society in course of time.

REFERENCES

Bakshi, P.M. (2004), *The Constitution of India,* Universal Law Publishing Co. Pvt. Ltd., Delhi.

Chakrabarty, Gurupada (2000), 'Development of SCs and STs: The Success So Far', *Social Change,* Vol. 30, Nos. 3 and 4, pp. 143-162.

Chatterjee, Sarajit Kumar (1996), *The Scheduled Castes in India* (Vols. I, II, III and IV), Gyan Publishing House, New Delhi.

Department of Justice, Committee on the Welfare of Scheduled Castes and Scheduled Tribes *(Second Report),* 1999-2000, Lok Sabha Secretariat, New Delhi.

Department of Personnel and Training, Committee on the Welfare of Scheduled Castes and Scheduled Tribes *(Sixteenth Report)*, 2001-2002, Lok Sabha Secretariat, New Delhi.

Department of Social Welfare, Report of the Scheduled Castes and Scheduled Tribes Commissioner, 1950-51 to 1979-80.

Dutta, Nalini Kanta (1991), *An X-Ray on Reservation Provision*, Anmol Publications, New Delhi.

Galanter, Marc (1962), *The Problem of Group Membership. Some Reflections on the Judical View of Indian Society*, 4 J.I.L. I 331 at 351.

Galanter, Marc (1984), *Competing Equalities: Law and the Backward Classes in India*, Oxford University Press, Delhi.

Gill, M.S. and A.M. Singh (1989), 'Reactionary Dissent by Caste Hindu Employees', *Social Change*, Vol. 19, No. 3, pp. 16-22.

Government of India, Census of India 2001, Primary Census Abstract.

Government of India, Report of the Backward Classes Commission, Vol. III, Delhi, Manager of Publication, 1956.

Gupta, P.K. (1991), *The Scheduled Castes and the Scheduled Tribes (Prevention Atrocities) Act, 1989*, Eastern Book Company, Lucknow.

Harold, R. Issacs (1965), *Indian Ex-Untouchables*, Asia Publishing House, Bombay.

Keer, Dhananjay (1981), *Dr. Ambedkar: His life and Mission*, Popular Prakashan, Bombay.

Kothari, Rajni (1970), *'Introduction: Caste in Indian Politics'*, In Rajni Kothari (ed.), Caste in Indian Politics, Orient Longman, New Delhi.

Majeed, A. and E.S.K. Ghosh (1989), 'Affective Syndrome Crisis in Scheduled Castes', Social Change, Vol. 19, No. 3, pp.90-94.

Narayanan, R.P. (1986), *'Reservation in Politics and the Scheduled Castes Elite'*, in V.P. Shah and B.C. Agrawal (eds.), Reservation: Policy, Programmes Issues, Rawat Publications, Jaipur.

Pandey, J.N. (1992), *Constitutional law of India*, Central Law Agency, Allahabad.

Prasad, Anirudh (1991), *Reservation Policy and Practice in India:* A means to an End, Deep and Deep Publications, New Delhi.

Ram, Nandu (1998), *The Mobile Scheduled Castes*, Hindustan Publishing Corporation, Delhi.

Ramaiah, A (1990), 'Reserved, but Restricted', *Mainstream*, January 20.

Rao, V.M. (2001), ' Development of the Scheduled Castes: A Systemic View', *Artha Vijnana*, Vol. XLIII, Nos. 1 and 2, pp.5-9.

Report of National Commission for Scheduled Castes and Scheduled Tribes.

Report of the Backward Classes Commission (Government of India Press, New Delhi, 1956), Vol. I, p.3.

Report of the Committee on the Welfare of Scheduled Castes and Scheduled Tribes, *(Sixteenth Report)*, 2001-2002.

Report of the Committee on the Welfare of Scheduled Castes and Scheduled Tribes, *(Second Report)*, 1999-2000.

Saha, R.K. (2002), 'How the Scheduled Castes are Distanced', *The Journal of the Anthropological Survey of India,* Vol. 51, No.3, pp. 1-26.

Sharma, Satish Kumar (1985), *Social Movements and Social Change,* B.R. Publishing Corporation, Delhi.

Singh, K.S. (1999), *The Scheduled Castes,* Oxford University Press, New Delhi.

Singh, Parmanand (1982), *Equality, Reservation and Discrimination in India: A Constitutional Study of Scheduled Castes, Scheduled Tribes and Other Backward Classes, Deep and Deep Publications,* New Delhi.

Suryanarayana, M.H. (2001), 'Scheduled Castes, Their Disadvantages and Deprivation: A rural All India Profile', *Artha Vijnana,* Vol. XLIII, Nos. 1 and 2, pp.84-97.

Upadhyay, H.C. (1991), *Reservation for Scheduled Castes and Scheduled Tribes, Anmol Publications,* New Delhi.

Uplaonkar, A.T. (1989), 'Protection discrimination and the Equality of Opportunity' *Social Change,* Vol. 19, No. 3, pp.3-15.

Wollheim, Richard and Berlin, Isaiah (1955-56), *Equality,* Part 1-2, p. 281.

Yadav, C.P. (ed) (2000), *Encyclopedia of Scheduled Castes and Scheduled Tribes* (Vol. I), Anmol Publications, New Delhi.

APPENDIX

The Government of India (Scheduled Castes) Order, 1936.
THE SCHEDULE

Parts	*Provinces*	*Scheduled Castes throughout the Provinces*	*Scheduled Castes Expect Provinces*
I.	Madras	Adi-Andhra, Adi-Dravida, Adi-Karnataka, Ajila,Arunthuthiyar, Baira, Bakuda, Bandi, Bariki, Battada, Bavuri, Bellara, Bygari, Chachati, Chakkiliyan, Chalvadi, Chamar, Chandala, Cheruman, Dandasi, Devendrakulathan, Ghasi, Godaga, Godari, Godda, Gosangi, Haddi, Hasla, Holeya, Jaggali, Jambuvulu, Kalladi, Kanakkan, kodalo, Koosa, Koraga, Mudumban, Kuravan, Madari, Madiga, Maila, Mala, Mala Dasu, Matangi, Moger, Muchi, Mundala, Nalakeyava, Nayadi, Pagadai, Paidi, Painda, Paky, Pallan, Pambada, Pamidi, Panchama, Paniyan, Panniandi, Paraiyan, Parvan, Pulayan, Puthirai Vanan, Raneyar, Relli, Samagara, Samban, Sapari, Semman, Thoti, Tiruvalluvar, Valluvan, Valmiki, Vettuvan,	Arnadan, Dombo, Kadan, Karimpalam, Kattunayakan, Kudiya, Kudubi, Kurichchan, Kuruwan, Malasar, Mavilan, Pano.

Contd.....

Parts	Provinces	Scheduled Castes throughout the Provinces	Scheduled Castes Expect Provinces
II.	Bombay	Asodi, Bakad, Bhambi, Bhangi, Chakrawadyadasar, Chalvadi, Chambhar, or Mochigar, or Samagar, Chena-Dasaru, Chuhar, or Chuhra, Dakaleru, Dhed, Dhegu-Magu, Dhor, Garode, Halleer, Halsar, or Haslar, Hulsavar, Holaya, Khalpa, Kolcha, or Kolgha, Kali-Dhor, Lingader, Madig, or Mang, Mahar, Mang Garudi, Maghval, or Menghwar, Mini Madig, Mukri, Nadia, Shenva, or Shindhava, Shinghdavor Shingadya, Sachi, Timali, Turi, Vankar, Vitholia.	Mochi, Kotegar.
III.	Bengal	Agaria, Bind, Bagdi, Bahelia, Bhumij, Binjhia, Baiti, Bauri, Bediya, Beldar, Berua, Bhatiya, Bhuimali, Bhuiya, Dhoba, Chamar, Dhenuar, Dosadh, Doai, Dom, Ghasi, Gonrhi, Garo, Halalkhor, Hadi, Hajang, Hari, Ho, Jalia Kaibartta, Jhalo Malo, or Malo, Kadar, Kan, Kaora, Kandh, Kandra, Kastha, Kapuria, Karenga, Khatik, Kaur, Khaira, Konwar, Koch, Konai, Kora, Kotal, Lodha, Lohar, Lalbegi, Mallah, Mech, Methor, Muchi, Musahar, Nagesia, Namasudra, Nat, Nuniya, Oraon, Paliya, Pan, Pasi, Pasi, Patni, Pod, Rabha, Rajbanshi, Rajwar, Santal, Sunri, Tiyar, Turi.	——
IV.	United Provinces	Agariya, Aheriya, Badi, Badhik, Chero, Dabgar, Dhangar, Dhanuk (Bhangi), Khatik, Kol, Korwa, Lalbegi, Baheliya, Bajaniya, Bajgi, Balahar, Balmiki, Banmanus, Bansphor, Barwar, Basor, Bawariya, Beldar, Bengali, Berya, Bhantu, Bhuiya, Bhuiyar, Boriya, Chamar, Dharkar, Dhobi, Dom, Domar, Gharami, Ghasiya, Gual, Habura, Hari, Hela, Khairaha, Kalabaz, Kanjar, Kapariya, Karwal, Kharot, Kharwar, (except Benbansi), Majhawar, Nat, Pankha, Parahiya, pasi, Patari, Rawat, Saharya Sanaurhiya, Sansiya, Shilpkar, Tharu, Turaiha.	Kori.
V.	Punjab	Ad Dharmis, Bawaria, Chamar, Chuhra, or Balmiki, Dagi and Koli, Dhumna, Od, Marija, or Marecha, Bengali, Barar, Bazigar, Bhanjra, Chanal, Dhanak, Khatik, Kori, Nat, Pasi, Perna, Sepela, Sirkiband, Megha, Sansi, Sarera, Gagra, Gandhila, Ramdasis.	

Contd.....

Parts	*Provinces*	*Scheduled Castes throughout the Provinces*	*Scheduled Castes Expect Provinces*
VI.	Bihar	Chamar, Chaupal, Dhobi, Dusadh, Dom, Halalkhor, Hari, Kanjar, Kurariar, Lalbegi, Mochi, Musahar, Nat, Pasi.	Bauri, Bhogta, Bhauya, Bhumij, Ghasi, Pan, Rajwar, Turi, Bhuiya.
VII.	Central Provinces and Berar	Basor, or Burud, Chamar, Dom, Ganda, Mang, Mehtar or Bhangi, Mochi, Satnami	Audhelia, Bahna, Balahi, or Balai, Bedar, Chadar, Chauhan, Dahayat, Dewar, Dhanuk, Dhimar, Dhobi, Dohar, Ghasia, Holiya, Jangam, Kaikari, Katia, Khangar, Khatik, Koli, Kori, Kumhar, Madgi, Mala, Mehra or Mahar, Nagarchi, Ojha, Panka, Pardhi, Pradhan, Rajjhar,
VIII.	Assam	Kaibartta, Bania or Brittial-Bania, Hira, Lalbegi, Namasudra, Mehtar or Bhangi, Bonshpor, Mali or Bhuimali, Dhupi or Dhobi, Dugla or Dholi, Jhalo and Malo, Mahara, Sutradhar, Muchi, Patni, Kaibartta or Jaliya.	———
IX.	Orissa	Adi-Andahra, Audhelia, Bariki, Bansor or Bavuri, Chamar, Burud, Chandala, Dandasi, Chachati, Dhoba or Dhobi, Ghusuria, Dewar, Godra, Godagali, Godari, Haddi, or Hri, Gokha, Ganda, Kandra, Irika, Jaggali, Kodalo, Katia, Kela, Madiga, Mala, Madari, Mangan, Mahuria, Mang, Mochi, Mehra or Mehtar or Muchi, Mhar or Bhangi, Paidi, Panchama, Panka, Relli, painda, pamidi, Siyal, Sapari, Satnami, Valmiki.	Pan or Pano, Dom or Dambo, Bauro, Bhumij, Turi, Bhuiya, Ghasi or Ghasia, Kori, Nagarchi, Pradhan.

10

GENESIS OF SCHEDULED CASTES AND CONSTITUTIONAL SAFEGUARDS FOR THEM

Sidhartha Sankar Laha and Anil Bhuimali

INTRODUCTION

The scheduled castes are the people who belong to the last Varna namely the Shudra or Avarna or Antyaja. The expression "scheduled castes" was first used by the Simon Commission and embodied in the Government of India Act of 1935. Before 1935 they were known as untouchables or exterior castes or depressed castes. They were, in fact, outside the caste (Varna) system. They were external in the sense that they were not allowed to live within the village settlement where people other than these group of people did live. Naturally they lived outside the village settlement. Mahatma Gandhi termed this caste 'Harijans' meaning people of God (Hari means God and Jans means people). They are being deprived socially, economically and politically for generations. In the traditional Indian society the deprivation of one section of people to another gave rise to social inequality. This still persists in our society and economy. The worst victims or sufferers are the scheduled castes or the dalits. The Constitution of India guarantees some of the privileges to this section which are also received by other citizens. The privileges include, among others, justice, social, economic and political liberty of thought, expression, belief, faith and worship and equality of status and opportunity. Some additional privileges in respect of education, employment and political participation are provided to the people belonging to the scheduled caste community.

The objective of the present article is to give an overview of genesis of scheduled castes in India and the constitutional safeguards provided to them since independence. This is, in fact, the review based on existing literature and all the analysis is primarily relied on the information/data collected from the secondary sources.

ORIGIN OF CASTES

Indian society is based on the institution of castes. Caste system in India is not a new phenomenon. Caste system in India was found in the traditional Hindu society. The institution of caste has survived in India in a far better form than any other country of the world. It is not an isolated phenomenon in the rest of the world. It is found in Egypt, in Polynesia, in Melanesia, in Fiji, in Somalia, in Rwanda and in many other countries. In ancient Greece and Rome too caste system was noticed in a comparable form. Traces of caste can also be found in Western Asia, China, Japan, America, Rome and tribal India.

A great diversity is found in the composition of the population of India. Variation exists in creeds, customs and colours. These variations among different sections of people have formed a multiple society which is barely found in the rest of the world. The racial elements in India have been divided into six different parts. These divisions are Negritos, Proto-Australoids (Pre-Dravidians), Dravidians (Mediterranean) Round-heads (Brachycephals-Alpenoid), Indo-Aryans (Nordic-Cancasoids) and Mangoloids. Negritos are not found in India. They are generally found in Malaya, the Philippines and in the Andaman and Nicobar Islands. In India they are rarely found among the Kadar tribe of the Cochin forest and among the tribes of the Rajmahal Hills, Bihar. They are also found in Burma. A small number of Negritos are found among the Naga tribes living especially in the Assam frontier. Proto-Australoids are aborigines of Australia. They are spread widely all over India.

Dravidians are a branch of the Mediterranean race (Smith) who came to India somewhere from East Africa. They came into India via Arabic and South Persia even before the stone age. There still exists a great debate in relation to their place of origin. Roundheads are also outsiders who came to India from the southern steppes of Russia through Iran. Most of the Roundheads settled in the Tamil and Telenga-speaking areas. Indo-Aryans are also outsiders who came to India for more than three thousand years back and settled in Punjab. The Mongolians occupied the higher mountains along the northern fringe of India. The Negritos, Pre-Dravidians, Dravidians, Roundheads, Indo-Aryans and Mongolians constitute the racial elements in the Indian population.

GENESIS OF SCHEDULED CASTES

The word 'caste' comes from Portuguese word 'casta'. This means breed, race or kind. Broadly speaking, a caste in India, signifies, total system of social stratification. The alternative words of 'caste' is 'Varna'. In India 'varna' represents four-fold division of society, i.e., Brahmin, Kshatriya, Vaishya and Sudra. This four-fold division of society was based on certain approved code of quality and action. The first three categories are also called dwija or born twice and the last category i.e., Sudra is called 'ekaja' meaning one born. Scheduled caste is a group of people who do not belong to the above mentioned sub-divisions. The British.government used the term 'depressed class' to identify so-called untouchable castes experiencing socio-economic-cultural discriminations at the hands of the upper caste people. In 1908 the then Viceroy of India Lord Minto advised to make a division of the Hindu population into three distinct categories, namely, Hindus, Tribals and the Depressed classes. In 1931, Ambedkar submitted a memorandum at the second Round Table Conference to change the term 'depressed class' into scheduled caste'. This was due to the fact that the erstwhile untouchables objected to the 'depressed class' term. The term 'scheduled caste' was adopted in 1935 to provide some social, economic and political safeguard to the section of people who were being deprived socially, politically and economically at the hands of the upper caste people. The constitution of India has also provided some safeguards to the scheduled castes and tribal population. Article 17 (see Appendix A) of the Constitution of India abolished the practice of untouchability and provided a legal basis for action against the practice of untouchability in the public life. The Untouchability (Offences) Act was passed in 1955 (see Appendix B) and it was amended in 1976.

SCHEDULED CASTES IN DIFFERENT STATES

Our Constitution has offered some social, economic and political safeguards to the section of people who belong to scheduled caste category. In this section we have tried to represent the list of scheduled castes in ten states and seven other North-Eastern states of India. Tables 1 to 11 show lists of scheduled castes of 10 states e.g., West Bengal, Bihar, Orissa, Gujarat, Rajasthan, Madhya Pradesh, Uttar Pradesh, Tamil Nadu, Karnataka and Kerala. Table 11 below gives an expression of scheduled castes in six sisters of North-Eastern states (Assam, Manipur, Mizoram, Nagaland, Tripura and Arunachal Pradesh) and lone brother Sikkim (the Hilly State). At present some 578 different castes have been enlisted in the category of scheduled castes.

Table 1
List of Scheduled Castes in the State of West Bengal

State	*Name of Scheduled Castes*	*Total*
West Bengal	Badi/Badhi, Bahelia/Baheliya, Baiti, Bauri, Beldar, Bhangi, Bhogta, Bhuimali/Bhuinmali, Bhuiya, Bin/ Bind, Muchia/ Muchi, Damai (Nepali), Dhoba/Dhupi/Dhobi, Doai, Doom, Doomna,/Dumna, Dosadh, Dusad/Dusadh, Ghasi/Ghasiya, Gonrhi, Hari, Jalia kaibartta/ jalia kaibarta/jalia, Jhalo Malo/Jhalo-Malo, Kandra, Kandara, Kondara, Kaora/Keora, Karenga/Karanga, Keot, Khaira, Khatik, Konai, Kotal, Lalbegi, Lohar, Mahar, Mal, Mundapotta, Namasudra, Nat, Nuniya, Paliya, pan, Pasi, Patni, Pod, Rajbanshi, Rajwar, Sarki (Nepali), Sunri (excluding Saha), Tiyar/Titar/Tiyor, Turi.	48

Table 2
List of Scheduled Castes in the State of Karnataka

State	*Name of Scheduled Castes*	*Total*
Karnataka	Adi Andhra, Adi Kamataka, Adiya, Ager, Baira, Bakad, Bakharia, Bandi, Bangara, Lambani/Laban/ Lambana, Bathada, Bedajangan/Budga, Jangam, Bellara, Bhambi, Asadaree, Bhambi, Machigac/ Machegar, Bhovi, Byagara, Chalavadi/Chalvadi, Chenna Dasac/Dardiga Dasar, Dakkal/Dakkaliga/ Dakkala, Dhor, Dom, Dombara/Dombar,Gantichore/ Gantichore, Godda, Halsar, Hulasvar/Hulsaver, Handi Jogis, Holaya/Holeya, Holaya/Holeya, Kembatti, Holeya Dasari, Kondara, Kosama, Kunchi Kosava, Kotgar, Kuravan/Sithanar, Madiga, Mahar, Mahyavanshi Varkar, Mang, Mehtar, Mour, Mukri, Nalkadaya/Nalkadeya, Nav Buddhist, Pole, Pambada, Parabar, Raneyar, Samabara, Sillekyathas/Sillekyatha, Sudugadu Siddha.	48

Table 3
List of Scheduled Castes in the State of Kerala

State	Name of Scheduled Castes	Total
Kerala	Arunthathiyar/Arunthatiyar, Ayyanavar, Baira, Bakharia, Boyan, Cheruman, Dom/Dombara, Domb; Dombar, Holaya/Holeya, Kadaiyan, Kakkalan, Kalladi, Kanakkan, Karimpalan, Kavara, Kootan/Koodan, Kuravan/Sidhanar, Maila, Malayan, Mannan, Mavilan, Nalkadaya/Nalkadeya, Nayadi, Padannan, Pallan, Palluvan/Pulluvan, Pambada, Panan, Paravan, Pathiyar, Pulayar, Samagara, Semman/Chemman, Jhandar, Valluvan/Valluvar, Vavuri/Bavuri, Velan,Churambu Velan, Veppur parayan, Vettiyan.	38

Table 4
List of Scheduled Castes in the State of Tamil Nadu

State	Name of Scheduled Castes	Total
Tamil Nadu	Adi Andhra, Adidravida, Adikamataka, Arunthatiyar/Arunthatiya/Arunthathiyar/Arunthatiyar, Ayyanavar, Bandi, Bhanumati, Chakkiliyan, Cheruman, Deverdrakulathan, Dom/Dombara/Domb, Domban, Godda, Holaya/ Holeya, Jambuvulu/Jambavulu, Kadaiyan, Koliyan, Kudumbar, Kurariar/kureri,Madgi, Mala, Munjhi, Mavilan, Paky; Thoti, Panan Pannadi, Panniandi, Paraiyar//Parayan, paraiyan/Parayan, Veppur Parayan, Paravan, Pulayan, Pullavan, Samban, Semman/Chemman, Thandan, Valluvan/Valluvar, Vettiyan.	37

Table 5
List of Scheduled Castes in the State of Orissa

State	Name of Scheduled Castes	Total
Orissa	Adi andhar, Amant/Amat, Badaik/Baraik, Bagbi, Banjara, Lambani/Laban/bambana, Bariki, Bauri, Bauti, Bedia, Chakli/Chakkoli, Chamar, Mochi/Muchia/Muchi, Chandala, Chandhai Maru/Charaimar, Cherua/Chhelia, Dandasi, Dewar, Dhamwar, Dhoba/Dhubi/ Dhobi, Dom, Dombo, Seddha Dombo, Dona, Duria/Duria Dom, Dom, Sikharia, Gardu, Ghantaghada Ghantra, Ghogia, Ghusuria, Godra, Gokho, Haddi/Hadi, Irika, Jaggali, Kandhera, Katia, Kelanalua/Naluakela, Kela, Sapua/Sapuakela,Kodalo/Khodalo, kori/koli, Kumonari/Kummeri, Kurunga, Mahuria, Murdapotta, Namasudra, Pan, Pano, Panka, Pap, Patial, Patratanti/Patratantia, Sabakhia, Samasi Sanei, Sauntia, Sinduria/Sindhuria, Siyar, Tamta, Tanudia, Tiyar/Tiar/Toyar, Turi, Turi betra, Ujla, Valamiki/Valmiki.	58

Table 6
List of Scheduled Castes in the State of Rajasthan

State	*Name of Scheduled Castes*	*Total*
Rajasthan	Aheri/Aheria, Badhik, Bagri, Bairwa/Berwa, Balahi/Balai, Bansphor, Baori, Baori, Bargi, Bowaria/Bauria/Bawariya, Bhambi, Rohit, Bhand, Chamar, Jatava, Jatava chamar, Jatav chamar/Jatav, Chamar, Regar, Regarh, Dabgar, Dhanuk/Dhanak, Dhoba/Dhupi/Dhobi, Garodo, Garo, Gavaria, Gingar, Kalbelia, Daliwal/Daliwal/Kalbelia, Kalbelia, Mewara/Mewara kalbelia, Kamad, Kanjar, Kapadia sansi/Khangar, Khatik, Kori/Koli, Madari, Mazhabi, Meghval, Mehar, Rawal, Saharya, Sansi, Santia, Sargura, Singiwala, Thori, Nayak, Tirgor	

Table 7
List of Scheduled Castes in the State of MP

State	*Name of Scheduled Castes*	*Total*
MP	Audheliya, Bagheti, Balahi/Balai, Bangali, Bansphor, Bargunda, Basor, Bawaria/Bauria, Bedia, Bedia, Bhuyiar, Boria, Chakali/Chakkoli, Chamar, Kuri/Chamar, Rohidas, Chidar, Dahait, Dewar, Dharkar, Dohor, Domar, Ghasi/Ghasiya, Gond, Habura, Hela/Hehtar, Holiya/Holia, Katia, Khairaha, Kharwar, Kol, Kori/Koli, Kuch bandia, Kumhar/Kumbhar, Mahar, Majhwar, Mang, Moghia, Parahiya, Patari, Rujjar	46

Table 8
List of Scheduled Castes in the State of Uttar Pradesh

State	*Name of Scheduled Castes*	*Total*
Uttar Pradesh	Agariya/Agaria, Badhi/Badi, Bahalia/Baheliya, Baiswar, Bajaniya/Bajania Nat, Bajgi, Balahar, Balahi/Balai, Bandi, Bansphor, Barwar, Basor, Bawaria/Bauria/Bawariya, Bedia/Beriya, Bhantu, Bhuiya Boria, Chamar/Chambhar/Chamar or Ramdasia, Chamar, Jatava, Jatav chamar/Jatav, Chero, Chura/Chuhra/Chuhre, Dabgar, Dhanuk/Dhanak, Dharkar, Dhoba/Dhupi/Dhobi, Dom/Doom/Dumar/Dun/Doom or Mahasha, Domar, Dosadh, Dusad/ Dusadh, Ghasi/Ghasiya, Gond, Habura, Hela/Mehtar, Kandra, Kandara/Kondara, Kapariya/Kaparia, Karimpalan, Khawar, Kol, Korama, Kunchi korava, Kori/Koli, Korwa, Lalbegi, Majhwar/Manjhi, Mushahar, Neo Buddhist, Pankha/Panika, Parahiya, Pasi, Saharya/Saharia.	49

Table 9
List of Scheduled Castes in the State of Gujarat

State	*Name of Scheduled Castes*	*Total*
Gujarat	Bhambi, Khalpa, Bhanbi, Rohit, Bhangi, Chamar/Chambhar/ Chamar or Randasia, Dangashia, Gardi, Garoda, Garo, Megh, Nadia, Neo Buddhist/Nav Buddhist, Thoria, Turi.	12

Table 10
List of Scheduled Castes in the State of Bihar

State	*Name of Scheduled Castes*	*Total*
Bihar	Bauri, Bhogta, Chamar/Chambhar/Chamar or Randasia, Chaupal/Choupal, Dom/Dombara/Dom, Domban/Dom or Mahasha, Dusadh, Dhari, Gharrami/Gharami, Kanjar, Mundapotta, Nat, Pan, Sawasi, Pasi, Turi.	13

Table 11
List of Scheduled Caste in the North Eastern States

State	*Name of Scheduled Castes*	*Total*
Assam	Bansphor, Bhangi, Bhuinmali, mali, Brittial/Bania/ Bania, Dhoba/Dhupi/ Dhobi, Hesi, jalkeot, Jhalomalo/ Jhalo-malo, Kaibarta, Namasudra, Patni, Sutadhar.	12
Sikkim	Damai, Kami, Sarki.	3
Manipur	Dhupi, Dhobi, Dugla or Dholi, Jalkeot, Yaithibi.	4
Mizoram	Bhuinmali or Mali, Bania, Dhupi, Dhobi, Dugla or Dholi, Jalkeot, Mehtar, Munchi or Rishi, Hira.	8
Arunachal Pradesh	Bansphor, Bhinmali or Mali, Dhor, Dugla or Dholi, Ghasi, Haddi, Hira, Jalkeot Jhalo, Malo, Patni, Sutradhar.	1
Tripura	Bhuimali, Dhoba/Dhupi/Dhobi, Gour, Jalia kaibarta/jalia Kaibarta/Jalia, Kahar, Kanda, keori, Koch, Kol, Mahisyadas, Mali/Malakar, Mundapotta, Namasudra, Patni, Sabar.	15
Meghalaya	People under this category were not found	NIL

Table 12
List of Scheduled Castes in Major States (India)

SI. No.	*Name of States*	*No. of Scheduled Castes*
I.	West Bengal	48
2.	Karnataka	48
3.	Kerala	38
4.	Tamil Nadu	37
5.	Orissa	58
6.	Rajasthan	38
7.	Madhya Pradesh	46
8.	Uttar Pradesh	49
9.	Gujarat	12
10.	Bihar	13
	Total	*387*

Source: Tables 1 to 12 compiled from Singh, K. S. (I999) : The scheduled caste, Revised edition, National Series Vol. II Oxford University Press.

The list of scheduled castes represented in Tables 1, 2, 3, 4, 5, 6, 7, 8, 9, 10, 11 and 12 show the population who enjoy constitutional safeguards in social, economic and political spheres. But many recent study (Bhuimali & Biswas, 2004) show that most of the benefits are enjoyed by the well-to-do scheduled caste families. The scheduled caste people, particularly living below the poverty line cannot utilise modern benefits of education, health, nutrition and other amenities. Naturally, they are not in a position to reap the fruits of reservation policy. Tables 1 to 12 represent the scheduled castes above a population of 10,000. There are at least twelve communities in a few states and one union territory who are not in a position to enjoy the benefits provided by the Central and State Governments. Table 13 below show these different twelve communities belonging to scheduled castes category, their respective states whose major components were studied elsewhere.

Table 13
Communities Whose Major Components were Studied Elsewhere

Sl. No.	*Community*	*State/ Union Territory*	*Total number*
1.	Ad Dharmi	Himachal Pradesh	15,098
2.	Adi Andhra	Andhra Pradesh	698,857
3.	Barahar, Basod	Madhya Pradesh	60,789
4.	Bhangi	Delhi	21,752
5.	Chakkiliyan	Kerala	29,001
6.	Holaya	Maharashtra	14,927
7.	Kabir Panthi	Haryana	31,503
8	Madari	Tamil Nadu	346,899
9.	Mala	Maharashtra	11,890
10.	Mallah	West Bengal	38,101
11.	Moger	Kerala	19,665
12.	Pallan	Tamil Nadu	993,070

Source: Compiled from the Census of India, 1981.

A COMMENT ON CONSTITUTIONAL SAFEGURARDS

In order to make the Indian society more egalitarian the Government of India since independence has been implementing various policies (see Appendix C) for the development of scheduled castes and scheduled tribes and other backward castes. The main object of such policies is to raise the social and economic conditions for the privileged section of the population of India. All the plans and programmes for the development of underprivileged people aim at improving the level of education, enhancing employment opportunities and after all raising their well-being. To provide educational opportunities among the scheduled caste population various facilities such as stipends, scholarships, tuition fees, book grants, etc. are being offered to them. Also there are provisions of reservation of seats in educational institutions (general courses and technical courses like medical, engineering institutes). Educated members in the scheduled caste community are provided job opportunities. The overall objective of such a policy is to improve educational conditions and the level of income of the people belonging to the scheduled castes community. Many studies show that literacy among scheduled caste population (along with scheduled tribes) has been rising steadily. But the rate of growth of literacy is not even in all the states and union territories. The literacy among the scheduled caste women are worse than the scheduled caste men especially in some states like Bihar, Rajasthan and Uttar Pradesh, To spread education among the scheduled caste community the Central and the State Governments have undertaken a number of strategies (in addition to those provided for them) such as Operation Blackboard, District Primary Education Programme, Shramik Vidyapeeth, Mahila Shiksha Kendra, Mahila Samakshya, Siksha Karmis, and many other non-formal education centres. To enhance the level of literacy two important steps, among others, have been taken. These are to increase the number of functioning schools and teachers and to ensure that the teachers really teach. To improve the level of income, employment opportunities are provided to the educated scheduled castes by way of reserving seats to government sector, educational institutes and other non-government sectors. The reservation policy in job has created ample scope of enhancing their income level. A development effort has been made to improve the economic lot of the scheduled caste community especially since 1978 through the announcement of a policy known as special component plan (SCP). This policy aims at securing the rapid socio-economic development of the scheduled caste population. It was designed to channelise the plan outlays and benefits in the areas of social and economic activity including agriculture, animal husbandry, poultry, provision for drinking water, electrification in the scheduled caste dominated areas, seiiculture, irrigation. There is also provision for plan outlays under the scheme in housing, link roads, self-employment schemes, social forestry, allotment of shops and stalls in public places.

CONCLUSION

The Constitutional safeguards (see Appendix D) provided to scheduled castes have been based on the values of equality, human dignity and social justice. But the measures adopted so far by the Central and State Governments are not sufficient enough to overcome the continued subordination most deprived section of the society. In India, the scheduled caste community lies at the bottom of the socio-economic ladder. The people in this category are virtually being bypassed from the market mechanism.

In the globalised market condition one thing is obvious: The rich becomes richer and the poor becomes poorer. Under the circumstances the scheduled caste community may be provided more protection. This needs a variety of positive interventions. This may assist the poor by way of a lot of interventions such as wage interventions and price interventions and creation of opportunities like employment creation, equitable share in socio-economic programmes etc.

REFERENCES

Abbasayalu, Y.B. (1972). "Scheduled Caste Elite", Hyderabad, Department of Sociology, Osmania University.

Aikara, J. (1980). "Scheduled Caste and Higher Education: A Study of College Students in Bombay, Poona", Distance.

Bakshi, P. M. [2004]. "The Constitution of India", Universal Law Publishing Co. Pvt. Ltd., Fifth Edition.

Basu K., P. Pattanaik and K. Suzumura (Ed.) [1995]. "Choice, Welfare and Development", Oxford, Clarendon,

Berreman, Gerald D. [1979]. "Caste and other inequalities: Essays on inequality", Meerut Folklore Institute.

Beteille, A. (1983). "The Idea of Natural and Other Essays", Delhi, Oxford University Press.

Beteille, A. (1991). "Distributive Justice and Institutional Well-Being," *Economic and Political Weekly,* (Annual Number), March.

Beteille, A. (1992). "Society and Politics in India, Essays in a Comparative Perspective", Delhi, Oxford University Press.

Bhuimali, A. (2000). "In Search of an Appropriate Reservation Policy for the Under-Privileged People of India", Lecture delivered at the UGC National Seminar on "Development, Deprivation and the Roots of Inequality" at University of North Bengal on 29-30 January.

Chakraborty G. [2000]. "Development of SCs and STs : The Success so far", *Social Changes,* Vol. 30, Nos. 3 & 4., Sept - Dec.

Chakraborty, Gurupada [2000]. "Development of SCs and STs : The success so far", Social Changes, Vol. 30, No 3 & 4, September - December.

Chalam, K. S. (1998). "Caste and Economic Reforms", *Seminar* 471- November, New Delhi.

Choudhary, K. (1988). "The Policy of Reservation: Need to Continue and Transcend." *Social Action,* Vol.48.

Daniwale S. M. [2003]. "The Political Mobilization of Backward Classes in India", *Man and Development,* September.

Dave, M. (1985). 'Backward Classes and Reservation' in Haroobhi Mehta and Hasmukh Patel (eds.), *Dynamics of Reservation Policy,* New Delhi.

Dreze, J. (1998). "Squaring the Circle", Seminar, 464.

Dreze, Jean and Amartya Sen [1995]. "Basic Education as a Political Issue", Journal of Educational *Planning and Administration,* Vol. 9, No.1, 1995.

Eighth Five-Year Plan (1992), *Planning Commission,* Government of India, Vol. II.

Foster J., J. Greer and E. Thorbecke [1984]. "A Class of Decomposable Poverty Measures", Econometrica.

Ghurye, G.S. (1994). "Caste and Race in India", Popular Prakashan, Bombay.

Government of India (1980). "Reports of the Backward Classes Commission", First Part (Vols. 1 & 2)

Government of India (1990). "B. R. Ambedkar, Castes in India", Speeches and Writings of Dr. Babasaheb Ambedkar, Vol. I.

Government of West Bengal (1999). "Annual Report of the Development of Higher Education", 1998-99.

Gupta, D. (1998). "A Question of Quotas", Seminar 471, November.

Judge Pranjit S. [2002]. "Religion, Caste and Communalism in Punjab" *Sociological Bulletin,* 51(2), September.

Kabra, G.D. (1984). "Development of Weaker Sections: Organisational Alternatives", Inter-India Publications, New Delhi.

Kamble, R. (1998). "Dalit Interpretations of Society", Seminar 471, November.

Mahapatra L. K. [1991]. "Development for Whom? Depriving the Dispossessed Tribals", Social Action, Vol. 41, No.3, pp. 271-287.

Mathew Zachariah [1972]. "Positive Discrimination in Education for India's Schedule Caste: A Review of the Problem 1950-70", Comparative Education Review, 16(1).

Nancharaiah, G. [1988]. "Land and Caste", Himalaya Publishing House, Bombay.

Narayan, S.S. (1998). "Gender Equality Through Reservation in Decision-Making Bodies", Social Action, Vol. 48. April.

Nayak Vijoy and Shailaja Prasad [1984]. "On levels of living of schedule castes and schedule tribes", *Economic and Political Weekly,* July, 28.

Panini, M.N. (1999). "M.N. Srinivas and Sociology", *Economic and Political Weekly,* January 22.

Pathy, Jagannath [1982]. "Politics of Tribal Welfare: Some Reflections", The Eastern Anthropologist, Vol. 35, No.4, pp. 285-300.

Patil, S. (1979). "Dialectics of Caste and Class Conflicts", *Economic and Political Weekly,* Annual Number, February.

Patnaik N. [1972]. "Tribes and their Development: A Study of Two Tribal Development Blocks in Orissa", National Institute of Community Development, Hyderabad.

Premi Kusum K. [1977]. "Privileges Given to the Schedule Castes in Education: A Critical Analysis", Paper Presented at Workshop on Alternative Educational Features, New Delhi, NCERT.

Puri, Harish K. and Pranjit S. Judge [2000]. "Social and Political Movements: A Reader on Punjab" Jaipur, Rawat Publications,.

Rao, C. Shankar [2003]. "Sociology Primary Principles", [3rd Revised and Enlarged Edition], S. Chand & Co. Ltd., New Delhi.

Roy, A. (1979). "Caste and Class: An Inter-linked View". *Economic and Political Weekly,* Annual Number, February.

Saggar Mridul and Pan Indranil [1994]. "SCs and STs in Eastern India, Inequality and Poverty Estimate" *Economic and Political Weekly,* March 5.

Sankaram S. R. [2000]. "Welfare of Scheduled Caste and Scheduled Tribes in Independent India— An Overview of State Policies and programmes" *Journal of Rural Development,* vol. 19(4), pp. 507-533.

Sau, R. (1999). "Human Development Index in View of Caste, Census 2001", *Economic and Political Weekly,* December 18.

Sen, A. (1987). "Commodities and Capabilities", Oxford University Press.

Shah, G. (1987). "Middle Class Politics: Case of Anti-Reservation Agitation in Gujarat", *Economic and Political Weekly,* (Annual Number), May.

Sheth, D.L (1987). "Reservations Policy Revisited", *Economic and Political Weekly.*

Singh Harbans (ed) [1996]. "The Encyclopedia of Sikhism", Patiala, Panjab University.

Singh, K. S. [1991]. "The Scheduled Castes", Revised Edition, National Series Vol. II, Oxford University press.

Srinivas M. N. [1966]. "Social Changes in Modern India", Bombay, Allied Publishers.

Srinivas M. N. [1987]. "The Dominant Caste and other Essays", New Delhi, Oxford University Press.

Srinivas, M.N. (1966). "Social Change in Modern India", Allied Publishers, Bombay.

Srinivas, M.N. and S. Seshaiah (1977). "Dimensions of Social Change in India", Allied Publishers, New Delhi.

Srinivash M. N. [1982]. "Caste in India and Other Essays", Bombay, Asia Publishing Co.

Sudarshan, R.M. (1998). "Where Are We At ?", Seminar 464.

The World Bank [1997]. "Primary Education in India", Manohar Publications, New Delhi.

Upadhyay, H. C. [1991]. "Reservation for Scheduled Castes and Scheduled Tribes", Anmol Publication, New Delhi.

Van Ginneken W. [1980]. "Some Method of Poverty Analysis, An Application to Iranian Data— 1975-70" World Development.

Wankhede, G.S. (1999). "Social and Educational Problems of Scheduled Castes: Some Critical Insights", The Indian Journal of Social Work, Volume 60, Issue 3.

Appendix A

Abolition of the Practice of Untouchability
(Article 17 of the Constitution of India)

"Untouchability" is abolished and its practice is any form is forbidden. The enforcement of any disability arising out of "Untouchability" shall be an offence punishable in accordance with law.

The main points under this section may be as follows:

(i) The removal of any disability, liability, restriction or condition with regard to access to shop, public restaurants, hotels and places of public entertainments, the use of wells, tanks, bathing ghats, roads and places of public resort maintained wholly or partly, out of State funds or dedicated to the use of the general public.

(ii) The throwing open the Hindu religious institutions of a public character to all classes and sections of Hindus.

(iii) The forbidding of any denial of admission to educational institutions maintained by the State or receiving aid out of State fund.

(iv) The setting up of advisory councils and separate departments in the State and the appointment of a special official at the Centre to promote their welfare safeguards their interests; and special provision for the administration and control of scheduled areas.

(v) Special representation in the parliament and the State legislatures for a period of twenty years.

(vi) The obligation of the State to consider their claims in the making of appointments to public services and reservation for them in case of inadequate representation.

Source: Baksi. P. M. (2004). The Constitution of India, Universal Law Publishing Co. Ltd. Fifth Edition.

Appendix – B
The Untouchability (Offence) Act of 1955

"(i) Committing any kind of social injustice, such as denying access to any shop, restaurant, public hospital, educational institution or any place of public entertainment. (ii) Preventing a person, on the grounds of untouchability, from entering a place of worship and offering prayers or fiom drinking water from a public well or spring. (iii) Refusal to sell goods or render services to a person on the grounds of untouchability is an offence punishable with imprisonment for six months or a fine upto Rs. 500 or both. (iv) Enforcing occupational, professional, trade disabilities in the matter of enjoyment of any benefit under a charitable trust, etc."

A criticism was raised regarding the purpose of the Act for which it was enacted. For wider applicability of this Act an amendment was made in the name of the Protection of Civil Rights Act which came into force with effect from 19th November 1976. The main features of the Amended Act are as under:

(i) Punishment for untouchability offences has been considerably enhanced, and both imprisonment and fine are simultaneously awarded for such offences.

(ii) Untouchability offences have been made non-compoundable."

(iii) Every offence, except where it is punishable with imprisonment for a minimum term exceeding three months, may be tried summarily.

(iv) Direct or indirect preaching of untouchability or its justification on historical, philosophical, religious or traditional grounds has been made an offence punishable under the Act.

(v) State Governments have been empowered to impose collective fines on the inhabitants of any area where such inhabitants are concerned in or abetting the commission of untouchability offences.

(vi) A public servant who willfully neglects the investigation of any offence punishable under this Act, shall be deemed to have abetted an offence punishable under the Act.

(vii) State Governments are required to take necessary measures to ensure that the rights accruing from the abolition of 'Untouchability' are made available to, and are availed of, by the persons subjected to any disability arising out of 'Untouchability'.

In sub-section (2) of section 15A of the Act, the State Governments have been directed to undertake *inter-alia* the following measures:

(i) Provision of adequate facilities, including legal aid, to the persons subjected to any disability arising out of 'untouchability' to enable them to avail themselves of such rights.

(ii) Appointment of officers for initiating or exercising supervision over prosecutions for the contravention of the provisions of the Act.

(iii) Setting up of special courts for the trial of offences under the Act.

(iv) Setting up of Committees at such appropriate levels as the State Government may think fit to assist the State Government, in formulating and implementing such measures.

(v) Provision for a periodic survey of the working of the provisions of the Act with a view to suggesting measures for the better implementation of the provisions of the Act.

(vi) Identification of the areas where persons are under any disability arising out of 'untouchability' and adoption of such measures as would ensure the removal of such disability from such areas.

Source: Upadhyay, H. C. [1991). "Reservation for Scheduled Castes and Scheduled Tribes", Anmol Publication, New Delhi.

Appendix – C
Policies Adopted for the Development of Privileged Class

There are a number of laws, both Central and State, which provide for safeguards to SCs-STs. Some of these emanate list of such laws in given below: -

(i) The Protection of Civil Rights Acts, 1955.
(ii) The scheduled castes and the scheduled tribes (Prevention of Atrocities) Act, 1989.
(iii) The Bonded Labour System (Abolition) Act, 1976.
(iv) The child labour (Prohibition and Regulation) Act, 1986.
(v) Act and regulation in force in different States to prevent alietion of land belonging to SCs-STs. In some States such provision exists in the Land Remote Code.
(vi) Act in different States for restoration of alienated land to SCs-STs.

Source: Government of India.

Appendix - D
Constitutional Safeguards for the Development of Weaker Section

(i) The abolition of 'untouchability' and the forbidding of its practice in any form (Art. 17);
(ii) The promotion of their educational and economic interests and their protection from social injustice and all forms of exploitation (Art. 46);
(iii) The throwing open of Hindu religious institutions of a public character to all classes and sections of Hindus (Art. 25);
(iv) The removal of any disability, liability, restriction or condition with regard to access to shops, public restaurants, hotels and places of public entertainment, use of wells, tanks, bathing ghats, roads and places of public resort maintained wholly or partly out of State funds or dedicated to the use of the general public (Art. 15);
(vi) The right to practise any profession or carry on any occupation, trade or business (Art. 19);
(vi) The forbidding of any denial of admission to educational institutions maintained by the States or receiving aid out of State funds. (Art. 29);
(vii) The obligation of the State to consider their claims in the making of appointments to public services and reservation for them in case of inadequate representation (Arts. 16 and 335);
(viii) Special representation in Parliament and the State Legislatures for a period of twenty years (Arts. 330, 332 and 334);
(ix) The setting up of advisory councils and separate departments in the State and the appointment of a Special Official at the Centre to promote their

welfare and safeguard their interests (Arts. 164, 338 and Fifth Schedule); and

(x) Special provision for the administration and control of schedule and tribal areas Art. 2 and Fifth and sixth schedules).

Source: Upadhyay, H. C. [1991]. "Reservation for Scheduled Castes and Scheduled Tribes". Anmol Publication, New Delhi.

Appendix - E
Protection of Civil Rights-Amendment Act, 1976

The salient features of 1976 Amendment Act, are :

(i) Imprisonment of not less than one month and not more than six months and also a fine ranging from rupees 100 to rupees 500 for all offences under the Act except for the unlawful compulsory labour where the imprisonment shall be from three to six months and also fine ranging from rupees one hundred to five hundred,

(ii) Employment in any job cannot be refused on grounds of untouchability.

(iii) No person shall be compelled on grounds of untouchability to do any scavenging or sweeping or remove carcass or to flay any animal or to remove the umbilical cord or to do any job of a similar nature.

(iv) No person shall be compelled to do acts mentioned in para.

(iii) Above on the threat of his social or economic boycott.

(v) No public officer shall willfully neglect the investigation of any offence punishable under the Act.

(vi) There shall be enhanced penalty for subsequent conviction for example, for a second offence the imprisonment may run from six months to one year and a fine of rupees two hundred to five hundred; for a third subsequent to the third offence, the imprisonment would be from one year to two years and also a fine of rupees five hundred to rupees one thousand.

(vii) Imposition of collective fine.

(viii) No application of the probation of Offenders Act. 1958 shall be available against conviction under this Act.

(ix) Duties of State Government: The Act enjoins on the State Governments certain duties relating to the enforcement and effectiveness of the Act. The duties may be summarized as under:

   (a) Provision of adequate facilities including legal aid to the persons subjected to any disability arising out of untouchability.

   (b) Appointment of officers for initiating or exercising supervision over prosecution for the contravention of the provisions of the Act.

   (c) Setting up of special courts for the trial of offences under the Act.

   (d) Setting up of committees at appropriate levels to assist the State governments in formulating and implementing such measures as are for the furtherance of the Act.

   (e) Periodic survey of the working of the Act.

   (f) Identification of the areas, localities and habitants where persons are, under such disabilities as are mentioned in the Act.

   (g) Adoption of such measures as would ensure the removal of disabilities mentioned in the Act.

(x) The office, which was compounded under the 1955 Act, shall no more be compoundable after the 1976 Amended Act., where the minimum imprisonment is less than three months. The offence shall be summarily triable.

(xi) Insulting or attempting to insult a member of a Scheduled Caste on the ground of Untouchability.

(xii) Commission of any offence against the person or property of any individual as a reprisal or revenge for his having exercised any right accruing to him by reason of the abolition of 'untouchability'.

Source: Upadhyay, H.C. [1991]. "Reservation for Scheduled Castes and Scheduled Tribes", Anmol Publication, New Delhi.

11

LITERACY RATE AMONG THE SCHEDULED CASTES WITH REFERENCE TO WEST BENGAL

Biplab Chakraborty

INTRODUCTION

One of the important indicators for development is education, especially for the backward people like Scheduled Castes and Scheduled Tribes. Since this section of our society has always been backward and deprived of basic rights, education has largely been far from their reach. Although our country could not come out from the darkness of illiteracy after the 58 years of independence, the socio-economic development of the Scheduled Castes and their integration with the mainstream is constitutional responsibility and a national goal. Achieving of this noble demands effective planning and implementation of the programmes for the development of the Scheduled Castes. The objective of planning in India right from the first five-year plan was acceleration of economic growth with justice. State has been assigned a crucial and active role in the process of economic development (Ahluwalia: 1991). In case of socially and economically deprived sections such as Scheduled Castes (SCs), variety of special development programmes have been launched in addition to different general development programmes. However, there is still a huge gap in the level of development between S.C. population and others. For fighting backwardness of the underprivileged classes programmes have been undertaken in the form of land reforms, redistribution of surplus land and wastelands particularly among S.C. agricultural labourers and marginal farmers. The state has also launched the programme of providing micro-credit to improve the agricultural productivity and to give financial assistance to improve their educational level [Nancharaiah: 2000]. Special consideration was accorded to SC families in the Integrated Rural Development Programme (IRDP). In the wage employment programme of Jawahar Rozgar Yojana, preference was given to SCs. The Government had taken different types of programmes in different times for the primary education viz. Operation Blackboard, Non-Formal Education (NFE) etc. For improving literacy and education level of these communities. In line with the policy of protective discrimination a number of incentives such as stipends, scholarship, and tuition fee and reimbursement of compulsory charges, and aid for books, uniforms, etc. are being offered to the members of the backward communities [Chakrabarty: 2000]. From the nature of the development policies it is not difficult to sense that educational development has been integrated with the policy of economic and social development of the SCs in the country and the state has assumed a key role in achieving the objective.

DATA BASE

Among the different indicators to measure development, we have chosen only literacy for the present paper. For simplicity of concept and easy availability of reliable data, we take only the Census data, which also make inter-state comparison easy and meaningful. To make the comparison we only consider those states, where Census data are available for the year of 1971, 1981 and 1991. For example, 1991 census excludes the figures of Jammu & Kashmir and 1981 excludes Assam where census could not be held due to disturbed condition prevailing there. In case of West Bengal there are 18 districts in 2001, but in 1981 and 1991 it had 16 and 17 districts respectively. Previously 24 Paraganas district was a single district, but it was divided in to two districts, namely, North 24 Paraganas and South 24 Paraganas by the time 1991 census was held. Similarly, West Dinajpur was also divided into Uttar (North) and Dakshin (South) Dinajpur districts in the early 1990s. In Table-5 we consider the Scheduled Castes literacy rates as reflected in 1981, 1991, and 2001 census. Whereas the figures for 1991 and 2001 exclude 0-6 year age group, the 1981 figures include 0-6 year age group. It is calculated on the basis of total literates divide by total population and multiplied by 100.

POSITION OF THE SCHEDULED CASTES IN INDIA

The Government has special concern and commitment for the well-being of the socially disadvantaged groups like the Scheduled Castes (SCs), as they still continue to lag behind the rest of the society due to their social and economic backwardness. These groups, which have passed through the process of welfare and development during the past four decades, will now be empowered to act as agents of socio-economic change and development. According to the Census data, the percentage of Scheduled Caste population to the country's total population was 14.82 per cent in 1971, 15.75 per cent in 1981 and 16.48 per cent in 1991. A large majority of them lives in rural areas. There has been an increase in the percentage of SC population to the total population from 1971 to 1991. They are dispersed all over the country, except Nagaland. In some states the presence of SC population is very low, viz. Meghalaya (0.51%), Manipur (2.02%), Gujarat (7.41%) and Kerala (9.92%). In the other states, the SCs constitute more than 10 per cent of their population. In a few states, the SCs constitute more than 20 per cent of the total of their population. Some of the states with larger share of SC population are Punjab (28.31 %), Himachal Pradesh (25.34%), West Bengal (23.62%) and Uttar Pradesh (21.04%).

The literacy rate among the SCs as per 1991 census was 37.41, while it was only 21.38 according to 1981 census. Within a decade, literacy rate increased by 19.03 percent. S.C. literacy rate was highest in Kerala (79.66 per cent), and lowest in Bihar (19.49 percent). In case of general 1iteracy rate Kerala took the highest position (89.81 per cent) and Bihar's position was the lowest *i.e.* 38.48 per cent. If we consider the state with relatively higher share of SC population viz. Punjab, Himachal Pradesh, Uttar Pradesh and West Bengal, we see that in all these states the SC literacy rate was more than 40 per cent. In Uttar Pradesh it was 26.58 per cent. The literacy rate of Uttar Pradesh was also very low, but the General literacy rate of the rest three states was higher than the National average.

According to 1991 census, the S.C population was 138.22 million, representing 16.48 per cent of the country's total population. Of these, 81 per cent live in rural areas. But the rural SC literacy rate was very low compared to the urban literacy rate. However, in Kerala, where General literacy rate as well as SC literacy was very high, the gap between rural and urban literacy was very low. In Uttar Pradesh the General literacy rate was low, and rural-urban literacy gap was also very high. But the other SC populated states viz. West Bengal, Uttar Pradesh, and Himachal Pradesh this gap was much lower than Uttar Pradesh

Although there has been a visible increase in the literacy rate of SCs during the last three decades the gap in literacy between the SCs and the General population still persists. But the female literacy rate among the SCs has increased substantially from 6.44 per cent in 1971 to 23.76 per cent in 1991. The most encouraging sign was the increase in the female literacy rates of the SCs and the General population during 1981 to 1991.

Table 1
Literacy Rate of SC among the Total Population

SI.No.	*State/Country*	*1981*			*1991*		
		Total	*Rural*	*Urban*	*Total*	*Rural*	*Urban*
	India	21.38	14.48	36.60	37.41	33.25	55.11
1.	Andhra Pradesh	17.65	14.05	37.70	31.59	26.08	54.10
2.	Bihar	11.40	9.11	24.27	19.49	17.49	39.23
3.	Gujarat	39.79	34.93	49.79	61.07	55.59	70.06
4.	Haryana	20.15	18.73	28.16	39.22	37.67	46.42
5.	Himachal Pradesh	31.50	30.42	50.69	53.20	52.00	70.32
6.	Jammu & Kashmir	22.44	21.36	30.69	-	-	-
7.	Karnataka	20.59	15.36	39.22	38.06	31.42	59.18
8.	Kerala	55.96	54.75	64.75	79.66	78.55	84.47
9.	Madhya Pradesh	18.97	15.37	35.48	35.08	30.22	52.26
10.	Maharashtra	35.55	30.21	47.13	56.46	50.27	67.07
11.	Manipur	33.63	31.84	42.63	56.44	56.69	56.22
12	Meghalaya	25.78	22.54	29.54	44.27	37.11	53.05
13.	Orissa	22.41	21.72	29.00	-	-	-
14.	Punjab	23.86	22.74	28.70	41. 09	39.55	47.04
15.	Rajasthan	14.04	11.26	26.75	26.29	22.06	43.35
16.	Sikkim	28.06	22.65	47.91	51.03	47.53	76.58
17.	Tamil Nadu	29.67	25.92	44.54	46.74	42.50	62.24
18.	Tripura	33.89	32.93	48.08	56.55	55.24	64.06
19.	Uttar Pradesh	14.96	13.51	27.39	26.58	24.76	42.30
20.	West Bengal	24.37	22.62	36.76	42.21	39.98	53.68

Source: Census of India 1981; Series-I: Primary Census Abstract, Scheduled Castes. Part-II-B (ii)
Census of India 1991, Series-1: Primary Census Abstract, Scheduled Castes. Part-II-B (ii)

Table 2
Literacy rate of SCs and General Population

	1971	*1981*	*1991*
General Literacy (including SC)	29.45	36.23	52.21
Scheduled Caste Literacy	14.67	21.38	37.41
Gap between SCs and General Literacy	14.78	14.85	14.80

Source: Census of India, Primary Census Abstract, Scheduled Castes. 1971-91

Table 3
Female Literacy Rate of SCs and General Population

	1971	*1981*	*1991*
General Female Literacy (including SC)	21.67	29.85	39.29
Female Scheduled Caste Literacy	6.44	10.93	23.76
Gap between SCs and General Literacy	15.53	18.92	15.53

Source: Census of India, Primary Census Abstract, Scheduled Castes 1971-91

POSITION OF SCHEDULED CASTES IN WEST BENGAL

States like Kerala, Maharashtra, Punjab, West Bengal a better response in education, but within the state, there are major regional and internal imbalances among the Scheduled Castes [Wankhede: 2001]. West Bengal located in the east of India and with a population of 80,176,197 in 2001, within this 18,452,555 was Scheduled Castes. The Government has been made some important institutional changes and a sharp acceleration in agricultural production in the 1980s and 1990s. Two major institutional changes takes place in the West Bengal since 1977. First one was the land reform, consisting mainly of tenancy reform and the distribution of agricultural and homestead land to the landless and poor households. The second major institutional change is associated with the establishment of a three-tier system of local government, known as panchayat system. West Bengal was the first state in India to establish a regular system of decentralized development administration.

Literacy rate of West Bengal still more than the National level. According to census 2001 all India literacy rate was 64.8 per cent, in West Bengal it was 68.6. The Scheduled Caste literacy rate in West Bengal was 59.04 per cent, which was much lower in compare to total literacy rate, but the Scheduled Caste Population was 23.02 per cent of the total population of West Bengal.

Table 4
Literacy Rate of Scheduled castes of West Bengal and India, 1961-2001

Year	*Male*		*Female*	
	West Bengal	*India*	*West Bengal*	*India*
1961	10.4	17.0	0.6	3.3
1971	25.5	22.3	9.2	6.4
1981	34.3	30.9	13.7	10.8
1991	44.4	40.2	23.3	19.0

Source: Census of India, Various Volumes

From the Table-4 it is clear that Scheduled Castes are deprived educationally since 1961. From 1971 the literacy rate of Scheduled Castes in West Bengal is higher than the all India S.C. literacy rate. But when we compare it to the West Bengal total literacy rate, which was much higher than the Scheduled Castes literacy rate in West Bengal.

Table 5
Literacy rates of Scheduled Castes in Different Districts of West Bengal

	1981			*1991*			*2001*		
	T	*R*	*U*	*T*	*R*	*U*	*T*	*R*	*U*
West Bengal	24.37	22.62	36.76	42.21	39.98	53.98	59.04	57.09	68.99
Koch Bihar	25.21	24.83	46.28	41.07	40.44	60.94	66.30	64.27	85.18
Jalpaiguri	23.05	22.32	31.71	41.34	40.52	47.74	61.87	61.13	68.37
Darjeeling	31.77	28.38	47.40	46.30	41.73	61.82	62.43	59.93	72.03
Uttar Dinajpur	20.03	19.19	36.33	33.05	31.43	53.84	50.06	48.31	69.34
Daxin Dinajpur	-	-	-				54.55	53.54	65.64
Maldah	20.41	19.93	38.00	33.89	32.94	50.56	51.17	49.99	67.69
Murshidabad	17.07	15.89	28.32	32.79	30.75	46.00	48.91	46.76	62.60
Nadia	27.51	25.99	37.82	45.32	43.04	55.71	63.09	61.77	69.21
North 24 Paragana	33.28	30.96	44.67	53.51	49.72	61.79	70.79	77.53	83.39
South 24 Paragana	-	-	-	49.79	48.75	63.27	59.01	56.15	73.70
Kolkata	42.59	-	42.58	56.53	-	56.53	70.54	-	70.54
Haora	28.80	25.68	38.73	44.87	39.91	56.12	61.13	57.16	70.39
Hugli	22.50	20.03	37.70	40.66	37.71	54.50	56.10	52.96	70.37
Medinipur	26.76	26.37	32.09	54.56	54.11	59.34	63.57	62.92	70.93
Bankura	14.93	14.37	23.80	26.96	26.16	38.15	42.92	42.22	54.78
Puruliya	18.46	17.95	23.40	31.81	30.80	40.33	45.15	44.47	50.08
Burdhaman	15.79	14.39	22.84	36.57	34.44	43.23	51.99	49.71	58.53
Birbhum	14.79	14.30	22.20	27.66	26.71	39.95	45.74	44.83	57.98

Source: Census of India, Various Volumes

From Table-5 it is clear that the literacy rate of Scheduled Castes increased sharply from 1981 to 200 l. If we compare it to the total literacy rate of West Bengal than it was much lower. Urban literacy is always much higher than the rural. In West Bengal, out of 18,452,555 Scheduled Caste populations, rural population was 15,524,925 and the urban population was 2,927,630. So, higher urban literacy is not indicating that the literacy rate was high. In the district of Koch Bihar more than 50 per cent of the people were Scheduled Castes, but the Scheduled Caste Literacy rate was not so low. But in Maldah, only 16.8 per cent people was Scheduled Castes, but the literacy rate also was not satisfactory. In case of Kolkata and North 24 Paragana the literacy rate was very high and more or less hundred per cent of people was urban people.

THE SARVA SHIKSHA ABHIYAN AND SC POPULATION

In accordance with the constitutional commitment to ensure free and compulsory education for all the children upto the age of 14 years, provision of Universal Elementary Education has been a salient feature of national policy since independence. Many numbers of schemes and programmes were launched to increase the literacy level and Universalisation of Elementary Education. These include the schemes of Operation Blackboard (OB), Non Formal Education (NFE), Teachers Education (TE), Mahila Samakhya (MS), state specific Basic Education Project like the Andhra Pradesh Primary Education Project (APPEP), Bihar Education Project (BEP), and the District Primary Education Programme (DPEP)

The Sarva Shiksha Abhiyan (SSA) is a historic step towards achieving the goal of Universalisation of Elementary Education (UEE) through a time bound integrated approach, in partnership with state. SSA, which promises to change the face of the elementary education sector of the country, aims to provide useful and quality elementary education to all children aged 6-14 years by 2010. To reduce literacy and provide basic education for all depends on community mobilization and also depends upon effective participation of Village Education Committee (VEC), Panchayats, NGOs, Parents, Teachers and Students [Madhusudan: 2001].

The West Bengal DPEP was formally launched in 1997-98, initially in five districts Bankura, Birbhum, Koch Bihar,

Murshidabad and south 24-Paragana. With the main objective to support the formal primary education system through their different interventions like Community Mobilization, Civil Works, Girls Education, Alternative Schooling etc. It also has programs to provide primary education for deprive urban children, disabled children and also for children from backward class [Human Development Report, W.B: 2004].

The main objectives of SSA are:

(i) All the children in School by 2003.
(ii) All the children complete five years of primary schooling by 2007.
(iii) All children complete eight years of schooling by 2001.
(iv) Bridge all gender and social category gap at primary stage by 2007 and elementary education level by 2010.

SSA gives special focus for the educational development of children belonging to the SC community. Every activity under the project must identify the benefit that wills acerute to children from the communities. Many of the incentives schemes will have a sharper focus on children from these communities. The SSA provides flexibility to local units to develop a context specific intervention. Some intervention could be as follows:

(i) Engagement of community organisers from SC communities with a focus on schooling needs from specific households.
(ii) Special teaching support as per need.
(iii) Ensuring sense of ownership of school communities by SC communities.
(iv) Training programmes for motivation for schooling.
(v) Setting up of alternative schooling facilities in unsaved habitations and for other out of school children.
(vi) Using community teachers.
(vii) Monitoring attendance and retention of children of weaker sections regularly.
(viii) Providing context specific intervention in the form of a hostel, an incentives or a special facility as required.

Sometimes the problems faced by the S.C children are often different from other children. For this purpose SSA have made the following provisions, specially for girls and S.C children's education.

I. Intervention for Early Childhood Care and Education.
II. Alternative facility like Education Guarantee Scheme (EGS) to be set up within one kilometer of all habitation
III. Special mainstreaming camps for out-of-school girls/S.C. children under the alternative and innovative education component.
IV. Provision for community participation with a focus on the women and S.C. participation.
V. Provision of context specific innovative intervention for girls education and education for S.C children upto 50 lakhs in a district in a particular year. This programme can include
    - Enrolment and retention drives.
    - Special campus and bridge course.
    - Setting up special models of Alternative Schooling.
    - Strengthening of madarsas and maktebs for formal education to girls.
    - Remedial/Coaching classes.
    - Providing a congenial learning improvement inside and outside the school.
VI. Training programme for community leaders to develop capacities for school management.
VII. Free textbook to all girls and S.C. children upto class VIII.
VIII. Mid-day-Meal programme to continue as at present.
IX. Incentives like uniform and Scholarship to be funded from state plan only.
X. At least 50% of the teachers to be appointed have to be women.

CONCLUSION

Dalits, particularly the SCs have been overwhelmingly engaged as agricultural labourers, and there has been no significant improvement in terms of their access to land despite land reforms and there is still a substantial gap in the level of development between SC population and non-SC population even after the fifty five-years of independence. The role of the states in implementing the programmes that improve their asset base and skills, particularly education should be strengthened. State should also provide necessary credit to enable the backward communities to increase the productivity of their economic assets and extend financial assistance to improve their education levels. Different types of special development programmes have been initiated and implemented for the economic development of SCs. As a result of these programmes, we see an improvement in the literacy status of the dalits. To reduce the gap with the general population the rural and urban gap has to be reduced and the gender gap too has to be reduced drastically. The urban people are privileged as that have access to the better facilities of urban centers but those who live in the rural areas find them in a disadvantageous position because the rural areas lag behind in terms of infrastructure facilities. Thus, the facilities of urban areas have to be extended to the rural areas too, because the major portion of the SC population lives in the rural areas and most of them work as agricultural labourers. The female literacy rate among the SCs also has to be increased drastically if we are serious in our fight against social inequality, backwardness and injustice.

Though the successful SSA campaign can achieve a lot for spreading literacy among the SCs the VEC the Gram Panchayats also have to come forward to achieve the task fast. Only the village people can easily understand the problems of the villagers and their active and committed participation in the state sponsored development programmes can ensure the uplift of the backward communities. In that case, the village people have to find out the problems of the poor, backward class people, and they have to utilize the opportunities created by the state through SSA. It would be no exaggeration to suggest that success of the state sponsored development programmes for the SCs would largely depend on the level of mobilization and collective initiative of these communities. The achievements could be sustained if the development initiatives assume the character of social movements.

REFERENCES

Ahluwalia 1.1, *Productivity and Growth in Indian manufacturing,* Oxford University Press, Delhi

Chakrabarty G.: *Development of SCs and STs:* The success so far, Social Change, September-December 2000, Vol.30 Nos. 3&4.

Chen Lincaln C. Education, *Equality and Security, Summary Commentary Revised,* Hotel Taj Bengal, Kolkata, January 2-4,2002.

Leclereq Francois: *Education Guarantee Scheme and Primary Schooling in Madhya Pradesh,* Economic and Political Weekly, May 10,2003

Maurya R.D.: *Impact of Special Component Plan On Socio-Economic Development of Scheduled Castes in Madhya Pradesh:* Indian Journal of Rural Development, 2000, Vol.20 (I), pp.131-151

Nancharaiah.G.: *Economic development of dalits and 50 years of Independence.* A macro analysis, *Social Change,* September-December 2000, Vol.30 Nos.3&4

Srivastava B.N. *Working of the Constitutional Safeguards and Protective Measures for the Scheduled Castes and Scheduled Tribes,* Indian Journal of Rural Development, 2000, Vol. 19 (4), pp.573-602.

Sankaran S.R. *Welfare of the Scheduled Castes and Scheduled Tribes in Independent India-An overview of State Policies and Programmes: Indian Journal of Rural Development,* 2000, Vol. 19 (4), pp.535-572.

Madhusudan J.V. *Network and Partnership in Education: A Case of District Primary Education,* Indian Journal of Rural Development, 2001, Vol.20 (4), pp. 769-778.

Rana Kumar *et al. Pratichi Siksha Pratibedan,* 2004, Vol. 1& 2, Day's Publications.

Ramchandran V.K, Swaminathan Madhura and Vikas Rawal: *Bariers to Expansion of Mass Literacy and Primary Schooling in West Bengal: A Study Based on Primary Data From Selected Villages:* Working Paper, 345

West Bengal Human Development Report, 2004, Development and Planning Department, Government of West Bengal.

Yadav Anil K.: *Disparities in the Growth of Primary Education: An Inter-State Comparison:* Labour and Development, Vol-8, No.102, December 2002.

12

HIS AND HER SYNDROME IN POLITICAL RESERVATION OF WOMEN: AN ANALYSIS IN THE PRESENT SOCIO-LEGAL FRAMEWORK

Biswajit Chatterjee

INTRODUCTION

The issue of women empowerment through political reservation has become a hypersensitive and controversial issue. The picture is more or less like the picture of uncertainty pointed in an old poem quoted by Lord Justice Cohen in a lecture at Cambridge;

> *"Mr, Leech made a speech, angry neat but wrong.*
> *Mr. Hart, on the other part, was heavy, dull and long.*
> *Mr. Praker made the class darker, which was dark enough without.*
> *Mr. Cook cited his book and the chancellor said.*
> *" I doubt"*[1]

Fifty-four years of constitutional experience shows that, we have done little for the women of our country. Women's empowerment gained currency throughout the world only in the late nineteenth century and in India we are now just debating some of its aspect. In the light of constitutional provision we have started thinking for the other half of the society who constitute nearly the half of India's population. We have, therefore, invented the principle of protective discrimination to enrich the concept of equality. Women, the weakest of the weaker section of the society still suffer from various kinds of discrimination.

This is the place, where the issue of political reservation of women gains primacy. But whether there should be reservation within reservation, that is whether, political reservation to women should also make way for the inclusion of scheduled castes/ scheduled tribe women? Whether they need some special treatment in this regard? The present Article discusses all these issues and reminds us of the need of the hour. In doing so it takes us to the glorious past when women of this country received respect to the fullest extent and points out the present dilemma and hesitation of the legislature in introducing the Women Reservation Bill and getting it passed by a thumping majority and thereby placing them in both Houses of Parliament and State legislatures.

WOMEN OF INDIA IN THE PAST

If we give a look into our past we will see how an important segment of the society has been marginalized so steadily and brutally. Progress of womankind has not always been in a single straight line; rather it has been on a zig-zag way. This is because, at every stage of this long journey there has been stiff opposition from various forces operating to produce disharmony in every framework of the society, be it social, political or legal. Vedic and Puranic tradition ascribe a divine status to women in terms of Lakshmi, Durga, and Saraswati. In the Rig-Vedic civilization, women enjoyed equal status with men. Women received education, observed Brahmachary and Upanayana and even studied the Vedas. Ghosha, Apala, Visharava, were composers of Vedic hymns. Gargi and Maitreyi were great women scholars during Upanishad period. But the Vedic period diluted the ancient concept and the position of women started dereriorating. They were denied the right to ownership of property and inheritance. A daughter began to be regarded as a curse. Even the earning of the women became the property of husband and sons. Dowry emerged as an institution during Gupta period; Sati became popular in the 7th century A.D. The period after A.D. 1206 saw the rise of female infanticide, child marriage, Purdah, Sati and other social evils[2]. It was the effort of some great people like Raja Ram Mohan Roy, Ishwar Chandra Vidyasagar and Mahatma Gandhi that the process of emancipation of Indian women started during British rule. After independence-several legislation were passed to remove the constraints hindering the progress of women. Inspite of this, women in India are still subjected to many discrimination and exploitation, whereas it is acclaimed by every civilized nation that women's empowerment is a condition for the advancement of equality, development and peace.

INTERNATIONAL EFFORTS

Advancement of the rights of women has been the concern of the world community since the end of Second World War. The preamble to the charter of the United Nations mentions the determination of the people of the United Nations "to reaffirm faith in fundamental human rights, in the dignity and worth of the human person, in the equal rights of men and women"[3] and to employ international machinery for the promotion of the economic and social advancement of the people. Similarly, provisions are also incorporated in the charter of the United Nations and other human rights instruments, which provide for the protection and advancement of the rights of women. Thus, we see the unequivocal acceptance of the following principle:

> *"Women empowerment and their full participation on the basis of equality in all spheres of society including participation in the decision-making process access to power are fundamental for the advancement of equality, development and peace"*[4]

> *"The full and complete development of a country requires the, maximum participation of women on equal terms in all fields; Women must have a equal stake in shaping societies"*[5]

> "Every one has the right to take part in the government of the country, directly or through freely chosen representative. A *proper representation of women in political affairs will ensure their views and needs reflected in public policies that affect their life most'*,[6]

CONSTITUTIONAL PHILOSOPHY AND MANDATES

The constitution of India guarantees equality of opportunity and status to women and men. It directs that women shall not only have equal rights and privileges with men but also that the State shall make provisions – both general and special for the welfare of the women. Despite the above constitutional guarantee, women in India who constitute nearly half the population are still subjected to many disadvantages, disabilities and inequalities in every sphere of their life. The reason is implicit in our traditional social economic and religious structure of the society. The patriarchy of traditional Indian society since times immemorial has viewed women as a product of history and based on this idea, the patriarchy has registered a milieu of mystification, whereas the reality is that women also actively participate in making history[7]. The patriarchy kept women illiterate economically unrecognized, socially inferior and legally helpless and their image in public life had been negatively influenced due to their unvalued and under valued work in economic terms, whereas the reality is that they also contribute in nations building.

The phrase *"equality before law"* finds a place in all most all written constitution that guarantees fundamental right. Our Constitution of India similarly has put an obligation on the state that it shall not deny to any person (including women) equality before the law and the equal protection of law will be given to all persons (including women).[8] Thus article 14 embodies the general principle of equality before law and prohibits unreasonable discrimination between persons. The concept of equality, which is embodied in, our constitution speaks for the rule that like should be treated alike and not that unlike should be treated alike.[9] The principle of equality must be read in the light of equality of justice. Our Indian judiciary has evolved for this purpose the theory of reasonable classifications to meet out the eventuality and to make the equality effective and in the real sense.

To make the equality clause more pragmatic the framers of the Constitution provided on the other hand that the state shall not discriminate on grounds of religion race, caste, sex or place of birth.[10]. In the same way the equality of opportunity in matters of employment or appointment to any office under the state is assured to all citizens including womens.[11] These provisions make it amply clear that both man and women will be treated equally. On the other hand founding father of our constitution were also conscious of the pitiable and miserable condition of the weaker of the society, therefore, they made some special provisions for them and empowered the state to make further provisions for the protection and welfare of women and children.[12] This means that some special care has been taken to provide a socio-economic framework of justice to equality in regard to women and children.[13] Finally, the state is under duty to see that no person is deprived of his life or personal liberty except according to the procedure established by law.[14]

In effect Article 14 embodies the idea of equality expressed in the preamble. The succeeding Article, that is Article 15 and 16 lay down the specific application of the general rule laid down is Article 14. While Article 14 places a duty on the state to follow the rule where by equal is to be treated equally. It also makes way for unequal treatment in unequal circumstances and provides the scope for reasonable classification. Besides incorporating the principle of natural justice and making it a essential component of law, Article 14 ensures fairness, equality of treatment and implies the absence of arbitrariness in every sphere of state action[15] while Art. 15(1) puts prohibition of discriminations only on grounds of religion, race caste, sex or place of birth, (implying that sex above not be made a ground of discrimination) Article 15(3) enables the state to make special provision for women and child (implying that protective discrimination is allowed in favour of women and child). Not only this, Article 16(1) further ensures equality of opportunity in matters of public employment. In the ultimate analysis these provisions besides upholding the concept of socio-economic justice, and many other thing also speak that there is urgent need to take special care for the protection and welfare of the women and there is room for that too. In other words, it can be said that the concept of equality and social justice enshrined in the Constitution long ago spelt out the need for political reservation of women. It was in consonance of the concept of equality and social justice that the policy of reservation in public employment for Scheduled Castes and Scheduled Tribes etc. has been brought into existence, long before the concept has been put in writing after an amendment of the Constitution.

POLITICAL RESERVATION

Women have been characterized as a 'suppressed majority.' In modern times this suppression has been fostered by the lack of political empowerment, arising out of lack of participation at the representative level (i.e. to say, to represent a constituency in a legislature) or at an individual level.[16] Moreover, the peculiar discriminatory caste system in India led to the growth of only a section of the society dominating the rest of the populace by depriving them of economic opportunities and equal privileges. For ages, castes women were kept under economic exploitation and it contributed to their backwardness. The Poona Pact was signed between Gandhiji and Dr. Ambedkar, who represented the Scheduled Castes, Scheduled Tribes and Depressed Classes. According to it, although separate electorates were not granted to the SC/STs, seats were reserved for them, which gave birth to the creation of joint electorates. As Chairman of the Drafting Committee of the Constituent Assembly. Ambedkar provided adequate scope for reservation of seats for the SCs. A law had to be passed to preserve the rights granted to the SCs and also to remove the shameful custom of unsociability. Thus, the caste factor was invariably an important item of the political agenda.[17]

The all round development of women is closely linked with their political empowerment. Therefore, the founding father of our Constitution incorporated certain provision. Article 330 and 332 of the Constitution provides for reservation of seats in the House of peoples[18] and Legislative Assemblies of the states.[19] Article 334 also makes a provision for the reservation of seats for SC/STs to the Lok Sabha for a period of ten years[20]. Thus by the eighth Amendment of the Constitution in 1960, it was prolonged for another ten years. In 1969, the 23rd Constitutional Amendment extended the reservation for a period of ten years till 1990. The SC/STs have 546 seats reserved in various state assemblies and about 291 seats in the Union territories. Inspite of these, Constitutional mandate there has not been any substantial representation of women in the Union Parliament as well as in the State Assemblies.

The unequivocal acceptance of women's right as human rights had been in our law books and the constitution for over decades. Ultimately some progress was made in the year 1992 through constitutional amendment. The reservation of seats for SC/ST women was inserted U/A243-D[21] and U/A 243-T[22] of the Constitution, respectively for Panchayati and Municipal areas. The 73rd and 74th Amendments to the Constitution of India popularly known as the Panchayati Raj and Nagarpalika Constitution Amendment Acts. These Amendments paved the way for women empowerment by providing that; (1) in every Panchayat and Municipalities seats shall be reserved for Scheduled castes and

Scheduled tribes. The number of seats so reserved shall be, as nearly as may be, in the same proportion to the total number of seats to be filled by direct election in that Panchayat or Municipalities as the population of the SC and STs in that Panchayat or Municipality areas bear to the total population of that respective area and such seats may be allotted to different constituencies in a Panchayat or Municipality as the case may be; and (2) out of total number of seats reserved under clause (1) not less than 1/3 seats shall be reserved for women belonging to SC and STs. Out of total number of seats to be filled by direct election in every Panchayat or Municipality as the case may be not less than 1/3 (including the number of seats reserved for SC and STs women) seats shall be reserved for women.

THE REALITY

The Act is most significant for the reservation for women including Scheduled Castes and Scheduled Tribe women. The Amendment sought to achieve such a political empowerment for women in the wider context of an attempt to promote local self-government and decentralized democracy. It heraled the ascent of nearly 8 lakh women (including those belonging to Scheduled Castes and Scheduled Tribes) to political position in the length and breadth of India at its rural grass root level, where the extent of patriarchy, illiteracy, poverty and socio-cultural norms are even deeper and more strangling than in urban areas.[23] Yet, these provisions need to be translated into reality. In fact practices of different states in this regard have not been satisfactory. A few states like, Maharastra, Kerala, Himachal Pradesh, Andhra Pradesh, West Bengal have given comparatively more representation to women in different tires of Panchayat as compared to other states.[24] The tragedy is, that the Panchayat system has thrown up aspiring women candidates who have no upward political mobility.[25] In most of the cases they can be found as proxies for powerful male politician.

Several factors inhibit the effective participation of women in the political process and institutional structure of democracy. Women's role in political process again has mainly been confined to the upper strata of our society. A broad based political participation of women has been limited due to various factors such as caste, religion, feudal attitude and family status. Despite several measures being taken up by the Government the scenario does not seem to have improved much. Barring a few exception women who constitute the half of India's population have not been adequately represented at the higher level.[26] Empirical data shows that the first Lok Sabha had 23 women while the 13th Lok Sabha has 49 women M.P.[27] Voices were raised by various women's organization demanding reservation of 33% legislative seats for women. It took fifty years for the women's reservation Bill to be introduced in Parliament for the first time in 1999. It took another four years for the elected representative of the people to re-introduce it and then shoot it down.[28] The honorable members of parliament committed to gender justice, did it again. They got together to block the Women Reservation Bill that was to have come up for discussion in the Lok Sabha in a manner that can only shame the nation. The acrimonious scenes in the parliament and arguments put forward by some parliamentarian in this regard only highlighted the double standards, if not outright hypocrisy, prevalent in the political class as a whole about the Women's Reservation Bil1.[29] The present Bill was criticized by the opposition on the ground that it was mere tokenism; it failed to include a quota for women from the OBC's, SC's, ST's and minorities.

We often hear that the Bill is an insulting handout that women who ask for it are admitting to their incompetence. But statistics prove that a greater percentage of women fielded win election than men.[30] In truth, women want reservation, not because they are incapable, but because they are shut out of the electoral process. The unprecedented victory of three powerful women in recent election held in four Hindi-speaking states is an indication in this regard. The victory of Sheila Dikshit, Uma Bharati and Vasundhra Raje, Sonia Gandhi, Sushma Swaraj, Rabri Devi, Jay Lalitha, Renuka Chowdhary, signals significant shift in paradigm of Indian politics.[31] This also proves that there is no harm in reservation of Legislative seats for women as because women are also aspiring to emerge as co-partners in national planning, policy making, and governance. It is also evident that they have proved that they are capable and fit for that position. But this should not be seen as resurgence of women's power in view of the fact that so far mostly men are on the centre stage of power politics. In fact, the presence of women in Parliament has come up from 4.4% to merely 7.97% in 1999.[32] The way Women Reservation Bill was beaten back is only indicative of the following facts;

1. Political parties are not practising what they are preaching;
2. As long as empowerment of women remains a politically loaded question in a largely male dominated political landscape, the situation is bound to be fractious as it is now;
3. There is a general fear amongst the male politicians that in a situation where tickets are distributed on merit, there is no doubt, women would pose a serious challenge to the entrenched patriarchal political order;
4. Male politicians think that gender balance, may reduce noisy scenes, walkouts, adjournment of proceedings, hangamas, horse-trading, corruption and specially criminalisation of politics, which is threatening the very foundation of Indian politics;
5. There is legislative gerrymandering of constitutional philosophy as far as the question of political reservation of women is concerned.

CONCLUSION AND SUGGESTION

The principle of equality and social justice, which are the corner stone of our Constitution, can be applied and extended to make way for political reservation of women. But the legislative lag, male chauvinism and gerrymandering of the constitutional policy by the successive Governments is really frustrating. The 73rd and 74th Amendments to the Constitution of India which is popularly known as the Panchayati Raj and Nagarpalika Constitution Amendment Act is a welcome step towards the political empowerment of women, but the provisions of this Act need to be translated into reality. As to the question whether women's reservation' should be made only for the women irrespective of caste, creed, or religion or it should also incorporate a quota for women from the OBC's, SC's, ST's and minorities; it can be said that the need of the hour is that there should be a broad based avenue for greater participation of women in decision-making. Having made a beginning with Panchayat and Municipal Committee, the next step should be to reserve one-third seats for women in the State Assemblies and Parliament. Those who are demanding an ironic divisive unity or a unity which is infact no unity at all, are not really practicing what they preach all the time.

Political parties supporting the Bill can make a much-needed beginning and consciously accommodate more women in the organisational structure. They can reserve the requisite 33% seats for women while allocating tickets for election. People who are demanding quota for women from the OBC's, SC's, ST's and minorities can also do the same at their organizational level. The time is now ripe for women N.G.O's, Mahila Morchas, Mahila Mandals, and other gender friendly groups to mount social pressure on the Government and the political parties to discuss Women Reservation Bill and arrive at some consensus. Let's all of us honestly try to place the other half of the society in both Houses of Parliament.

REFERENCES

Quoted from V. R. Krishna lyer *"Judicial Justice – A new focus"* (Bombay N.M.Tripathi), 1985, at pp. 118-119.

Rashmi Singh, *"Towards a Gender Just Indian Society"*, Women's Link, April-June 1999, Vol-5, at p. 17.

Charter of the United Nations, 2nd Preambuler Paragraph.

The Beijing Declaration.

Preamble of C.E.D.A.W, 1979.

Article 21 of the Universal Declaration of Human Rights 1948.

D.K. Sarkar *"Decentering Women's Development; Politico administrative and Economic Agents for re-construction", in A. Bhumali ed. "Education employment and empowering women" Serials Publications,* 2004, at p. 313.

Dr. R.N. Sharma *"The problem of working women and her economic independence in Indian society,"* in Shamsuddin Shams - edt. *"Women law and social change"* at p. 116.

Dr. V.N. Shukla - *"Constitution of India"*, 9th ed. 1994, at p. 38.

Art. 15 (1)-States that-the state shall not discriminate against any citizen on grants only of religion role, caste, sex place of berth or any of them.

Art. 16 (1) States that – There shall be equality of opportunity for all citizens in matters relating to employment or appointment to any office under the State:

Art. 15 (3) States that – "Nothing in this article (Art 15) shall prevent the state from making any special provision for women and children."

Dr. R.N. Sharma *"The problem of working women and her economic independence in Indian society"* in Shamsudd Shams - edt.[11] *"Women law and social change"* at p. 117.

Art. 21 of the Constitution of India..

E.P. Royappa V. State of Tamil Nadu AIR 1974 SC 555; Maneka Gandh IV. UOl AIR 1978 SC 597; R.D. Shetty v. Airport Authority AIR 1979 SC 1628.

B. Shivaramaya: *"Women and the Law"*, Vol-XXIX, Annual Survey of Indian Law, (1993), at p-145.

Dr. Kamala Jain, *"Panchayati Raj and Participation of Women"*, Vol. – X, Legal News and Views, at p. 28-29.

Article 330 of the Constitution reads:

"Seats shall be reserved in the House of Peoples for-

The scheduled castes

The scheduled tribes...

The scheduled tribes in the autonomous districts..."

"The number of seats reserved in any state.. ..for SC/ST under clause (1) shall bear, as nearly as may be the same proportion... as the population of SC/ST in the state..."

"Notwithstanding anything contained in clause (2) The number of seats reserved in the House of people for the ST....a population not less than the population of the ST in the said autonomous district..."

Article 332 of the Constitution says:

"Seats shall be reserved also for SC/STs in the Legislative Assembly of every state "Seats shall be reserved for autonomous district. . "

"The number of seats shall bear the same proportion to the total number of seats. . . Bears to the total population of the state.

"The number of seats reserved... Shall bear to the.. .not less than the population of the district bears..."

"The Constitution for the seats reserved.. .not comprise any area outside that district..."

Article 334 states that:

"Notwithstanding anything in the foregoing provisions, the provisions of this Constitution relating to. The reservation of seats for SC/ST in the House of People.

And Legislative Assemblies of the sate.. .and shall cease to have effect on the expiration of a period of fifty years from the commencement of this Constitution.. ."

"Article 243-D of the Constitution deals with reservation of seats for SC/ST and Women. As regards SC and ST.. .the number of seats reserved for them. ..as the population of SC and STs in a Panchayat area bears... Not less than one-third of the total number of seats so reserved, shall be reserved for women belonging to SC/ST as the case may be."

"Article 243- T provides for the reservation of seats for members of SC and STs in every Municipality. The number of seats reserved for them...in same proportion..."

Directory on Panchayati Raj and Women in India, Centre for Development Studies and Action, New Delhi, 2001, at p-23.

Leena Prasad, "Women Reservation: Some burning Issues" Women's Link, July 2002, Vol- 8, at p-27.

Staff Reporter, Times of India, 7th March 2003.

Suman Krishnan Kant, " *Women's Development and Mutual Co-operation in the Family,"* Women's Link, April 2001, Vol- 48, at p-3.

Women M.P in 13th Lok Sabha, Source: Election Commission of India.

Editorial, Asian Age, 8th May 2003.

Id.

Staff Reporter, Times of India, 7th May 2003.

A. K. Nikore, *"Gender Scape of Indian Politics Some Reflection"*, Legal News and Views, February 2004, at p-4.

Leena Prasad, *"Women Reservation: Some burning issues"* Women's Link, July 2002, Vol. - 8, at p. 28.

13

SCHEDULED CASTE WOMEN IN DECISION-MAKING: A STUDY OF DARJEELING MUNICIPAL ADMINISTRATION

Padam Nepal, Namrata Pariyar

INTRODUCTION

Mankind's experience over the millennia in the planet reveals that women have lived in two parallel worlds ever since the first community habitation, shelter or villages, They have occupied positions of eminence and authority and even gone into battles. They have also been objects of repression, uncalled for violence and the petty tyrannies of the male bread winner (Bhan and Singh: 2001). An enigma to be desired, mankind has ever been willing to give women everything but equal status in every domain, including the political. Women, which forms the bulk of the society had, and, to a significant extent, still have been alienated from the political domain. In reviewing the history of recent socia-political dynamics specially in the Third World countries, one observation which stands out clearly is that irrespective of the change of regimes, sexual inequalities in households, field and factory persists with little modifications; wage and educational differences continue unabated; women are oppressed and exploited in various ways as ever, and the special needs of women are postponed or put aside as trivial items (Black and Contrell: 1981) despite several national and international instruments striving to put an end to such a discrimination. The Universal Declaration of Human Rights states that everyone has the right to take part in the Government of his/her country. The empowerment and autonomy of women and the improvement of women's social, economic and political status is essential for the achievement of both transparent and accountable government and administration and sustainable development in all areas of life. The power relations that prevent women from leading fulfilling lives operate at many levels of society, from the most personal to the highly public. Achieving the goal of equal participation of women and men in decision-making will provide a balance that more accurately reflects the composition of society and is needed in order to strengthen democracy and promote its proper functioning. Equality in political decision-making performs a leverage function without which it is highly unlikely that a real integration of the equality dimension in government policy-making is feasible. In this respect, women's equal participation in political life plays a pivotal role in the general process of the advancement of women. Women's equal participation in decision-making is not only a demand for simple justice or democracy but can also be seen as a necessary condition for women's interests to be taken into account. Without the active participation of women and the incorporation of women's perspective at all levels of decision-making, the goals of equality, development and peace cannot be achieved. Hence, all states across the globe have been striving of late to empower women through various constitutional and extra constitutional means to enable them to participate meaningfully in political process and the decision-making institutions, and India is not an exception to this general rule.

However, Indian scenario is somewhat different. It is obvious that the problem converge on caste, class and gender. Caste has several implications for access and entitlement. The higher the caste, the greater the access and entitlement to land, other resources, and to policy making institutions and political processes. For historical reasons, scheduled castes have faced considerable discrimination, which is reflected in the poor level of human capital development, especially among women. Thus, the scheduled caste women face a double jeopardy: first as a scheduled caste that is discriminated due to historical reasons; and second, as women. Being a scheduled caste women amounts to suffering multiple discriminations and deprivations as is historically revealed. Despite abolishing untouchability, prejudice against the scheduled castes in general still persists in one form or the other, be it overt, covert, or subtle in expression. It is reckoned that only those policies designed and made by the women belonging to these communities will have a substance that will help them come out of such jeopardy. Therefore, their participation in decision-making is encouraged at different levels of administrative hierarchy at all levels of local, regional and national administration. In this backdrop, the present study aims to evaluate the participation of scheduled caste women in the decision-making process of Darjeeling Municipal Administration in West Bengal.

METHODOLOGY

The objective of the present study is to assess the extent of access of the Scheduled Caste women to the urban local level decision-making institutions. It also purports to examine whether adequate representations are made from these communities in such bodies in terms of their population, etc. and also to evaluate the nature and magnitude of the influence these participants exert on the making of the local level decisions after they have been elected to the said decision-making body. To this end, the author has carried out this study through primary data collected from the universe of study through the interview schedule that was administered to the respondents (the scheduled caste women representatives in the Darjeeling Municipal Boards of 2000 and 2004) and from the informal discussions and interviews, which were used to elicit further information. Secondary data obtained from various sources are also used extensively for the analysis and, accordingly, the conclusions have been drawn.

SCHEDULED CASTE WOMEN IN DECISION-MAKING PROCESS: THE CONSTITUTIONAL PROVISIONS

Decision-making is an analytical concept, which involves a set of questions or categories in the light of which concrete institutional realities are identified, described and compared [Macridis: 1964]. It is a social process that selects alternatives for implementation and execution from among the many that may be available. It denotes the dynamic process of interaction among participants who determine a particular policy choice. However, for the present purpose, decision-making shall be taken in its widest connotation, as understood in the Country Report for the Fourth World Conference on Women, Beijing, 1995 [GOI : 1995].

Women's role in decision-making is one of the most important questions for consideration in the movement for their empowerment. Urban local self-government has offered the Indian women in the post-independent period, a 'space' to actively participate in the decision-making process. The 74th Amendment to the Indian Constitution seemed as a major breakthrough towards ensuring women's equal access and increased participation in political power structures. This amendment has also initiated a powerful strategy of affirmative action for providing the structural framework for women's participation in women's political decision-making and provided an opportunity to ring women to the forefront in municipal development and administration, and develop new grassroots level leadership at the urban local levels. Thus, the women belonging to the Scheduled Caste (along with the Scheduled Tribe women) who constitute the peripheral groups among the Indian women got a considerable opportunity to participate in the decision-making process in urban local administrative institutions especially in the aftermath of the 74th Constitutional Amendment Act, 1992. Let us now examine the provision of the 74th Constitutional Amendment Act, 1992 [GOI: 1993].

The 74th Constitutional Amendment Act, 1992 added part IX-A in the constitution, entitled *'the municipalities'*. The Act also gives details of the reservation of seats for Scheduled Castes and Scheduled Tribes, women and backward classes under section 243- T of the Act which may be summarized thus: -

1. Under clause [2] section 243-T states that not less than one-third of the total number of seats reserved under clause [1] shall be reserved for women belonging to Scheduled Caste, or as the case may be to the Scheduled Tribe.
2. Clause [3] states that not less than one-third (including the number of seats reserved for the women belonging to the Scheduled Caste and Scheduled Tribes) of the total number of seats to be filled by direct election in every municipality shall be reserved for women and such seats may be alloted by rotation to different constituents in the municipality .
3. Clause [4] provides that the office of the chairpersons in the municipality shall be reserved for the Scheduled Caste and Scheduled Tribe women in such a manner as the legislature of a state may by law provide.

4. Clause [5] provides that the reservation of seats under clause [1] and [2] and the reservation of offices of chairperson (other than the reservation of women) under clause [4] shall cease to have effect on expiry of the period specified in Article 334.
5. Clause [6] provides that nothing in the part shall prevent the legislature of a state for making any provision for reservation of seats in the municipality or offices of chairpersons in the municipalities in favour of backward class of citizens.

These provisions of the 74th Constitution (Amendment) Act constitute a welcome gesture having a far-reaching consequence in the political and social life of women in general and the women belonging to the depressed sections of the society, that is, Scheduled Caste (and Scheduled Tribe women) in India. But such a constitutional directive in itself is not sufficient to ensure the meaningful participation of women in political process and in decision-making unless the institutions in which they are represented do not create mechanisms through which they can exert influence to produce the resultant decision in their favour.

Hence, in the following sections we endeavour to make a particularistic analysis of the situation as it exists in Darjeeling Municipal administration in West Bengal, a state that is known to have kept the Panchayat and municipal bodies very active in pursuance of their goals and objectives

THE DARJEELING MUNICIPALITY CASE

A Profile

Darjeeling Municipality is the oldest Hill Municipality in West Bengal. The Municipality has a patrilineal, patriarchal and patrilocal society with a total population of 107,197 heads spread over 17,247 Households, sizing somewhere around 6.2 people per household on an average in 32 different wards of the Municipality. The entire population is urban and its population structure is such that out of the total population stated above, 12,747 are scheduled tribes and the scheduled castes population in the Municipality Stands at 7150 persons. Literates account for approximately 83.97 per cent of the total population and the remaining 16.03 per cent of the population is illiterate (Census of India: 2001). The

Municipality is administered by a Municipal Board constituted every five years having 32 members in it as elected representatives of the people hailing from different wards. Each ward has one seat in the Board, which is filled by the candidate who wins the party based elections from the ward.

The History

Although popular participation in civic administration actually started in 1847 in Darjeeling Hills, the Britishers established in Darjeeling Municipality on July 1,1850. Originally, the municipality had area of 138 sq. kms, comprising of the entire area of land ceded by the Raja of Sikkim. Today, Darjeeling covers an area of 1065 sq. kms, extending from Ging Bazaar to Jorebunglow. Its population in 1869 was 22607 people but today it stands, as according to the present Darjeeling Municipality Records, at 107, 197 persons. Till 1994, the municipality was governed by Bengal Municipality Act of 1932. Today, it is under the jurisdiction of Bengal Municipality Act of 1993, which came into force from July 1994 in the aftermath of the 74th Constitutional Amendment Act.

As regards the constitution and election of the municipality, it was in its inception, placed in the 1st schedule along with Khulna, Hazaribagh, Muzzafarpur, Dharbanga and Bhagalpur in which the commissioners were appointed by the local government, and also placed in the 2nd schedule with Burdwan, Hooghly, Nadia, Hazaribagh etc. in which the chairman was to be appointed by the local government. During the British period, no adult franchise was applicable in the election. Only tax and ratepayers were eligible voters. The first general election on the basis of adult franchise was held only on March 23rd, 1964 (Govt. of West Bengal: Order, 1963).

However, only three elections, 1994-1999 and 2000 present day have been held on party lines in the aftermath of the implementation of the 74th Constitutional (Amendment) Act, which provides among others, reservation of seats for women in Urban local bodies.

Scheduled Caste Women in Decision-making in the Municipality

Despite the attempt to social reforms by stalwarts like Ram Mohan Roy in Bengal (of which Darjeeling was and is a part) and persistent efforts to empower women, the exercises invariably failed to bear fruitful result. Women seldom saw themselves as significant actors in the public space prior to the mechanism developed to this end by the 74th Amendment Act in India in general, and in Darjeeling in particular. One is, although constrained in any research attempt on Darjeeling Municipality owing to the unavailability of data as the documents were gutted by fire on 20th November 1996.

Leave aside the representation of the Scheduled Castes women; the election of women in general to the Municipal Boards constituted prior to the implementation of the 74th Constitution (Amendment) Act was rather insignificant and inadequate. The number of women representatives increased only after the adoption of the constitutional mechanisms to this end by the 74th Amendment Act in 1993. This has been illustrated through Table 1 given below:

Table 1
Percentage of Elected Women of the Total Elected Representatives in the Municipality (Before the Implementation of the 74th Amendment Act).

Sl.No	Year	Total Members	Nominated	Elected	Male	Female	% of Elected Female
1.	1951	31	8	23	23	0	0
2.	1952	29	6	23	23	0	0
3.	1960-64	28	0	28	28	0	0
4.	1965-70	28	0	28	27	1	3.57
5.	1984	28	0	28	28	0	0

Source: Darjeeling Municipality Records.

From the above table it is evident that over the years after independence, the Municipal Boards were formed. But there were some nominated members in the board for a decade. With the introduction of adult franchise in the 1960s, all members were elected representatives. However, upto the mid 1960s, no woman

Table 2
Percentage of Elected Women to Total Elected Representatives in the Municipality [After the implementation of 74th Amendment Act]

Sl. No.	Year	Total Members	Elected	Male Elected	Female Elected	% of Elected Females
1.	1994-1999	28	28	27	1	3.57
2.	2000-2004	32	32	20	12	37.50
3.	2004-	32	32	19	13	40.62

Source: Darjeeling Municipality Records

was represented in the Darjeeling Municipality. One woman was elected in the board consisting of eight members in 1965-70, but it was purely incidental. Again the board that was constituted in 1984 conspicuously had no woman representative.

Table 3
Number of Elected Scheduled Caste Women in the Municipality

Sl.No.	*Year*	*Total Members*	*Total Male Representatives*	*Total Women Representatives*	*S/C Women Representatives*
1.	1994-99	28	27	1	0
2.	2000-04	32	20	12	3
3.	2004-	32	19	13	1

Source: Darjeeling Municipality Records.

From the above tables (that is, tables 2 and 3) it is seen that unlike the previous Municipal Boards constituted prior to the 74th Amendment Act, 1992, the Boards constituted in the aftermath of the said Act have incorporated more women in general and the scheduled caste women in particular see especially the Board formed in 2000 which shows a higher level of representation given to women belonging to the Schedule Caste communities in particular. The last Board shows that 9.37% of the total membership of the Board constituted of schedule caste women, which is 25 per cent of the total women representatives in the Board. The Municipal Board constituted in 2004, however, has a different story to tell. Although the percentage of women increased from 37.5% to 40.62%, the number of scheduled caste women representatives showed a decline from 3 in the past Board to just one in the present Board. Consequently, no significant programme or policy is made by the municipality in the direction of empowerment and development of women belonging to the schedule caste and schedule tribe communities.

It is quite interesting to note that despite the growing population of the Scheduled Caste population in general and of the scheduled caste women in particular in the area under study, there has not been a proportionate increase in the number of their representatives in the Municipal Board. Whereas there were three Scheduled caste women in the previous Board, the present Board has only one scheduled caste women representative. From table 4 below it is revealed that only one member belonging to the scheduled caste women category has been elected to the Municipal Board in 2004 out of the 32 representatives. Few wards in Municipality, viz. Ward No.7, 12, 14, 15, 23, 25, 26, 29, 31 and 32 have more scheduled caste women than men. However, there is no single Scheduled caste representative from these wards in the Municipality. There are only two members belonging to scheduled caste community elected to the Board, one male from ward 1 and one female from ward 3. But percentage wise it is an adequate representation to the Board, because the Scheduled caste community forms approximately 6.7% of the total population and the percentage of the scheduled caste representatives in the Board comes to around 6.25%, which is commensurate to their number in terms of population.

A discussion with the scheduled caste women representatives in the Municipal Boards (2000-2004 and 2004-) revealed that they belonged to the ruling GNLF party in Darjeeling Hills. The party had filed the scheduled caste women candidates for contesting the elections in the ward as envisaged in their party programme, which gave them the opportunity to come out as representatives in the decision-making forum. In the present Board too, both the SC candidates, male from Ward No.1 and female from Ward No.3 belong to the GNLF Party. It implies that the political parties also have subscribed to the constitutional directives and are encouraging women to participate in political dynamics and decision-making arena.

However, this does not imply that the scheduled caste women have been able to influence the decisions of the Municipality and have led to policy adoptions that are visibly contributing to the welfare of the scheduled caste women. The Board, unlike in the municipalities in the neighbourhood (Siliguri etc.) does not have a separate committee within it for the welfare of the Schedule Caste Communities. Within the territorial jurisdiction of the Municipality, the welfare and development schemes for the scheduled caste women are adopted and implemented by the West Bengal Schedule Caste and Schedule Tribe Development and Financial Corporation; and in this direction several continuous programme are adopted (Gupta: 1998). However, the fact remains that the Municipal Board, despite having a significant and adequate representation of the women belonging to the scheduled castes has conspicuously failed not only to design and implement women's empowerment programmes, but have too miserably failed to even constitute a committee etc to this end. This is a pointer to the fact that the women

Table 4
Population Structure of the SCs in different Wards and Their Representatives in the Municipal Board (2004-)

SI. No	*Word No.*	*Total Populat-ion*	*SC Populat-ion*	*Proportion SC to Total Population (%)*	*Sex Ratio of the Scheduled Castes 2001 Census*	*SC Women Representatives 2004 Board*
1.	1	4153	242	5.8	936	No
2.	2	2604	91	3.5	820	No
3.	3	3119	142	4.6	945	YES
4.	4	3515	117	3.3	1053	NO
5.	5	2389	46	1.9	840	NO
6.	6	4359	71	1.6	340	NO
7.	7	3957	206	5.2	1081	NO
8.	8	3858	231	6.0	848	NO
9.	9	2804	114	4.1	932	NO
10.	10	2314	52	22	1000	NO
11.	11	2810	11	0.4	375	NO
12.	12	3278	275	8.4	1331	NO
13.	13	1545	13	0.8	625	NO
14.	14	5499	595	10.8	1066	NO
15.	15	1281	72	5.6	1182	NO
16.	16	4526	29	0.6	933	NO
17.	17	4882	627	12.8	894	NO
18.	18	4187	365	8.7	984	NO
19	19	3519	251	7.1	961	NO
20.	20	1663	3	0.2	500	NO
21.	21	1022	10	1.0	667	NO
22.	22	2358	256	10.9	925	NO
23.	23	3249	364	11.2	1116	NO
24.	24	1288	105	8.2	694	NO
25.	25	1766	240	13.6	1284	NO
26	26	2279	485	21.3	1127	NO
27.	27	3423	195	5.7	806	NO
28.	28	7076	457	6.5	835	NO
29.	29	5604	395	7.0	1047	NO
30.	30	3920	147	3.8	838	NO
31.	31	4794	467	9.7	1113	NO
32	32	4156	476	11.5	1097	NO
Total	All	107,197	7,150	6.7		ONE

Source: Census Abstract, 2001.

play but a pseudo-effective role in determining the policies and the decisions of the Municipal Board. The present study has explored some reasons as to why the scheduled caste women have failed to exert desirable amount of pressure in the Board to constitute committees etc for the upliftment of their counterparts who elected them to power from the wards.

CONCLUSION

The fact that the Government has established multi-tier decentralized administrative structures to ensure the participation by the marginalized groups cannot be denied. For the empowerment and development of women in general and women belonging to scheduled caste community in particular, reservation of seats at various administrative levels has been made through constitutional mechanisms. Municipal bodies are one such administrative units where such reservation is sought for their empowerment through participation in the decision-making process. However, despite assuming leadership at the grass-root level governance, their influence in the decision-making process is still insignificant. This owes to a plurality reasons some of which are pointed below:

- The respondents feel that there are barriers for the scheduled caste women to enter political arena in general and to the decision-making bodies in particular. Amalgams of reasons are cited as constituting barriers or constraints. They include management of the household, male dominance, and the traditional attitudes prevalent in the society about women.
- Secondly, lack of political will in women also has constrained them from entering the decision-making and political domain. The lack of political will, as understood from the opinions expressed, owes to the fact that the society does not consider politics as a territory suitable for women.
- A mixed response was obtained on the question that whether vulnerability of women constituted a barrier for them to enter the 'public' sphere. Whereas some strongly expressed the view that it did, others held the view that as society is our own; such a threat perception may be ruled out.

As regards the domain of decision-making, the respondents cited a few reasons as to why the policies do not adequately reflect changes after they have entered the decision-making bodies. Some important findings in this regard are:

- That despite being a women or a member of a depressed class, as soon as one becomes a member of such an institution as the Municipality, the interest of the Municipality becomes primary. They opine that they need to work exclusively within the jurisdiction of the municipality, which renders them difficult to bring about desired radical changes in a short period of time.
- It was also found that the women belonging to the scheduled caste community who get elected to the municipality do not have a good knowledge about the rules, procedures and technicalities involved in the process of decision-making. This has resulted in their inefficiency as most of them seemed to belong to the first generation representatives and have no prior experience about dealing with multidimensional urban development, civic issues and their complexities.
- Thirdly, it was observed that the lack of desired and adequate support from the senior male members, poor organizational structure and the paucity of resources of the municipality also limited their scope of striving for radical policy shifts towards the betterment of scheduled caste women.
- Finally, passivity of women in general is yet another constraint that limits their effectiveness in the decision-making domain. Only those who had prior political experiences at the ward level or in other party hierarchies as active members are more active vis-a-vis the others who have directly got elected without much political activism in the past.

Therefore, what is needed for their fuller empowerment in the decision-making sphere is to train them timely on the related complexities that they are supposed to cope with. However, it should also be remembered that a single training is quite unlikely to help them build their capacity in the sphere of decision-making. A continuous process of monitoring and evaluation would produce better results, if it is coupled with proper and timely institutional supports. Hence, the need of the hour is their orientation, capacity building, information updating and counseling. This done, it is not quite unlikely that the perception of women especially belonging to the schedule caste communities in our society will change, bringing about greater social justice as they form the anchor of society. And therefore, every step towards empowerment of Schedule Caste women is likely to give a boost to social justice, at least in an incremental way, making the Indian democracy more democratic for the dalits to live prestige, dignity and honour.

REFERENCES

Bhan, C and Raj Singh. (2001): "Women's Empowerment for Gender Equality. A Functional Analysis", *Kurukshetra,* Vo1.49, No. 11.

Black, N. and A.B. Contrell (eds.)(1981). *Women and World Change: Equity Issues In Development,* London, Sage.

Darjeeling Municipality, *Darjeeling Municipality Records.*

Government of India (2001), Census Abstracts, Census 2001.

Government of India (1995), *Country Report: Fourth World Conference on Women, Beijing,* Department of Women and Child Development, Ministry of Human Resource Development, New Delhi.

Government of India (1993), 74th Constitutional Amendment Act, 1992.

Government of West Bengal (1963), Order, 1963.

Gupta, Lalan P (1998), Tribal Development Administration, Classical Publishing Company, New Delhi.

Macridi Roy C (1964), *The Study of Comparative Government,* Random House, New York.

INDEX

A

AP, 3, 8, 29, 62, 67-69, 72, 97, 121, 122, 124, 128-131, 141

AP Primary Education Project, 8, 121, 183

Aksharan Shankranti, 8, 121

Ambedkar, BR, Dr. (Baba Saheb Ambedkar), 7, 74-80, 84, 85, 95, 139, 191

America, 161

American & French Revolutions, 26

Andaman & Nicobar Islands, 141

Aquinas, Thomas, St., 15

Aristotle, 15

Arunachal Pradesh, 141, 163

Aryans, 101

Asia, 161

Assam, 87, 163

Australia, 161

B

Bacon, Francis, 15

Backward Classes, 142, 143

Backward Commission, 135

Baluch, 79

Bangladesh, 79, 106

Brahmins, 79, 80

Bihar, 29, 62, 6, 68, 70, 72, 73, 91, 163, 168, 183, 194

Bihar Education Project (BEP), 183

Bonded Labour System (Abolition) Act, 1976; 145

British Govt., 76

British India, 151

British Raj (British Rule), 74, 78, 189

Buddhism, 28

Burma, 161

C

Chaduvula Pandga, 8, 121

Chaos Theory, 18

Chhattisgarh, 14

China, 35, 161

China's Agrarian Policy, 35

Christianity, 80

Christians, 80

Chinese Economy, 35

Colony Health Centre, 112, 113

Common Minimum Programme (CMP), 121
Constitution of India (Indian Constitution), 28, 96, 102, 117, 119, 135, 136, 138, 140, 143-145, 152, 160, 191-193, 196, 203
Constitution of India 73rd & 74th Amendments, 193, 196, 203-207;—23rd Amendment, 193
Consumer Price Index for Agricultural Labourers (CPIAL), 70
Convention on Elimination of All Forms of Discrimination Against Women (CEDAW), 14, 30
Country Report for Fourth World Conference on Women (Beijing), 202
Covenant on Civil & Political Rights, 30
Covenant on Eco., Social & Cultural Rights, 30

D

Dalits, 212
Darjeeling Municipality in W.B., 204-207
Developing Countries, 6
Directive Principles of State Policy, 144
District Primary Education Programme (DPEP), 8, 121, 168, 183
Dravidians, 161, 162; —Pre-Dravidians, 161, 162
Durkheim, 19

E

East Africa, 16
Education Guarantee Scheme (EGS), 185
Egypt, 161
Engels, Friedrick, 19

F

FGT Index, 65, 66, 72
Female Literacy, 87, 88, 108; —Rates, 35, 36
Five Year Plan (First), 177
France, 18
Fundamental Rights, 137, 191

G

GNLF, Party, 208
Gandhi, MK (Gandhiji), 7, 74-79, 95, 102, 160, 189, 193
Gandhism, 75
Gender Inequality, 29, 45; —Economic, 31; —Education, 35
Gini Coefficient, 61, 62
Globalization, 33, 95
Govt. of India Act of 1935; 2, 139, 151, 160
Govt. of India (SCs) Order, 1936; 2
Gram Panchayats, 186
Greece, 15
Green Revolution, 37
Gujarat, 3, 67, 70, 72, 73, 87, 91, 97, 163, 170

H

HDI, 59
HDI, Survey, 61, 62, 72
HP, 179, 180, 194
Harizans, 102, 135, 160

Haryana, 141
Hindus, 74,. 76, 78, 102, 145, 162
Hinduism, 75, 76, 102
Hobbes, Thomas, 15
Human Rights, 25

I

IDRC, 61
ILO, 55
IRDP, 14, 178
Indian Democracy, 212
Indian Judiciary, 191
Indian Social System, 117
Indian Society, 76, 80, 85, 117, 161, 167
Indo Aryans, 161, 162
Inequality, 11-13
Intellectual Achievements of 17th Century, 15
Iran, 161
Islam, 28, 78

J

Jawahar Rozgar Yojana, 178
Jinnah, 7, 74, 75, 77, 79

K

Karnataka, 3, 97, 141, 163
Kerala, 3, 87, 88, 91, 97, 163, 181, 194

L

Lakshadweep, 141
Land Reforms, 34
Lock, John, 15
Lohia, EVR, 80

M

MRTP Act, 31
Madhya Pradesh, 62, 67, 71, 73, 87, 195
Maharashtra, 62, 67, 68, 71, 73, 97, 174, 181, 194
Mahila Morchas, 147
Mahila Samakshaya, 168
Mahila Shiksha Kendras, 168
Malaya, 161
Male Literacy, 108, 109;
—Rate of, 109
Manipur, 141, 163, 179
Marginal Farmers, 178
Marxian Theory of Social Development, 19
Meghalaya, 141, 179
Mid-Day Meal Scheme, 8, 121
Millar, John, 18
Minto, Lord, 162
Mizoram, 87, 88, 141, 163
Mongolians, 161, 162
Municipal Boards, 206, 207
Muslims (Indian Muslims/ Muslims of India), 74, 77, 78
Muslims Unit (Hindu-Muslim Unity), 77, 79

N

NACO Report, 113
NCAER, 62, 66, 69, 70, 72
NGOs, 4, 97, 183
Nagaland, 141, 163
Naik, VP, 150, 152, 159
New Eco. Policy, 94
Non-Formal Education (NFE),178, 183

North-Eastern States, 163
North Indian States, 3, 97

O

OBCs, 3, 96, 97, 196
Operation of Black Board Scheme, 183
Orissa, 62, 67-72, 163

P

PCR Act, 14, 119, 136, 147, 149, 154
Pakistan, 74, 76, 77
Panchayat & Municipal Committee, 193, 196
Panchayat System, 194
Persia, 161
Philippines, 161
Phooley, Jatirao, 84
Planning Commission, 61
Primary Schools, 129
Probation of Offenders Act, 1958; 150
Public Sector Enterprises, 32
Public Service Commission, 147
Puna Pact of 1932; 76, 151, 192
Punjab, 141, 162, 179, 181
Pushtuns, 79

R

Rajbanshis, 102, 103
Rajasthan, 87, 91, 168
Report of Human Rights Watch, 13
Report of National Commission for SCs & STs, 13
Report of UNAIDS/WHO, 114
Reservation Policy, 3, 5, 98
Rights of Women, 190
Rome, 15, 161
Round Table Conference, 76, 162
Rousseau, 15, 16
Roy, Ram Mohan, 85, 189, 205
Russia, 161

S

SC Agricultural Labourers, 178
SC Boys, 124, 128
SC Children, 121, 124, 135, 184, 185
SC Families, 134
SC Girls (SC Females), 118, 124, 134
SC Literacy, 180;—Rates of, 86, 87, 179-183;—Female, 122; —Male, 122
SC Population, 108, 120
SC Teachers, 131
SC Women, 202, 203, 207, 208, 212
SC/ST Household, 62
SC/ST Population, 62, 140, 141, 177, 179, 181, 183, 185, 186, 207
SCs/STs (prevention of Atrocities) Act, 1985; 28
SHGs, 49, 53-56
Sachs, Wolgang, 33
Sarva Shiksha Abhiyan, 8, 9, 121, 184, 186;—Campaign, 186
Scotland, 18
Sen's Poverty Index, 65, 66, 72
Shiksha Karmis, 168
Shramik Vidyalay, 168
Simon Commission, 2
Smith, Adam, 18

Social Discrimination, 27
Social Movements, 23
Somalia, 161
South Asian Countries, 79
Special Component Plan, 168
Spencer, Herbar, 19
Spencer, Oswald, 20
State Specific Basic Education Project, 183

T

Tamil Nadu, 3, 62, 67, 97, 141, 195
Tarijot Colony, 106, 108-111, 114
Teachers' Education, 183
Theory of Social Evolution, 19
Third World Countries, 200
Toynbee, Arnold, 20
Tribal-Sub Plan, 84
Tripura, 162
Turgot, Jacques, 18

U

UN, 190
UNDP, 42, 59, 61
UNFPA, 61
UP, 88, 141, 163, 168, 179, 180
Untouchability, 27, 148, 149, 201
Untouchability (Offences) Act, 1955; 28, 136, 147-149, 162
United Nations Commission Committee, 14
Universal Declaration of Human Rights, 25-27, 30, 200
Universal Elementary Education, 183
Universalization of E. Education, 183
Uttaranchal, 141

V

Varna System (Caste System), 2, 160, 161, 192
Vidya-Volunteer Scheme, 8, 121
Vidyasagar, Ishwar Chandra, 85, 189
Village Education Committee, 182, 186

W

WB, 67-73, 105, 163, 179-183, 194, 202, 204, 208
WB Distt. Primary Education Programme, 183
WB SC & ST Development Financial Corpn., 208
Weber, Max, 19
Women's Equal Participation in Decision-making, 201, 203
Women's Empowerment, 188
Women's Reservation Bill, 189, 195, 197
Women's Pol. Reservation (Pol. Reservation to Women), 188, 189, 194, 196